BLINK

Ian MacDonald was born in Glasgow and spent much of his youth in approved schools and prison. He ran a successful bar before being jailed in 1993 for a failed bank robbery. He has now turned his back on crime and lives quietly in his home town.

David Leslie worked for the *News of the World* for more than four decades before retiring and is now a freelance journalist and author. His other titles include the bestselling *Crimelord*, *The Happy Dust Gang*, *The Gangster's Wife* and *The Hate Factory*.

Blink

A Journey Through Gangland Mayhem

IAN 'BLINK' MacDONALD with DAVID LESLIE

MAINSTREAM
PUBLISHING

EDINBURGH AND LONDON

First published in Great Britain in 2012 by
MAINSTREAM PUBLISHING COMPANY
(EDINBURGH) LTD
7 Albany Street
Edinburgh EH1 3UG

ISBN 9781780575759

A catalogue record for this book is available
from the British Library

Printed in Great Britain by
CPI Group (UK) Ltd, Croydon, CR0 4YY

1 3 5 7 9 10 8 6 4 2

Acknowledgements

ANYONE WHO HAS been in prison knows the value of friendships: that friendly face at visiting time, the writer of a letter and, once freedom comes, the importance of the offer of a helping hand, a word of encouragement, even just a chat to lift you from the despair that all too often beckons. I have been luckier than most, not only in the number of my friends but in the quality of their kindness, and one motive for writing this book was to be able to tell them that without their support I would not have made it.

So I want to place on record my sincere thanks to: Patricia McGarrigle, who sadly died before the book could be published, her husband, Dick, daughter Laurine, son Ralph and Uncle Charlie; Tommy O'Leary, Caff and Sammo; Ross Campbell and Big Davie for a yachting trip I shall never forget; John Stark, Leighanne and Darren Lyttle; Big Obbs from the Arches; Horsey and Logie; Adam and Claire from Stepps, who gave me such help after the bomb incident; Alan, Sharon and Stuart in Durham; Steff Lennox; John Coyne; Jake Clark; Thomas Duffy and his sisters Marie and Diane; my cousins Brenda and Catherine; Tam McGrattan and Betty from Blackhill; Ross Birnie and his nephew Alexander; Big Mark and Rosco; Paul and his dad, Willie, and pal Joe; my friends among the Travelling People who pestered me to tell my story, especially Ward Bateman and Asa; Robert Kingsley and Clive at Blackpool, who made sure I found peace and quiet to write when I went caravanning; Andy and Nan Wilson, for such happy memories of being taken by them to Ibrox, and their son Andrew, who died in tragic circumstances; that excellent photographer Brian Anderson for his spontaneous generosity; my son Daryl, for burning the midnight oil with me as I remembered and wrote. Rab Scullion, Alan Love, Jim Brown, Star Keenan and John Lynn are brilliant guys who have always been there for me when I've needed help. I have been lucky, too, in having very skilled and patient lawyers. My thanks go to Andrew Gallen and Joe Shields in Glasgow and Vicky King in London.

I have been especially saddened to learn, while writing this book, of the death of Michael Carroll, who finally lost a very long and brave fight against illness. RIP Michael.

But I want to dedicate *Blink* to two very special people whose example in fighting adversity has been my constant inspiration: my dear friend David Brisbane Fitzsimmons, who passed away in January 2010, and, dearest of all, my ma, whose love has never wavered.

Ian MacDonald

Contents

Prologue

IT WAS A hot day, but I felt cold. Outside, Londoners bustled about their business in the summer sunshine. In a cell below the Central Criminal Court – the Old Bailey – my thoughts were solely on a dozen men and women in a room just a few feet above me. It was Tuesday, 10 August 1993 and they were the jury deciding whether I was guilty of taking part in a crazy attempt to rob a bank.

With my five Glaswegian accomplices, I had been hating the very thought of this day. Twenty-seven months earlier, we had used a shotgun to try to get our hands on six million pounds. It had all gone wrong, and while some of us had escaped, the coppers had tracked us down. That was just the start of more madness. Trials began and were scrapped. Jurors suddenly went sick, a barrister was caught talking out of turn, we rioted over corned-beef sandwiches and were betrayed on the eve of a plot to take hostages at pistol point and flee. So the show was moved to the Old Bailey, and in the end it was the lawyers who became rich, not us. Of course I'd been part of the gang, but there was no way I was going to put my hands up and be meekly led away to miserable years in prison. The police wanted us jailed, so it was up to them to convince the jury we were guilty.

Guilty. How I dreaded the sound of that word. I wondered how many others had waited in this same windowless box over the years. Ruth Ellis shot dead a lover; mass murderer John Christie bricked his victims up in his house. They both heard a jury foreman say 'Guilty' and were led off to be hanged, like spies and sheep stealers before them. So did poor teenager Derek Bentley – and he'd only tried pinching from a sweet warehouse. We'd thought we'd get six million pounds.

A million each, more than enough for me to take my little son, Daryl, and his mum, Sheila, to start a new life in Spain. 'If you can't do the time, don't do the crime' was the old lags' motto, one I often repeated to myself, but this had looked as if it was going to be so easy. I'd robbed before, although nothing on this scale, and knew you needed a bit of luck. But we had none. Nor did the manager of the Chinese restaurant in Glasgow where I was tucking into bang bang ji with Sheila when the police jumped on me. He was left waving an unpaid bill and the police the gun they'd found in my pocket. So off I was dragged to face the music, to the accompaniment of punches and kicks. I had come to expect treatment like that.

And so here we were after trial number four, the final episode in a long-running saga and one that would have had a television audience in stitches. A Judas witness had turned up with his own Bible, men in wigs from London's posh cocktail belt struggled to understand Glaswegian accents and mentalities, and we thought about crushed dreams, the pistol and the grass who gave the game away.

The jury took their time, and no wonder. They were given two nights in a luxury hotel to think about their decision while we sweated among lice and cockroaches in grim Belmarsh nick. Of course it all had to end, and it did on the third day. It was Tuesday, VE Day, Verdict Day.

London commuters were forced to step aside for our prison van, sandwiched between Range Rovers packed with police holding sub-machine guns. Motorcycle outriders halted traffic and in the sky above a police helicopter circled. Inside the van, we were shackled. At court, we walked through a corridor of armed policemen into the holding cell below the dock that we had come to know so well.

After what seemed an eternity, there was a sudden rattle of keys, the door opened and a guard was telling us, 'Right, lads, the jury are coming back with a verdict.' So this was it. Was I going back to Scotland or being confined for the best years of my life in top-security jails as a high-risk Category Double-A prisoner, a danger, a threat, a potential escaper?

The dock was an island in a sea of uniformed police. In front of us, our QCs and lawyers turned round, trying to give encouragement. But these were desperate moments. It's supposed to be a good sign if the jurors look at you once they've come to a decision, and we craned our necks for some reaction as they shuffled into their places. But there was nothing. Only silence. Then I heard it. 'Guilty.' 'Guilty.' 'Guilty.' On and on it seemed to go. Now it was the turn of the jury to be shocked as they heard that I and three of the others were already serving prison sentences. And the length of time they had spent deliberating suggested there were those among them who had wanted to find us not guilty.

In May of that year, Thomas Carrigan and Robert Harper had been given seventeen years each for three bank robberies in Norwich. Mick Healy had been serving ten years in Shotts prison, Lanarkshire, for a bank robbery when he'd escaped in a butcher's van and, while on the run, had linked up with us for our big job. He got a further two years for the escape. I'd already been jailed for taking the gun into the Chinese restaurant.

The eminent judge Sir Lawrence Verney, the Recorder of London, was clearly not a man who wasted time on niceties, not with us anyway. 'Each of you is convicted of a very serious conspiracy to rob,' he said, as if we didn't already know that. 'The law requires me to say – it seems absurd in the circumstances – that only a custodial sentence will suffice.' Then came the numbers. James Healy was first. He got 16 years. I was given 16 years for the bank job and another 6 months for escaping. The toll mounted, the years adding up as though they were mere figures and not chunks of our lives. Michael Carroll, 18 years; Robert Harper, 16 years; Thomas Carrigan, 16 years; and Michael Healy, 19 years, to start when his 10 was finished.

BLINK

At least we took it on the chin. Nobody flinched, complained, screamed insults or threats. We'd done the crime, now came the time. All of us had known the risks. When finally the judge told our guards, 'Take them down,' we stood up, raised our thumbs in the air and started singing 'Always Look on the Bright Side of Life'. We were still singing as we walked down the steps from the dock to start our journey through the depths of England's toughest jails. But inwardly I was asking, 'How did I get here? Where did it all go wrong?'

1

Colonel Blink

WE MACDONALDS ARE a feisty lot. It's said we descend from Conn of the Hundred Battles, an Irish king who slashed and stabbed those who stood in his way about 2,000 years ago. Maybe I inherited something from his genes, because my philosophy has always been to stand no nonsense from anybody. I know about Conn because one of my great pleasures is reading, and circumstances have meant that over the years I've had plenty of time to study the history of the clan.

Of course, mention the name MacDonald and many people automatically think of the Glencoe Massacre. I am fascinated by accounts of that terrible incident on 13 February 1692 when, in the early hours of a freezing morning, nearly 80 MacDonald men, women and children were slaughtered by militia whom they had earlier wined and dined, generously sharing their meagre supplies. According to one version, the MacDonalds were being punished for thieving. Whatever the motive, it was a dreadful act of betrayal by those the victims had entertained. I suppose that many elements of the Glencoe tragedy have been mirrored in my life, one in which stealing, persecution and betrayal have all played a part.

One of the first to die at Glencoe was the MacDonald leader, Alasdair Maclain. Nowadays, we would term him the local Godfather, but it would be a twentieth-century Godfather who would want to influence me. His name was Arthur Thompson and he lived in Provanmill Road in the East End of Glasgow. I had just reached my teens when we became near neighbours to the Thompsons. Most people in Glasgow remembered how Arthur's mother-in-law had been killed right outside their home when somebody planted a bomb beneath his car. That was in August 1966, when I was aged five. Years later, I would come to know how Arthur must have felt. But that was for the future.

The famous Rottenrow Hospital in Glasgow is closed now. Sadly, many people remember it as the birthplace, in 1938, of the Moors murderer Ian Brady. It was also where I was born, on 2 March 1961. I wasn't the first child for my ma, Margaret, and dad, John. They had had a son, John, on 1 June 1959, but tragically my brother caught a virus and, despite brain surgery, died at just 14 months. So I appeared on the scene and settled into life in a tenement in Lenzie Street, Springburn, in the north of Glasgow. No bathrooms for the likes of us in those days, and 16 months later I found myself sharing the communal tin bath with younger brother Gary. This time, Ma, like many of her friends, chose to have her baby at home rather than go to hospital, and he came along on 29 July 1962. With the family expanding, we moved to a different flat in Lenzie Street and not long afterwards, on 12 May 1965, Gary and I were joined by another brother, Alan.

Among my earliest memories of growing up in Lenzie Street are trips to Woolworths in busy Springburn Road when I was around five. I can remember Ma smacking my hand every time we went into the shop because I would automatically reach into the pick 'n' mix and try to put the sweets into my pocket without anybody noticing. Sometimes Gary and I would sneak out from our house to Woolies to fill our pockets. Looking back, I suppose that shoplifting sweeties was my very first criminal act. It would not be the last.

When I was five, I started at Albert Primary School in Springburn. Everybody knew it as 'the Wee Albert'. It was just a five-minute walk from home. My ma's sister Chrissie also stayed in Springburn, in Wellfield Street, with Billy, my uncle, who was a steel erector and a fierce Celtic supporter. They had three girls – Anne, Margaret and Brenda – and a son, George, who was the eldest. Chrissie worked in a launderette. Around the corner from Aunt Chrissie's was a swing park, and not long after starting school I slid down a chute and tore my face. It left a scar that I still have.

The flat was overcrowded and we moved to a four-in-a-block house, upstairs with two bedrooms and, lo and behold, a bath and inside toilet, and a huge, grassy back garden. I couldn't believe this change in luck and we felt as though we had come into a fortune. It was magical, completely out of the blue – to go from a tenement flat to a 'Big House'. We had moved four miles, to Drumpellier Street in a district in the East End of Glasgow called Blackhill. I later learned that Blackhill was one of the most deprived areas not just in Glasgow but in Europe. But to us, compared to our tenement close in Springburn, this was heaven. Close by was Barlinnie prison, a place I would come to regard as a hell on earth, while around the corner lay Provanmill and the home of the Thompsons, where the bomb went off under the Godfather's car in August 1966.

I'd barely had time to get to know my classmates at the Wee Albert before I was waving goodbye to them. Moving house meant starting at a new school, Riddrie Primary, where I was soon friends with Brian Graham, James Brocket, Elaine Sneddon, Carol Morrison and Jackie Henderson. Riddrie was a Protestant school and I am a Protestant, but Blackhill was mainly a Catholic area. Most of my neighbours in Drumpellier Street were Catholics, which made things awkward as far as Da was concerned. The reason was simple. In Glasgow, there has long been a huge divide between Catholics and Protestants. Sectarianism and bigotry are almost a way of life for a lot of Glaswegians, and nowhere is this shown more dramatically than in football and the two teams known as the Old Firm: Celtic is the Catholic club and Rangers the Protestant one. So it was never a good thing to walk around shouting about your love for your team. People have been killed for doing that. Da, though, couldn't have cared less. He was a diehard Rangers supporter, the kind who would have bled blue if you'd cut him open. He was very proud to support his team and didn't care who knew it. He used to take me to Ibrox when I was five to see the team play. And although I was living among and playing with many Celtic fans, most of whom tried to persuade me to switch allegiances, my loyalties were already ingrained. They lay firmly with Rangers.

In September 1970, we three boys had a surprise when we were joined by a sister, whom our parents named Tracy. Since Gary and I were older, we explained to Alan that a big stork had flown by and dropped her in our back garden. 'Well, why do we need to take her, then?' Alan complained. 'The Mundays downstairs only have two boys, why do they no take her?' Alan was jealous when Tracy appeared, because it meant he would no longer be getting special treatment as the baby of the family. But then it became obvious he was not the only jealous one. Da was unhappy with the amount of time and attention Tracy was getting from Ma and soon we noticed he was drinking a lot more. Then the shouting and anger started. We were nervous and unsure of what to do, and then we began hearing Ma crying and realised he was beating her.

It wasn't fair. Raising kids in a place like Blackhill wasn't easy; there were gangs and widespread violence, features of a lifestyle that most people around us accepted as normal, and Ma did her best to make sure we boys didn't get involved in that. She made sacrifices so we never wanted for much and tried her best to spoil us rotten whenever she could. She was only trying to be a good mother, a good person. At the time, she was working in the canteen at Foresthall Hospital, which had at one time been the Springburn poorhouse. Her sister Chrissie, having left the launderette, was the cook, and her other sister Madge also worked in the kitchen. When she finished her shift, I'd see Ma staggering along the street towards our home, clutching bags filled with goodies from the hospital kitchen. And this was the ma that that bastard was hitting. It was terrible listening to her cries. One night when I was ten, Alan, Gary and I decided we could no longer listen to the violence. We ran into the living room and, as we were still very small and Da was a good six feet tall, stood on the couch then jumped onto his back to take his attention away from Ma.

He would sometimes come home drunk singing 'The Sash', a Rangers song. That was a crazy thing to do in Catholic Blackhill, and Ma would send us brothers to drag him into the safety of the house. There were times when I found him sitting sobbing, his head in his hands, drowning his sorrows in a bottle.

The first time this happened, not understanding what was wrong, I asked Ma, 'Has Granny MacDonald died?'

She told me, 'Rangers just got beat today, that's all.'

'Naebody's dead,' I would tell my brothers. 'He's greetin' cos Rangers lost,' and they would look at me in astonishment and disbelief that a grown man, and not just any grown man but our da, was howling and shouting because of football.

The boozing and violence became so bad that police were regularly appearing at weekends to arrest Da for domestic abuse. After court on a Monday and a fine, he'd try to get back in the house. Ma would tell him he wasn't welcome, pass his belongings out to him in black bin bags and he'd go off to stay in a hostel with dossers and alcoholics.

Money was short and I started up a paper round to help out, eventually building up 30 customers and trying to make sure I went for the money just after they'd opened their pay packets. Ma's da, Granda Muir, who was known as 'Big Jocky', kept the cash for me. I was saving up for a Chopper bike. He had a heart of gold, just like Granny Muir, who sometimes took me and my cousin Catherine to Butlins holiday camp in Ayr. Ma's younger brother, my uncle Charlie, was a Royal Marine who often brought back presents from foreign postings like Singapore and Hong Kong.

From time to time, Ma would take Da back after he promised to stay off the booze. But the pattern was always the same. He'd reform for a little while, then the violence would start again, Ma would take us to stay with Granda and Granny Muir, then Da would be making promises to behave. And so it went on.

Despite this, we children still enjoyed ourselves. We'd spend hours roaming the streets and playing our favourite game, Two-Man Hunt, in which two of us would be the hunters having to find the others, who hid out in back courts, gardens and even the local graveyard, Riddrie Cemetery, two miles away. Maybe the tricks I learned then about lying low helped me as an adult when I had the law chasing me. Sometimes Gary and I and pals who included Eddie and Billy Munday, George McGuigan, John and Wullie Gibson and Wullie Cox would go collecting birds' eggs down at the canal at Blackhill. The spot later became part of the M8 motorway. These were great, fun times. Around then, a gas pipe exploded under a local café, the Golfers' Rest, scattering sweets, biscuits and cakes, and as soon as we heard what had happened we youngsters made a beeline to forage for free goodies. In the summer, I would stay with Aunt Chrissie and make more friends, like Tam McNab and George Meiklejohn. Years later, I bumped into George at Shotts prison.

When I was 12, I started at Smithycroft Secondary School, which lay in the shadow of Barlinnie jail. At times, I'd wonder what it was like to be locked up, but mostly my thoughts were on the opposite sex and football. I'd find myself staring not only at the older girls but also at the better-looking female teachers. That wasn't my only reason to be cheerful, because in May 1973 Rangers won the Scottish Cup in front of 122,714 fans at Hampden Park, beating a Celtic side that included Kenny Dalglish 3–2.

Two more of my friends at this time were Joe MacAree and James McCuley (known to pals as 'Codgie'). Both were in the Army Cadets and I'd often see them looking smart in their uniforms. I said I was thinking about joining too and they talked me into it, with promises of going on holiday with the Cadets. What they omitted to tell me was that these holidays involved assault courses, staying in old army billets and hiking cross-country through mud in pouring rain. There were about 15 boys from Blackhill and Provanmill in the Cadets, including Arthur Thompson junior, son of the Godfather. Arty was only a year older than me but even at that young age he was fascinated with guns. He was easily one of the quickest at stripping the old rifles we used for weapons training. Guns would come to shape his future.

2

Schoolboy to Bad Boy

I WAS STILL ONLY 14 when I started hanging around street corners, mixing with locals who were stealing cars and breaking into shops. While one half of me was dying to join in, the other was telling me to stay away. As Da was a strict disciplinarian, my brothers and I didn't want to get on the wrong side of his violent temper. Neighbours like Gilly Martin and his wife – who had a son, John, and daughter, Maureen – were always telling me to stay out of trouble, but I never listened to their good advice. I thought the lads on the street corner had a far more exciting lifestyle than me, and they impressed me by bragging about their crimes. My life seemed boring in comparison. I gave up the Army Cadets, ignoring the pleas of Joe and Codgie for me to stay in. Soon I was a passenger in stolen cars, then breaking into shops through the roof and stealing cartons of cigarettes and drink. I gave up my paper run, too, no longer needing it, as I was making far more money from crime. At school, I was becoming less and less focused on lessons, instead concentrating my efforts on chatting up girls. I was also growing and looking forward to the day when I'd be big enough to batter Da, avenging the pain and misery he'd inflicted on Ma. But she beat me to it, finally deciding she had had enough and throwing him out for good.

With Da no longer on the scene to keep me in order, my recklessness worsened. Things at school came to a head one day when I got into a fight with another boy and accidentally punched a PE teacher as he was breaking it up. As a consequence, I was expelled. Now I had time to run with older boys in a local gang. Inevitably, because I wasn't even 16, the police started picking me up, and Ma would have to collect me from their custody. In 1976, after a few of these episodes, the Children's Panel sent me to Larchgrove Remand Home in Edinburgh Road, Glasgow, where an assessment was to be made as to whether I had learned my lesson and could return home or was a nuisance to society and should be sent to an approved school.

The regime at Larchgrove was horrendous and should have put me off offending for life. I was put into a dormitory with seven other boys, including 'Dainty' McDade from Blackhill. Some boys escaped after their mates on the outside jemmied wide the iron bars across the windows. I wasn't so lucky. The Panel sent me to Kibble Approved School in Paisley for a year. The pipe-smoking governor was known as 'Plastic Arse' because rumour had it he'd been shot in the backside during the Second World War. I was kept there over a miserable Christmas and New Year and made a promise to stay clear of crime.

Sadly, I didn't keep my pledge. At the end of January 1977, I was told that because I had behaved myself I could spend a weekend at home. I went out with pals that night, having carefully listened to Ma warning me not to get into trouble. I did as I was told, but things went badly wrong the following night when a pal invited me to a party in Provanmill. It sounded good and a couple of my pals were eager to hear all about my adventures in Larchgrove and Kibble. They seemed to think I'd been on some sort of a holiday. 'It's no all burds and sunshine,' I told them. 'Try dark nights spent in a dormitory listening to boys crying for their mas and days spent in a field nearly getting frostbite picking turnips while Plastic Arse smokes his pipe to his heart's content.'

Things got better when I started chatting with a stunning blonde whom I'd known at Smithycroft school. The record player was belting out a Rod Stewart hit of the day, 'Tonight's the Night', and I wondered if that might be an omen. It was, because the blonde and I ended up alone together in one of the bedrooms and before the party broke up she agreed to see me a month later, when I reckoned I would be due another home leave from Kibble. I was on such a high that instead of going home I joined some pals in a stolen car and we found ourselves being chased by the police.

Abandoning the motor, we took to our heels. I was determined not to get caught, but I became tangled up in a barbed-wire fence in a back garden and suddenly the pursuers were on me. Instantly, the beating started. I received repeated painful blows to the back of my head. At first, I thought I was being punched or kicked, and then I realised they were using truncheons. My head felt as if it had burst and I was tossed into the back of the police van like a rag doll.

At the police station, the charge was car theft and two police assaults. I'd been warned by others what the form was in those days. You'd be beaten till you could barely remember your own name then charged with assault, allowing your tormentors to get a couple of weeks off work and enough money in compensation for their injuries for a week in Spain. I wasn't to know it at the time, but that was the first of many beatings I'd receive from men in uniforms.

On Monday morning, I found myself at court in Ingram Street, Glasgow. Nowadays, the building is a plush bar and restaurant, the Citation, and when I'm there I allow myself a wry smile as I think back to how on my first visit I was dragged inside in handcuffs. In a tiny cell, crammed in with nine others, I waited to hear my fate. There was a bowl stuck to the tin wall in which we had to urinate. The smell was terrible. At midday, we were given a plastic cup of lukewarm, weak tea, two pieces of Spam and the luxury of a chocolate digestive biscuit.

I was sent to Longriggend Remand Centre at Greengairs near Airdrie while the authorities decided my fate. Gary had sadly followed me into lawbreaking and his misbehaviour resulted in his being sent to Oakbank Approved School in Aberdeen. At Longriggend, I first met Steven 'Star' Keenan from Royston, the beginning of a friendship that is as strong now as ever. Star was a year older than me. We went to the gym regularly and played five-a-side football, and Star, a really good player, made sure I was in his team.

Just before I appeared in front of a sheriff in Glasgow, I was told there were three alternatives: a detention centre, a secure unit called Rossie Farm or borstal. Representatives from Kibble encouraged me to choose Rossie Farm, telling me horror stories about the brutality that went on in borstals. My view was that, as it was inevitable I'd be sent to borstal at some stage in my life, I might as well get started now. So borstal it was, and I knew what to expect. But before then, I'd experience even worse: I was remanded to Barlinnie for three days before being transferred to a hall for new borstal inmates in Polmont near Falkirk.

Anyone spending their first night in Barlinnie can expect a frightening and daunting experience. For me, at the age of sixteen years and three weeks, it was terrifying. I had heard stories about Barlinnie, Bar-L, the Big House – everyone had – and was scared by the thought of how tough you needed to be to survive in there. On arrival, I was ushered to a table in the reception hall by a screw who asked my name and sentence. When I hesitated, he shouted, 'You think you're a hard man, you little shit? What's your fucking name and sentence?' There was barely a second to utter a word before, all of a sudden, he jumped up from his chair, grabbed me by the ear and pulled me round a corner. He opened the door to a tiny, almost miniature cell, which I would come to know was termed a 'dug box', and pushed me inside. 'This is the Big Hoose,' he said ominously. 'It's for men, not skinny little fuckers like you. If I hear a word, I will personally come in there and kick the shit out of you.' And with that the door was slammed shut and the key turned in the lock.

I was shaking with fear. The screw looked like a giant. I'd only had a few minutes to consider the prospect of how bad this prison might be when the door opened again and more warders started shouting abuse. 'Think you're a wee ticket, son, battering police officers, aye? Should we find out how hard you are, then? Come on, ya skinny wee runt, let's see how hard you are now. Your mammy's no here to help, boy.' I started to wonder if I'd walk out of Barlinnie alive. I looked at a sea of uniforms stretched over broad shoulders and muscle. Feeling sicker by the second, I wondered how they knew I'd assaulted police officers. They didn't need to batter me to leave me speechless with fright. I heard them laughing as they clanged the door shut, leaving me to pray the days would pass quickly. I couldn't wait to transfer to Polmont, away from this hell. I had been at Barlinnie less than an hour and was already a wreck.

They left me to cower for another half an hour, then the door was opened and another warder, one I hadn't seen before, looked in and said, 'Right, borstal boy, let's be having you to see the doctor.' He didn't seem as angry as the others, and I followed him into a room where other prisoners sat on wooden chairs. The screw walked off, leaving me confused and still petrified. One of the inmates looked at me. 'Wee man,' he said, 'you look as if you need yer mammy.' While the others began taking an interest, he carried on, 'Did those arsehole screws give you a fright or something? You look awfully white, son.' I couldn't even move my lips. Now all the prisoners burst out laughing. They were much older than me and would already have been 'jail wide'. I figured they could see how young I was and had guessed what the screws must have been like with me in reception.

Finally, I had the courage to mumble, 'They know I'm in for police assault. I thought I was gonnae get a tanking off them.'

Another of the guys, who looked to be in his mid-30s, leaned across and told me, 'Aye, they would have seen the charges on your sheet when you came into reception. Keep your head down and you'll be all right, kid.' He seemed to know what he was talking about and I guessed he was a Barlinnie regular.

Suddenly, a door opened, a screw in a white jacket shouted 'next' and one of the prisoners jumped up and disappeared with him. As the door was closing, I heard the warder yelling, 'Name and number for the doctor.' Now a new fear hit me. What number? I didn't have one. I turned to one of the prisoners sitting next to me.

'Here, do I need to give a number or something?' I said.

He had a long beard and an evil look. 'You don't know yer number, wee man?' he asked.

Now I started to panic. 'Will it be the same one I had at Longriggend?' I asked, and the room erupted with laughter again. If I wasn't so worried, I might have been annoyed.

'Don't be daft,' was the reply. 'You're no in that kids' playground any more, son.'

I was on the verge of tears, not helped when another con smirked, 'Aye, you're gonnae get your cunt kicked in if you've not got your number.'

My asking 'How can I get it, then?' simply produced more mickey-taking.

Somebody clearly fancying their chances of a career as a stage wit piped up, 'Mate, my ma has more chance of getting her numbers up in the bingo the night than you have of getting yours for the doc in there.'

It was obvious they were having a good time at my expense. A voice behind me said, 'The poor wee fucker hasn't got a clue. Wait till he gets to the halls.'

I thought, 'Please just let this be over with so I can get home to Ma. I swear I'll never be in trouble again, never.'

The screw who had led me in appeared and asked if I had seen the doctor. He looked at me with fury and disgust when I told him no and snarled, 'That will be "No, sir" when you talk to me, MacDonald.' I could tell he was showing off. He ordered me to jump ahead of the others in the queue, calling me 'borstal boy' again, which raised yet another laugh at my expense.

This was starting to irritate me, but at that moment the door opened and I was pushed in to see the doctor. The screw in the white jacket shouted, 'Name and number, boy – and stand up straight.' In desperation and expecting a knock on the head, I gave my name and the number I'd been allocated at Longriggend. But no blow, no screamed insults. Instead, the doctor began asking all sorts of questions: had I got this or that wrong with me, did anyone in my family have TB? I wasn't sure what TB was but answered no. Then White Jacket began examining my hair with one hand while shining a lamp on me with the other. I realised he was checking for head lice. Meanwhile, the doctor was still droning on. Did I have diabetes? Had I ever tried to kill myself? I answered no to both.

White Jacket finished his probing. 'Drop your trousers, MacDonald,' he said, and I was convinced I'd heard him wrong.

'Wh-what did you say?' I asked, not sure if I wanted to know.

He repeated himself in what I thought was a sinister tone. 'I said drop your trousers now, boy.'

The doctor's questions were still continuing and, as I assured him there was no history of any heart condition in my family, my mind was reeling. Drop my trousers? It was the very first time I'd been asked to do that by anyone – well, except for a girl, but that was different – and the fact that White Jacket was still holding the lamp didn't make me feel any better. 'He's going to examine your pubic hair for crabs,' the doctor said, and I felt a little more at ease, though I was still wary.

So I dropped my trousers but was still ready to put up a fight. White Jacket bent down to shine his light and look for the 'seaside nippers'. I thought back to the blonde in the bedroom and recalled her telling me she hadn't been with many guys, but was still relieved that all appeared well. Remembering her made me determined to see her again, if I got out of this nightmare alive.

Then I was shocked out of my daydream as the doctor pronounced, without even bothering to look up, 'You're fit and healthy to be transferred to Polmont.' He had continued writing throughout the questioning and now I prayed he was signing my passage out of Barlinnie.

Outside the examination room, I was taken back to my kennel, where a few moments later a passman (a prison trustee) handed me my dinner: a bowl of Barlinnie stew. It was disgusting, but I forced it down me in quick time. I was starving, having had only the few pieces of Spam and the chocolate digestive in court earlier in the day.

Then it was off to the shower with the white Windsor soap with which I would become familiar over the years, it being the standard-issue soap in prison at the time. I was given prison-issue clothing (which was always either too big or too small), then taken over to one of the halls and put into a cell.

By now, it was lock-up, and I heard a screw going by checking all the doors. I made up my bed, clambered in, the lights went off and I was alone with my misery. I lay in darkness for a few minutes, letting my eyes adjust, unable to get comfortable, the rough blankets itching my skin. A thin beam of light shone through the solitary barred window and I knew it came from the same moon that hovered above the house where Ma sat safely. She was just a few hundred yards away, but it might as well have been a thousand miles.

I became conscious of a background noise and realised I was listening to the sound of traffic speeding along the M8 motorway. I thought, 'That used to be the canal. Now it's paved over with concrete and tarmacadam. It's as if they've buried our good times under there.' In cars and buses, happy people were speeding to parties or home, to see friends or simply drive about. They'd be laughing, singing, chatting. Boys would be with their girlfriends, others with their mates. My thoughts drifted to the time when I was six and we'd lived in another Big House. I remembered how happy me and my brothers had been having lots of space, our own bathroom, even a back garden! I thought about the canal and all the fun I'd had walking along it with my pals. Those happy days had been taken for granted. Not so long ago I had been a carefree kid. Now the good times were gone. I flashed forward ten years from those days to where I was now, a borstal boy at sixteen. It was hard to take in how fast my childhood and early teens had gone by. My old school was just yards away and Ma's house only a stone's throw off. Now I was in the Big House. It didn't take a lot of thought to decide where I'd rather be.

3

Bunny Hop

DURING THE THREE days I spent at Barlinnie, I said little to anybody, deciding silence was a virtue. The ordeal of that hellhole ended when I and three others were driven in a prison van to Polmont. There I would be housed in the Allocation Hall, known as 'Ally Cally', while the authorities decided where I should be placed next.

I was surprised to be greeted by a couple of guys in suits, and at first wondered if they were CID officers. Then I realised they were warders, that the staff didn't wear uniforms but everyday clothing. Any hopes I had that this was a sign of a more relaxed regime were instantly dispelled when, as though reading my thoughts, one of the suits stepped forward. 'Surprised, are we, lads?' he asked, with a horrible crooked smile that didn't quite reach his eyes. Then, gesturing in the direction of a row of cells, he added, 'Just because we don't wear uniforms in here doesn't mean we're a soft touch, so get in those fucking boxes and get your gear off now!'

At the time, the Scots sprinter Alan Wells was the fastest runner in Britain. He went on to win an Olympic gold medal in 1980. But in the race to the dug boxes that day he would have finished a poor second behind me. We emerged wearing red striped shirts and coarse black trousers that itched. As we four new arrivals lined up, a screw told us we would spend eight weeks in Ally Cally after which, depending on our behaviour, we would either stay at Polmont or be moved to an open borstal.

'Right, ladies,' said the suit as he showed us to our cells, 'when you get up in the morning, and you'll get up exactly when you're told to get up, you will make your bed and fold your sheet and blankets.' He introduced us to another inmate, a veteran of a month at Polmont, who was to show us the ropes. 'All right, mate? You look a bit lost,' he said to me. 'Don't worry, we're all like that when we first come in.'

I watched him folding the bed-sheets and blankets into a square. 'That's what you call a bed block,' he said. 'You've got to do that first thing in the morning when you get up.' I told him that didn't seem too bad, but his reply shattered my optimism. 'Yeah, but you get up at half six and either go straight to the gym or get dragged there. Listen, you don't ask in here. You wait to be told what to do. It's like being in the Army, and the suits don't take any messing about.'

The next morning, I discovered he was right. I was still struggling to make my bed block when a set of muscles wearing shorts and a T-shirt and with a whistle hanging round its neck screamed at me to, 'Get fucking out now.' Before I knew it, I was falling in line behind everyone as they were hopping – yes, hopping – along the landing, hands behind heads. I had just been introduced to the notorious 'bunny hop'. By the time I reached the gym, my legs were killing me, I was out of breath and sweat was pouring from me. The bunny hop was only for starters. There followed a nightmare of running, jumping and carrying each other around, all at full speed. At breakfast, I wondered how long I'd have to endure this before I could just go home and get on with my life. I daydreamed about the blonde I'd met at the house party and wondered how Gary, Alan and Tracy were getting on and if Ma was doing OK.

Suddenly one of the suits screamed out, 'MacDonald.'

'Aye, that's me,' I said, and instantly knew from his look I'd made a mistake.

'"That's me, sir", you little fucker,' he told me.

I was literally pushed into the office of the governor, who looked at my file and told me, 'You are here because you are a nuisance to society and it's our job to rehabilitate those who are nuisances. Maybe we can make you into a good, law-abiding citizen and you can go back to your community and no longer be such a pest to everyone.' He closed the file. The interview was over and I was made to run back to my cell.

The early rises, bunny hops and ridiculous sprinting around the gym were bad enough. The food was worse, a tasteless slop of three courses slapped onto a metal tray and eaten with plastic cutlery. The afternoon was spent scrubbing corridors, resulting in painful knees, adding to the discomfort of already aching muscles. Another inmate, a friendly guy who introduced himself as 'Aikey', explained the routine for the remainder of the day and demonstrated again how to make up the bed block. That evening, during the two-hour free period, I looked in on the recreation room, but it was Thursday and the seats around the television were crammed with boys watching *Top of the Pops*.

I couldn't wait to be locked up that first night. Already, I was sick of Polmont and the boot-camp regime. The next morning, the routine was repeated. And so it went on, day after day. Until I went to Polmont, I had never been much of a reader, but one of the boys gave me *Papillon*, the true story of a guy wrongly convicted of a murder in France and sentenced to a life of hard labour. I became so immersed in the book that I found myself looking forward to lock-up, when I could open its pages. Reading about the exotic locations and passionate women he described was an escape for me from the boredom and grind of Polmont. My new-found enjoyment of books would serve me well over the years.

After two weeks, I was visited by Ma, Alan and Tracy. On the way to the visiting room, one of the guys told me his girlfriend was coming with their two-year-old son. 'You have a son? You don't look old enough,' I said, and he told me, 'I'm 18, mate, just turned 16 when he was born.' At that time, I was 16, and it was strange to think of having a child.

Tracy came running towards me, smiling and shouting my name. One of the suits stepped towards her, waving his hands. 'You're not allowed in this area,' he told her. 'Please go back to your table.' She ran past him and I lifted her up, telling her how much I had missed her, but the suit, clearly furious, stormed up, shouting, 'Put her down and get over to your table.'

'My boss is having a bad day,' I whispered to Tracy as I put her down. It would become an in-joke in later years, when I would tell my son, niece and nephews that I was 'working in the Big Pub' to explain my absence from their lives.

All too soon, the visit was over. When the family left, I felt down. They had reminded me what I was missing back at home. It was easy enough to take my mind off the outside world when I was bunny-hopping, tearing around the gym or scrubbing corridors. But when those you love are sitting right in front of you, you can't avoid that feeling of knowing you're missing everything that's happening outside. So many prisoners go through a horrible black hole of depression and emptiness after visits from the family.

In the weeks that followed, however, I felt I was getting into the swing of things, coping better. In the seclusion of my cell, I would write the occasional letter to Ma or Gary. Over the years, Ma would clock up more miles than Marco Polo, travelling all over Britain to visit Gary and myself in some of Her Majesty's institutions.

I met guys from all over Glasgow, like Frank Ward from Possil, Big Lurch from the Calton and Muiry from Milton. I got to know them when I was down at recreation or at the gym, when we were allowed to take a breather. Then there was Shug O'Donnell from Barlanark, who was older than me. I would meet him again many years later, when he had become a successful businessman and professional gambler and racehorse owner. Eventually, I became good friends with his sister Christine, who lives in the East End of Glasgow.

During my stay in Ally Cally, waiting to be assessed, I kept out of trouble. I was truthful when the time came for me to appear before the Allocation Board, and I told them, 'I know what I did was wrong. I just really miss my family, and I want to go home as soon as possible.' My honesty must have impressed them, because

BUNNY HOP

I was moved to an open borstal at Castle Huntly near Dundee.

The Castle was so different from anywhere I had been before. The atmosphere was relaxed and the suits didn't give me such a hard time. By June 1977, I had been there a month and had served more than three months of my borstal time. I was working in the cookhouse but hoping for a job in the gardening party, so I could be out in the country. One of the perks of starting work in the cookhouse was that I was moved into a single cell, as I had to be up half an hour earlier than the rest of the borstal population in order to help with preparing breakfast. At first, I didn't like working in the kitchen. My job was washing pots, pans, trays and everything else used to feed more than 100 hungry borstal boys. But another perk was that at one o'clock I could have a shower and a rest in my cell, either reading or getting in a quick sleep, while the rest of the lads were busy in the workshops. Since we were now into the summer months, I was allowed to walk in the grounds and around the football pitch, and I would sometimes spend an afternoon lying on the grass sunbathing. I would then return to the kitchen at four to face a pile of kitchenware that needed to be scrubbed and thoroughly cleaned.

While I waited for my move to the gardening party, I was promoted to the fruit and vegetable table, where the job consisted of cleaning these eatables then chopping and slicing them for cooking by others higher up the chain. Clearly, my work impressed, because after another month I was again promoted and trusted with the task of making porridge, rice and custard. I was taught to mix the ingredients in huge containers, which I would watch over till the food was ready. It was easy once I had the hang of doing it, and gave me more free time in the afternoons to sunbathe. In fact, it was such a good number that when I was eventually offered a job in the gardening party I asked to stay in the cookhouse. I didn't tell the bosses that yet another perk of the cookhouse was that I could more or less eat as much as I wanted and sneak out food for my friends, who by now included a few of the boys from Paisley like brothers Basil and Bonzo Burns, Big Hendy, Budgie and Mailley. I always made sure my pals got extra chips from the serving hatch and I regularly smuggled sandwiches and cakes out for guys to eat in bed at night. In return, I was given Mars Bars, soap, toothpaste and shampoo.

In August, the borstal laid on an open day, when families could visit the inmates. There was food for everyone and a seven-a-side football tournament. That sparked a lot of interest, but not so much as the transfer that month of Kenny Dalglish from Celtic to Liverpool for a British record of £440,000. He'd been a Rangers fan in his younger days. For some, though, the highlight of the open day was the chance to disappear into the bushes and trees with their girlfriends for a few whirlwind moments of passion. That was the same month that Elvis Presley died, his health shattered by years of drug abuse, a problem that would in the years to come account for some of my friends.

Soon, the time came for me to appear before another board, which would decide if I would be allowed privileges such as home visits during the next few months. A good result would mean my exchanging the red shirt for a blue one. A blue shirt meant that you were an old hand who was being prepared for ultimate release. Yet again, I'd tried to be on my best behaviour, but there was one black mark against me that could have set back my chances of staying at Castle Huntly. Not long after I'd arrived there, a guy from Dundee had decided to bully me. I couldn't let this continue, because to do so would have been a sign that I was a coward and vulnerable to becoming a whipping boy for all and sundry.

So I offered him a square go, a fist fight. Because he was three years older and bigger than me, he poked fun at my challenge, but then I walked up, kicked him in the face and when he went down punched him again and again. I began seeing him as Da. I actually believed for a few minutes, in the haze of my temper, that this guy was Da, who'd battered poor Ma senseless. Now I was getting payback. The officer on night duty heard the fuss and broke it up. When the governor asked what had happened, I stayed silent, but my opponent blamed it all on me, and as a result I was given an extra 28 days on my sentence. But once the other guys learned how the bully had grassed me up, he became the whipping boy.

The board decided the extra 28 days was punishment enough. I didn't get my blue shirt that day, but I received it a month later. Now I could smell freedom.

On her next visit, Ma gave me the news that Gary had escaped from Oakbank in a stolen car with two friends and was being hunted by the police, who had been to her house looking for him. She hadn't wanted to tell me about this in a letter, thinking I already had enough of my own worries. In fact, the opposite was the case. I was doing my time well enough but always worried how Gary was coping.

My second Christmas away from home was approaching, but by now I was well settled into life at the Castle and nine months into my borstal. Wee Aikey, who I'd met in Ally Cally and who had been such a help, was due for release and went, leaving me still there. But I had lots of other friends, and in January I was allowed four hours of freedom in Dundee with my family.

It was great to get out of jail clothes and back into civvies and trainers for my big day out. Ma, Alan and Tracy arrived early by train and bus, and our first stop was a café, where I ordered my favourite ice cream, a knickerbocker glory. This was pure heaven. I'd had visions of a vodka and coke, but the other inmates had warned me that if I was caught drinking alcohol I could end up in serious trouble and it might even hinder my release, which had been set for the last week in February, a week before my 17th birthday. Sure enough, back at the Castle I was given a strip search. Staff had expected me to smuggle in drink or cigarettes, but I had none. They even smelled my breath to check for alcohol, and I realised the guys had been right to warn me off taking a drink. All the checks showed up was a chocolate-stained mouth from my ice cream.

Now there were just six weeks to go. I had heard the term 'gate fever' used for the first time while I was in Castle Huntly. It was an expression with which I would become familiar. It simply meant someone was coming to the end of his sentence and couldn't stop thinking of the day he would be released. That day finally came for me at the end of February. After saying my farewells, and with a train ticket for Glasgow in my pocket, I was driven off, convinced I would never see the place again. Little did I know that a quarter of a century later I would once again be driven up that sweeping path to the Castle reception, as a 42-year-old hardened criminal. For now, though, I was turning 17 and the world was my oyster.

4

Sweaty Socks

NIGHT AFTER NIGHT when I was locked up, I had imagined a reunion with my beautiful blonde. Now my dreams were about to become reality. I'd become a regular at the Open Arms pub in Riddrie, meeting up with pals from my schooldays, including Davie Beattie from Blackhill, and the Stoddards, Brian and Joe. I would also see Andy Breen and was friendly with his brothers, Robert and John. My life seemed back on track; things were looking up.

Freed from Castle Huntly, I had gone back home to Ma – who was still working at Foresthall Hospital – Alan and Tracy. Gary was now in another approved school, Geilsland in Beith, Ayrshire, having been caught after a month on the run. I was determined to stay out of trouble and luck seemed with me, because a couple of weeks after my release Ma introduced me to Duncan Lightbody, one of the bosses of a heating engineering firm based in Maryhill, Glasgow. Even though Ma was frank about my past troubles, about how I'd gone off the rails after I was expelled from school, to my surprise, he asked if I would be interested in working for him. Everyone deserved a second chance, he said. He had a partner, George McKerracher. The firm was called McKerracher and Lightbody Heating Engineers, and Mr Lightbody said I could start there the following week. So I began my very first job since the paper round of my schooldays. Most nights when I came home from work I would be knackered and, after having my tea, would fall asleep on the couch. But I was still learning and enjoying my trade. Furthermore, it was all legal, and at weekends I felt entitled to go out and spend the money I'd earned legitimately.

That's how I happened to be at the Open Arms. There was a disco and I was singing along to the Abba hit 'Take a Chance on Me' when I heard someone say my name and felt a tap on my shoulder. I turned to see a gorgeous face smiling at me. 'Don't you recognise me?' she asked. Of course I did. I'd seen her face in my mind a million times since I'd been sent to borstal. It felt like I'd just been struck by a bolt of lightning. It was the blonde from the party. She wore a figure-hugging black dress that started just above her knees and her blue eyes sparkled. She seemed impressed when I said I now had a job, and as we talked the night whizzed past.

We parted with a kiss on the cheek and the promise of a date the following week, when I took her to the cinema then sneaked her into Ma's house, where we were soon naked in bed. While I recovered from the best sex I had known, she told me she hoped I would never see the inside of a prison cell again. Then she added, 'My uncle doesn't want me to see you. He says you're no good and you'll always be no good.'

Was he being prophetic? That November, after a drunken night out with pals in Glasgow city centre, we stupidly decided it might be fun to steal a car. The inevitable result was that I was arrested by police in Royston Road after a high-speed chase and was packed off on remand to Longriggend. I cursed myself for what I had done. I wasn't forced into that car; it was my own choice. I couldn't understand why I kept allowing myself to get into these situations. I spent the time sulking, knowing my job and the blonde were gone.

At Glasgow Sheriff Court, I pleaded guilty and was sent to a young offenders' institution for three months and disqualified from driving for five years. The sentence was backdated to when I'd been arrested, so I was freed in January 1979.

To my amazement, Mr Lightbody offered me my job back, but I knew I would be too embarrassed to face people who had given me such a huge chance to turn my life around, and nor could I trust myself not to fuck up once more. So I decided that never again would I work another nine-to-five job. Instead, I'd start a career as a full-time criminal.

It wasn't long, therefore, before I was breaking the law again. This was the path I'd chosen. My life as a professional crook began with visits to Glasgow city centre with a girl I knew who was skilled at shoplifting. We would emerge from big department stores like Marks & Spencer and British Home Stores carrying bags full of clothes, which were always easy to sell on. Security then was lax and I could comfortably double or treble the money I had earned as a heating engineer.

As I became more adept, my confidence grew and I widened my area of operations. I would go to Blackpool, for instance, for a three-day rampage and head back with a car boot packed with clothes and video recorders, which were very much in demand then. Others joined me on these sprees, but it all ended in disaster during a trip to Blackpool with two friends from Provanmill, one of them Brian Martin, and a girl from Govan. We were tailed to our digs by police, who found a couple of video recorders and bags of stolen clothes from shops in Preston and Blackpool. We three boys were remanded to a notorious haunt, HMP Risley, better known as 'Grizzly Rizzly', near Warrington in Cheshire. The place was full of guys on remand, mostly from Liverpool. Most of the windows in this tip had been smashed by rioting inmates. It was a real dump.

From the very start, I was noised up by a section of guys on my landing just because I was Scottish, and for the first time I heard a phrase they used for us down there: 'sweaty socks', cockney rhyming slang for 'Jocks'. One guy in particular was forever annoying me. Something needed to be done, and one day I walked into his cell carrying a sock with a battery inside and repeatedly smashed it over his head as he lay on his bed reading. He started screaming and alarm bells sounded. I made myself scarce, but within an hour a crowd of warders manhandled me to the segregation block, calling me a 'typical Scottish bastard' and asking if I was from the Gorbals. That night, the Scousers were singing, 'The Jock's in the block, the

Jock's in the block, ee aye addio, the Jock's in the block.' They went on for hours, but I laughed to think that while they'd call us sweaty socks, it was with a sock that I'd meted out rough justice to their loudmouth bully pal.

When I appeared before Blackpool magistrates on 11 June 1979, I was sent to a young offenders' institution for six months. Brian was given three months' detention while the other guy and the girl got suspended sentences, allowing them to go home. I was dubbed up in the infamous Walton jail to await a transfer to an institution and found myself next to Donny MacDonald from Cambuslang, who soon became a good friend.

I was much cheered by a visit from Gary, who had finished his time at Geilsland. With him came Colin and Pat Friel, our mates from Provanmill. It was obvious they had been drinking. Pat was wearing a kilt, and when he walked into the visiting room he spotted me and yelled, 'There's McHaggis!' At one stage, he asked a screw, 'Want to know what a true Scotsman wears under his kilt?' He kept jumping on our table and shouting, 'Hoots, mon, get it up, yes!', and inevitably my visitors were thrown out. 'All you Jocks are mad,' a warder told me.

My move to a young offenders' institution never happened, and instead I was told I was being returned to Scotland to face an outstanding charge at Glasgow Sheriff Court of being in a stolen car. This came as a pleasant surprise, because it would mean being near my family and away from any revenge attacks for my battering of the Grizzly Rizzly bigmouth. Donny was to be transferred north of the border, too.

But then came disturbing news. In a letter, Ma told me that Alan had been sent to St John's Approved School in Edinburgh Road, Glasgow. It was virtually next door to my first institution, Larchgrove. Now all three of us brothers had been to approved schools and I felt sorry for Ma, who must have been embarrassed when meeting up with her sisters, my aunts Chrissie and Madge, knowing no one in their families had been in trouble. I worried about whether Alan could handle himself and about the effect of this on Ma.

SWEATY SOCKS

Donny and I were moved together, and our journey north was broken by a five-day stay at Low Newton Remand Centre, Durham. I was just 18 years old but had already seen the inside of three jails in England alone. This would not be my only visit to the historic town of Durham. I didn't know it then, but I would be returning. Eventually, we arrived at Glenochil Young Offenders Institution in Stirlingshire. A kindly screw arranged for Donny and me to be in adjoining cells, and the other boys in our section made us feel welcome. They asked the usual questions. Where are you from? What's your sentence? What are you in for? How long are you in for? And I would ask exactly the same. Every first conversation in prison began like that.

The sheriff gave me a paltry six weeks to run consecutive to my six months, which meant I'd be released in November. Donny wasn't so lucky. He thought he had done a deal to get a shorter sentence of around nine months but instead was given another two years. After that, his mood changed and he told warders he would not be going to work.

'You'll not get paid, then, or be allowed into the recreation room,' was the response.

'I can handle that,' Donny replied.

He started a silent protest, so he couldn't be accused of causing disciplinary problems, and spent the majority of his time in his cell. I tried to make him see that what he was doing was pointless, because he was hurting only himself, but it was to no avail.

As my liberation day neared, Donny and a few of the other boys in the section had a booze-up one Saturday afternoon. The others had been secretly making hooch and reckoned it was now ready for drinking. By this time, I had made lots of good friends, boys like Wee Mo Morrison from Govan and Sammy Ralston, 'Sammo the Bear', from Cranhill. Sammo is a really good pal to this day. In 1987, he was involved in a riot at Peterhead prison in Aberdeenshire in which a warder was taken hostage. Prime Minister Margaret Thatcher sent in the SAS, the first time these elite soldiers had been used to end trouble in a British jail.

Before we were locked up at five o'clock, I took four one-litre

41

bottles of hooch into my cell to share with Donny. I'd pass him his share on a makeshift line, made from shoelaces, running between our windows. I had been boozing most of the day and was already half drunk and heading for the kind of drunkenness that leads to violence.

In between quaffing the home-made sherry, Donny and I had booze-fuelled blethers out of the windows. We were having the time of our lives and, like the drink, the hours flowed by. But it all started to go wrong when he began to trash his cell, throwing what little he had out of the window, encouraged by other inmates. He ripped up his mattress and smashed the ceiling light. Things became really serious when Donny began shouting threats against the screws. I tried to calm him down, but the noise was deafening and it was only a matter of time before they arrived in force.

And they did, but what happened was to leave me with a horrible sense of injustice. Screws started running down the corridor and one of the inmates screamed to Donny, 'You're getting a beating.' But it was my door and not his that clicked open. Why? I thought. Then a sickening realisation came to me. Donny's second name was MacDonald, the same as mine. The screws had the wrong cell, but it was too late to do anything about it, to explain they were making a mistake. They piled into my cell and I started swinging my fists, hoping to catch a few of them, but I was dragged to the ground and felt sharp blows all over my body. Somebody grabbed my wrists and pulled me out into the hallway. The solitary confinement unit was linked to our cell block by a long corridor known as 'the Russian Front'. It was the main artery of the prison and seemed to stretch for ever. I was dragged along the whole length of it, kicked, punched and beaten every agonising inch of the way. My ordeal only finished when I reached solitary at the end of the Front and was thrown into one of the tiny cells, coughing, wheezing and gasping for breath. It was a struggle just to stand up.

I was stunned and could not believe they had opened my door. OK, so Donny and I happened to have the same second name, but doubtless others shared it. A noise interrupted my thoughts and I heard Donny crashing into the cell across from mine, having received similar vicious treatment. My feeling of injustice strengthened with each hour and I told myself, 'They'll realise their mistake and in the morning they'll be coming in here to apologise.' Of course, that was a pie-in-the-sky hope. Like others before and since, I discovered that authority does not know how to say the word 'sorry'.

The events of the next morning, when it came, left me convinced that anyone hauled into the governor's office on a disciplinary charge could forget any prospect of receiving an apology, an admission they had been wrongly or unfairly treated. Through the years, I have learned that prison governors all over Britain don't accept not-guilty pleas by inmates to allegations that they have broken the rules. I learned a lesson that day that would serve me well on my many future visits to governors' offices. No matter what the circumstances, expect absolutely nothing but a guilty verdict. What took place left me bitter and disgusted, feelings that remain.

The night of the disturbance, I heard footsteps heading down the Russian Front in my direction. The cell door opened and a warder appeared, but not to apologise. Instead, he told me, 'MacDonald, you will be appearing in front of the governor tomorrow.'

I was staggered and demanded, 'What for? I've done nothing.' But I could tell he wasn't in the least interested in anything I might want to say.

'You've been shouting abuse out of your window and were spotted throwing things.'

I had been bashed and bruised. Now I was to be stitched up by the battering squad, expected to take the blame for their mistake and their brutality towards me.

Next day, with my body still throbbing and aching, I appeared before the governor and pleaded not guilty to breaching discipline. Two screws said they had heard me shouting and seen me throwing things from the cell window. I tried putting up a defence, protesting that they had the wrong man, pointing out that Donny and I had the same surname. But it was clear I was wasting my time. They went through the formality of listening, then announced I was guilty and would have seven days added to my sentence, to be served in 'the digger', the solitary confinement unit. Later, I heard Donny had received double this punishment.

I did my seven days quietly. There wasn't much I could do, apart from pacing up and down for hours on end, taking four steps in one direction, then turning and repeating the drill over and over. It is a routine I have never been able to shake off. To this day, I still do a lot of pacing, wherever I am.

My punishment over, I served the remaining few weeks of my sentence in another wing at Glenochil. It was good to spend Christmas and New Year at Ma's instead of being banged up. None of the festive cheer that hung around Glasgow, in the city lights, the Christmas shopping, the carol singers, extended to prison.

That year, the movie *The Deer Hunter*, starring Robert De Niro and Christopher Walken, was released. It was about American soldiers in Vietnam being captured and forced to play Russian roulette. Walken caught my eye and I followed his career avidly over the next few decades. He made a film that is one of my all-time favourites, *King of New York*, in which his character is released from prison and steps into a limousine. The significance of that scene to me was not lost on my family.

horseback waded in with their batons to try to break it up. As usual, the police took a heavy-handed approach, smashing innocent people across the head. This riot led to an alcohol ban that still prevails in Scottish football to this day.

In June that year, my pal Joe Steele's two brothers, John and Jim, from Garthamlock, and their friend Archie Steen escaped from Barlinnie prison while there for visits from Peterhead. They got onto the roof from the shower room just before breakfast on a Sunday morning and tied a rope to the chimney. Somebody was waiting on the other side of the prison wall to tie the other end to a screw's washing pole. The three abseiled to freedom and in the process highlighted the brutality against prisoners in Peterhead. One of my friends, who was in the same Barlinnie hall as the escapers, later told me he would be forever grateful to them, as he ended up getting their breakfasts – three boiled eggs.

Gary, meanwhile, had stabbed someone in Barmulloch one night, and was sent to borstal in Polmont. 'Doing your share of the bunny hops, then?' I'd ask him on visits. Alan was released not long after Gary went to Polmont. It seemed one of us would be freed just as another was going to jail. This went on for some time.

I started going about with a guy I'll call Jack Woods and Paul Ferris. I'd known Paul for a few years, because he used to hang around with Alan. One day we were playing pool at Jack's home with a friend, Tam Malloy, when the CID arrived. We assumed they were on the lookout for Paul, who was on the run from the police, who wanted to interview him about minor offences, so Jack opened up the little compartment inside the table into which the balls ran. Paul was so wee and skinny then that he managed to climb inside the pool table and stay there until the police left.

Paul delivered booze to pubs and clubs and said the job made him around £50 a week. Although he was sixteen and three years younger than me, I respected him as a very game boy. Also from Blackhill, he had fought with the local Welsh family. He knew I had graduated from shoplifting to jewel thefts and that I was forever running around Hogganfield Loch to keep fit, but he didn't know how the two activities were connected. He was aware, from Alan – 'Alco' to his friends by now – that I was usually pocketing £500 in cash, although a really good haul could make me a couple of thousand pounds.

One day, Paul asked, 'Blink, I'm working in this job for peanuts compared to what you're making. Alco's told me what you're doing. Can I join up with you?' I liked Paul and knew he was game enough, so I agreed to take him on and show him how it was done. I explained how I dressed well, spoke politely to whoever was serving me, planned everything minutely and knew exactly where I was heading after snatching the tray. I emphasised to Paul, 'Don't mess about, because if you do then that's when your bottle will go.'

He was still keen, so I took him to Dunfermline and said, 'Watch this.' I told him, 'See your fifty quid? You're going to make five hundred today, at least.' That was a lot of money in 1980.

Fergie was amazed at the detail of the planning. I told him, 'Sit in the car and wait for me. I won't be long – ten minutes maybe.' I was back in nine minutes, a £3,000 tray of rings hidden beneath my coat. Pulling open the car door, I jumped in and told him, 'Right, drive.'

He did, and as we made our getaway I opened my coat to show him the haul. 'Fucking hell,' said Paul. We went to a resetter in Glasgow who would usually give me a third or a fourth of the face value and left his home with £1,000, of which I gave Paul half.

'You're doing the next one,' I told him. And he did.

I took him to a jeweller's and pointed out a tray in the window filled with rings worth thousands of pounds. We'd carefully worked out his escape route, and while I waited in the car he came up trumps. Fergie leapt triumphantly into the motor, shouting, 'Right, drive,' and off we went. He thought it was great.

And so Paul became my apprentice. What he knew, he learned from me and I suppose I started him in a career as a criminal. He was right up for the jewellery grabs. Jack came along sometimes, but he had a different technique, and one that inevitably meant a bigger prize. Not one for subtlety, he preferred the 'smash and grab' approach, which involved using sledgehammers to smash in the windows and, during the commotion, grabbing as many trays of rings, watches and bracelets as we could carry, before making our way back to the car, usually a stolen motor, where Paul would be sitting waiting to drive us away to safety.

Smash-and-grabs were incredibly profitable, and the three of us ventured all over Scotland and down into England in search of suitable targets. Money just seemed to roll in. It was never a problem offloading the goods because there were plenty of fences in Glasgow at that time who were happy to take the booty off our hands. If we got a tray of diamond rings, say, valued at £40,000 retail price, we could look to be getting £10,000.

Throughout my life I've never been one for keeping money in the bank. After all, banks get robbed, don't they? And I should know. 'Have it, spend it' has been my philosophy, and so it was in those early days. My money bought me a good time – frequenting the city centre, splashing cash on drinks, clothes and women. I wasn't into drugs then, though as I got older I would find myself succumbing to them. Now and again, Jack and I would give a girl a diamond ring as a present to try to win her heart. To us, it was nothing more than a gesture, as if we were buying her a drink. What was the odd diamond or two to us when we were stealing thousands of pounds' worth of them every fortnight?

Paul and I became really good friends. We'd socialise together, going out purely with the intention of having fun. We used to visit clubs like the Jamaica Inn in Glasgow, and one night Fergie challenged me to a contest to see who could down a pint in one go, no stopping for breath. I was older and bigger than him, but whereas I couldn't finish mine, he emptied his glass.

At the same time, Paul and I were building up a reputation for ourselves, not just as jewel thieves but for serious violence. We would carry Stanley knives, and when we got into trouble at bars or clubs in town or elsewhere, full of drink, we would pull out our Stanleys and start assaulting those who'd offended us. At that time, I probably cut about a dozen people myself, and that's how the tag 'Blink' was given another meaning. It was said I could slash somebody before they had time to blink. But this is not a version that I have ever endorsed. As for the victims, I didn't feel anything, certainly not sympathy. That's how it was then. Some of these people were trying to hurt me; I was simply trying to get in there first.

Sometimes I would have a few drinks in the Provanmill Inn, and I would often see Arthur Thompson in there, because it was Arthur's local. I didn't take special notice of him. He was older and I respected him, and that was it. But I would discover he had been taking notice of me.

Ma, meantime, had started a job in the Manx Bar, across from the Royal Infirmary in Glasgow. She worked downstairs in the lounge. I went to see her occasionally and one night bumped into an old friend from Longriggend, Star Keenan. He was with his friend Gall and Gall's brothers Bobby and Dessy, from Royston.

Ma was seeing James McGill on a regular basis and one night, while they were drunk, I picked up James's keys to his taxi and went out for a spin. I never turned on the 'for hire' light; I just drove into the city for a while and back up the road again. It was immense fun, particularly when a few people tried flagging me down by putting their arms out, hoping to get me to stop. When I got back to Ma's home, neither she nor James had realised I'd borrowed his cab. However, while I'd been driving about in the hackney, my mind had clicked into gear and a plan had started to form. As usual, it involved making money. When I confided to Jack and Fergie what I had in mind, they were both amazed but enthusiastic. So we scouted about the city centre and clocked a few shops in which we were interested. They were packed with the most fashionable gear of the day: suits, leather jackets, designer shirts and denims.

That weekend, at one o'clock in the morning, while James was asleep at Ma's house, I took the keys to his hackney cab. My accomplices were waiting at Fergie's home and it was obvious from their expressions that the pair of them couldn't believe the plan was really happening as I drove up, pumped the horn, pulled down the driver's window and told them to get in. They climbed into the back as though they were fare-paying passengers. 'Told you I'd get it, no problem,' I said.

We headed into the centre of Glasgow and they jumped out at the shop we had decided to rob. I parked around the corner, waited until I heard the alarms go off, then drove back and we filled the taxi with stolen suits and leathers. I reckoned we had two minutes before the police arrived, but that was all we needed. 'Right, boys, time up,' I shouted, and they piled in clutching more gear. As we drove off, I saw a police car, its blue lights flashing, heading towards us and ordered the pair in the back to duck down. The police shot past, clearly seeing me as a late-night cabbie on his way home. We roared with laughter and Jack took us to a lock-up garage where we stashed our loot. Then I drove my passengers home.

We used the 'hackney raiders' plan a few more times before James tippled that something was going on. He mentioned to Ma that he'd been noticing how the level of the diesel gauge seemed to mysteriously drop. Because of my age, if I'd driven up to a garage in a black cab and filled it up, it would have attracted suspicion. So we gave up the taxi trade, but we'd had a good run out of it. And then Fergie went off to work for Arthur Thompson – but that was by no means the end of our relationship.

6

Stanley Gang

THERE ARE TIMES when I feel most of my life has been spent looking into the eyes of a good-looking girl or out through the bars of a prison window. I've never been able to resist a smile from soft, red lips. Women have brought me a bewildering mixture of pain, pleasure and occasionally trouble.

It was 1980, and I was regularly turning up at the Provanmill Inn, 'the Provy', where Arthur Thompson would sit at the bar noting everything that happened and everybody who came in. I'd been dating one of the barmaids, Patricia McLaughlin, a stunning brunette with a lovely and lively personality. The Provy had a reputation as a Celtic pub and one night two of the players, Charlie Nicholas and Danny Crainie, came along for a function. Charlie was making his name in the first team by this time, scoring in nearly every game. He scored that night, too, with Patricia. Afterwards, everyone would chant 'Charlie is your darling' when she walked by. But by then she wasn't my darling.

Gary's luck with women was even worse. At the start of 1981, I was arrested for driving while disqualified and remanded to Longriggend, where I met George Madden for the first time, along with Toaly, Big Gibby and Tony McGurn, who were from the Springburn area. I also got to know Big Cux from Ruchazie and Des McKeown from Hamilton, who were in for a shotgun murder. They eventually got life and served about 18 years each. Anyway, not long after I arrived I was caught fighting with another boy and

52

put into a section for unruly inmates known as 'the Dog Leg'. While I was in there, Frank Ward told me he'd seen Gary – 'Gash' to his friends – arriving at reception. The next morning, another pal, Terry Curran, discovered why Gary was there, and his news devastated me. Gary was accused of attempted murder.

I behaved myself to get out of the Dog Leg so I could talk to Gary and find out what had happened. It was all over a woman, he told me.

'I nipped a burd at the St Roch club and asked her to come back to Ma's. She told me to come to her sister's. But when I get there this guy answers the door, points to her and says, "That's my burd."'

Gary's date had fallen out with her bloke and taken Gary along to spite her boyfriend and make him jealous.

'What happened?' I asked.

'He was too cheeky, so I just cut his throat with a Stanley,' said Gary.

I felt gutted for him and helpless. Not half as sorry as the guy with the cut throat, of course.

I kept making polite requests to be housed beside Gary, but these were fobbed off with excuses, and I was becoming increasingly frustrated about the fact that nobody seemed prepared to listen to me. This led to a fierce argument with a warder who came to my cell one day. 'Address me as Mr MacDonald from now on,' I told him, and flicked his cap off. When he tried locking my door, I jammed it with my foot then pushed him flat on his backside, and he screamed for reinforcements. The next day, I was hauled in front of the governor and sent to solitary for seven days. The other boys shouted encouragement when they spotted me alone in the exercise yard, calling, 'Go on yersel', Blink! Keep the heid up!' I'd been in the digger six days when a warder wound me up, saying there'd be no exercise that day because it was raining. He found some excuse why I couldn't exercise indoors and I was locked back up. I banged and kicked at the cell door, with the result that I was given another seven days' solitary. I'd had enough. I decided it was time to have some fun and noise up the warders.

At exercise the next day, I shinned up a drainpipe and clambered onto a roof. 'MacDonald, come down!' warders were shouting, while other inmates yelled support and banged on their windows. My mind was made up; there was no turning back now. I felt on top of the world and started giving the warders abuse, pointing out that they'd be in trouble for letting me slip away from them, then ripping up slates and hurling them at screws. I spotted a particularly unpopular one, a bully known as 'the Pie Man' because he used to pinch our food, and took careful aim. He had to duck and weave his way to cover. After a while, I was knackered, my hands bleeding, but the adrenalin was pumping.

The governor showed his face after an hour. 'Just come down, Ian,' he said. 'You'll get a hot dinner and I'll review your case.'

That was shorthand for more time in the digger. I lobbed slates in his direction and told him, 'You're wasting your time. Get the fuck away.' When the bill came for the damage, he'd have to explain all this to the Scottish Office in Edinburgh.

I stayed there for nine hours, ripping up three-quarters of the roof, giving up just before midnight. I had been promised there would be no beating, and in my cell I was kindly given a cup of tea and a sandwich. I didn't touch either, suspecting that what was in them wasn't milk or brown sauce.

I lay back on my mattress – there were no beds in solitary confinement – and fell fast asleep. But my rest lasted only a couple of hours. I was woken by a commotion, shouting and swearing. Someone was pushed into the next cell and the door slammed shut. It was Wardy, who told me that he and Gary had smashed up their cells while a dozen inmates threw furniture out of their windows and others started fires. I felt proud that the mutiny had been in support of me. Wardy said he was naked and still handcuffed. Minutes later, Gary was dragged into an adjoining cell. 'You all right, Gash?' I shouted, and heard him yell back, 'Aye, but my baws are killing me.' That made me and Wardy laugh. We knew that whatever had been done to Gary it hadn't destroyed his spirit or sense of humour.

Later that morning, we were driven to the dreaded Barlinnie, taken to D Hall and read the riot act. They told us that if we kept out of trouble and acted like men, we would be treated as such. If not, we could expect every bone in our bodies to be broken. So we kept our heads down.

Gary's trial was set for May 1981, and that month Scotland went to Wembley and came away with a win, John Robertson scoring the only goal of the game. We wondered if that might be a good omen, but a few days later Gary was jailed for eight years. We had hoped he might get no more than four, and I was shattered, wondering how he would get through such a sentence.

He was to be transferred the next day, but a kindly warder let us have a few minutes together.

'Did the guy and the burd grass you in?' I asked.

'Of course they did,' he said.

At the end of June at Hamilton Sheriff Court, I received three months in a young offenders' institution, backdated to include the time I'd already served, which meant I was released later that night, after returning to Barlinnie for the paperwork to be finalised. It felt great to be free and walking the short distance to Ma's house.

I started going back out to the city centre, usually with Jack Woods. Fergie would come along too, but most times he would get a knock-back from the guys on the door because he was baby-faced and looked underage. The bouncers shouldn't have argued with us. We'd follow them when they finished their shifts and, with our faces covered by balaclavas, attack them with baseball bats and coshes, as well as my favourite weapon, the Stanley knife. I always made sure there was a new blade in before I slashed their faces. We became known as 'the Stanley Gang'.

I was only 20, but I would take cheek from nobody, no matter what their reputation. One night, I was with Jack and one of his pals in Ultrateque disco in Wellington Street in the city centre. A few months earlier, somebody had smashed the window of Jack's dad's home, poured in petrol and set it alight. Jack's dad and his girlfriend were asleep and lucky to escape alive. The same culprit had carried out a similar attack on the uncle and aunt of a pal of mine who lived in Shawlands. We spotted the arsonist, and it was decided that, because he didn't know me, I would be the one to avenge those dreadful attacks. As he emerged from the toilet, I followed him across the dance floor then slashed his face. Jack dragged me away as my victim lay bleeding. We believed we had done a good turn, that we'd probably saved another family from a night of terror.

A while later, though, I was the one hoping for a favour. Alan, Fergie and I, together with another pal, 'Pickles', had been arrested after police stopped a car in which I was a passenger and some tools were found in the boot. We were remanded on the grounds of being a 'known thief', a Mickey Mouse charge the police would use to hold you if you had previous convictions and they couldn't charge you with anything else. I knew there were no problems for Alan and he'd be freed, but the potential consequences for me were serious, because I was also wanted for an alleged assault and could be facing two years' jail.

While we waited in a cell at court for our appearances in front of the sheriff, I turned to Alan and asked, 'Could you do me a massive favour? If the police come to the door and shout for me, will you go in my place?' Alan told me, 'No chance,' but I went on, 'You won't get the jail and it means I can get out. Just tell them my date of birth and they'll believe you.'

Fergie backed me up, saying, 'Alco, it's your brother. You can't see him go to jail, come on,' while Pickles said, 'Just do it, Alco.'

Then came what I hoped was my masterstroke. 'Look, I'll even give you five hundred quid if you do this,' I told Alan. Still he hesitated, so I reminded him, 'Just say it was a mistake. Tell them I made you do it. I'm your brother, for fuck's sake.'

The door opened and two uniformed cops demanded, 'Who is Ian MacDonald?' I shoved Alco forward. 'You Ian MacDonald?' he was asked. He nodded, then gave my date of birth, and off they went. A few minutes later, a turnkey asked for Alan MacDonald and I stood up to be told I was being released without the need to appear in court. I signed for Alan's belongings and went off in a taxi.

Later, I found out Ma and Fergie's dad, Willie, had been in the public gallery waiting for us to appear. When Fergie told them I had got out in Alan's name, Willie, a lovely man, was in stitches at the fact that I'd got one over on the authorities and done a runner. Alan told me all hell had broken loose when the switch was discovered. He'd been interrogated and beaten but had refused to say I had made him pretend to be me. I was happy to increase his compensation.

I stayed on the run until December, when I met up with Fergie one night and told him I was going into the city centre in a stolen car. There were already fake number plates on it. He warned me not to drive, but I ignored him. Later that night, giving a girl a lift as a favour, I crashed into a lamp post near Arthur Thompson's house, breaking my leg. The girl was thrown head first through the windscreen. I knew I would be in trouble, because there was a warrant out for my arrest over the assault allegation and the escape, but I didn't help my cause by kicking one of the cops who tried to help me. That got me a beating in return before I was taken to hospital and then on to prison. 'I've crashed into Barlinnie,' I told a friend.

Two months later, in February 1982, at Glasgow Sheriff Court, I was sent to a young offenders' institution for nine months and found myself back at the Russian Front in Glenochil. My 21st birthday was just a month away, but the only key to the door I saw was the one used by the screw who locked me up.

I spent a lot of time in the gym, trying to get my leg back to normal, and met Andrew Gibson from Royston and Cal Connors from Germiston. Willie Bennett, who worked in the gym, and his pal Gandhi were other fitness fanatics. Sammo the Bear was at Glenochil, too.

When I reached 21, I was categorised, in prison terms, as an adult and sent back to Barlinnie, where I was classed as an escapee. There I met, for the first time, Ernie Barrie from the Gorbals, who was serving two years for assisting two inmates to escape from Perth jail. Any man who'd done that for friends was going to be a friend of mine.

I'd been in the Big House about a month when a pal in a different hall sent word he was being badmouthed by another inmate. I decided to mete out appropriate punishment and made myself a blade – a toothbrush with a disposable razor blade melted into it. I slashed the target in the toilet, disposed of the blade, went to my cell and closed the door. I had told no one what I was going to do. An investigation began and, because I was a suspect, I was moved to another cell, where I found myself next to Tam Moffat. He told me he and his brother James, both of them from Castlemilk, had just been sentenced to 18 years after being convicted in May at the High Court in Airdrie of a spate of armed bank jobs, including one at the Clydesdale Bank in Bridgeton, Glasgow, that the prosecution claimed had netted them £47,000. There were two other brothers in the family, George and Albert.

The screws never discovered the identity of the slasher, but in June I was jailed over the car smash and the assault on the police at the scene. Then it was back to Barlinnie, where I stayed cool until my release in September.

Back on the streets, I began dating a girl from Barmulloch called Lorraine Burns. Jack, meantime, had been arrested after a smash-and-grab in which diamond rings worth £200,000 had been stolen and never recovered. An off-duty policewoman had said she'd seen him with a sledgehammer and had picked him out in an ID parade.

Jack was determined to escape and during a visit I slipped him a centre punch, a tool used for punching holes in metal. The plan was that on the prison bus taking him to court he would use it to smash a window. A close pal promised to follow the bus in a car to pick Jack up once he was out and drive him to freedom.

Things did not go well. Unfortunately, the screws handcuffed Jack to another prisoner, who was only told at the very last minute what was to happen and never asked if he wanted to go along with the escape. It turned out he didn't. What was more, Jack saw a car following the bus, but it was the wrong one. His pal had slept in. Although Jack legged it, dragging his reluctant partner with him, they were soon caught hiding in a garden in Stepps.

At least the escape was good news for another inmate. In the bus, Stephen MacDonald realised what was about to happen, slipped his handcuffs, followed them through the window and disappeared, although he was caught later.

Back in Barlinnie, Jack got a battering and then four years' jail.

Gary was having no luck either. At Glenochil, he punched a warder because his breakfast egg wasn't hard enough. It turned out neither was the screw. The upshot was that Gary was transferred to Jessiefield jail at Dumfries, a move that would spell trouble for me.

A friend whom I'll call Brian Buchanan and I teamed up and raided the odd jewellery shop, and I asked if he would come with me to visit Gary, who had been joined by Jack. At Jessiefield, the warder who took us to the visiting room seemed pleasant enough, and I managed to sneak Gary a lump of hash. On the way home, Brian suggested stopping at Moffat Woollen Mills to get ourselves sheepskin coats, which were really in fashion then. It was easy. We walked in wearing smart suits and out wearing nicked sheepskins over the top. Putting them in the car boot, we headed for Glasgow, intending to show them off that night when we went clubbing at the popular Warehouse in Dunlop Street.

We never made it. When we were nearing Motherwell, a police car stopped us and the copper wanted to know if we'd been to Moffat. We told him no, but then he insisted on looking in the boot and found the coats. Brian said we'd bought them earlier that day in Yorkshire, but the uniform showed us the tags with 'Moffat Woollen Mills' on them. I had the passenger window down and thought about doing a runner but quickly realised an escape wasn't on. 'I can't believe you never took those tags off,' I told Brian. Reinforcements arrived and we started back to Dumfries, handcuffed in the back of a police car.

When we got there, I asked the police what put them onto us and was told that an elderly lady had gone into the Mills and told an assistant, 'I think two young gentlemen have stolen coats from here.' The store said nothing was missing, but she persisted. 'They were smartly dressed in suits and ties. They were in and out in five minutes, and they were wearing sheepskin coats when they left.' The assistant had a look and found two empty coat hangers. 'Did you get a good look at the gentlemen?' she asked, and the lady not only obliged with a description but had also written down our registration number.

We were charged and locked up, and instead of living it up in Warehouse I lay on a thin, stinking mattress, thinking of my lost date and how Gary would be off his nut by now on the best Pakistani black hash I'd given him earlier.

In court the next day, we decided to plead guilty and take a fine. But they clearly didn't like Glaswegians in Dumfries, because the sheriff remanded us in custody for two weeks for reports. We were taken to Jessiefield, not as visitors this time, and by chance the same warder we'd spoken to the previous day met us. He had to look twice to confirm it was us and started laughing. 'Back to stay this time, lads?' he asked, and went off to tell his pals over in the hall where Gary was probably still recovering from his trip on my hash.

7

Godfather Summons

MY TEETH WERE fine, at least I thought so, but I put in a request to visit the prison dentist. So did Brian. We had been asking to meet up with Gary and Jack Woods but were continually refused. They were in another part of Jessiefield. Then came a stiffie (prison jargon for a smuggled message) telling us that we should complain of needing dental treatment. Gary and Jack would do the same, allowing us to see one another in the medical centre waiting room. Anybody who has seen the film version of *Porridge*, the comedy series about prison life featuring Ronnie Barker and Richard Beckinsale, will remember Harry Grout, the prison Godfather, making a similar arrangement as part of an escape plot.

So Brian and I duly reported sick for the next five days in a row, telling the doctor we were suffering from toothache, and were booked to see the dentist the following week. Gary and Jack had done the same and turned up early to wait for their appointments.

As they reached the waiting-room door, where Brian and I sat trying to look in pain, they found themselves surrounded by warders, who told them, 'You're not to go in there – governor's orders.'

Jack protested, demanding, 'What the fuck has the governor got to do with it?' but was merely told, 'We're under strict instructions to keep you both away from here.'

Gary said, 'Well, tell the governor he's a prick,' and Jack chipped in with, 'We're not in the fucking Stone Age. Let him see his brother. We're not mass murderers.'

Of course, the screws had worked out what was going on. 'Listen, MacDonald,' Gary was told, 'the governor is behind this decision. Think we're idiots? We know your fucking teeth are OK.' They were sent back to their cells.

I'd known something had gone wrong when I'd turned up, and now I reckoned it was time to throw in the towel. However, as a result of my prolonged complaints, I was told I had to visit the dentist.

'I hear you've got bad toothache. Open your mouth and I'll have a look,' he said as I seated myself in his chair.

As I opened my mouth, I tried to explain, 'No, no, I'm feeling OK now,' but the man regarded his job with zeal.

'A couple of your teeth have gone bad,' he said after an examination. It was news to me, but before I knew it I'd been given a jab in the gums and the offending pair had been yanked out.

As Brian sat waiting his turn, he saw me emerge holding a blood-spattered cloth to my mouth. Before his name could be called, he vanished in the direction of the safety of his cell. That night, I shouted from my window to a guy who knew Gary and Jack, 'Tell those pair of cunts to come up with a better plan next time, eh?' I told him, 'My fucking mouth is killing me.' The only consolation was a piece of hash a sympathetic pal smuggled to me. It helped ease the pain and get me off to sleep.

While we waited for the sheriff to decide just how heinous was the crime of stealing a couple of sheepskin coats, I met a lot of boys from Glasgow who were being held at Jessiefield. Among them was Mick Healy, who was doing a five-year stretch for robbery. Mick would come to play a major role in my story. Gary Moore was there too. This was late 1982 and just 18 months later he would be making headlines. I'll tell you why shortly. Willie and Pat Watson from Parkhead were also in Jessiefield. They were good friends of mine, and Gary always spoke especially highly of them.

In October, when we turned up to be sentenced, Brian and I

were told by the sheriff, 'You are a pair of rogues and it is my duty to see that you remain off the streets for as long as possible. I'm only sorry the law does not allow me to give you much longer than three months.'

Free at last a few weeks later, my payment to society made, I joined up again for a time with Lorraine, but I didn't want a long-term relationship. My mind seemed always to be on things like clubbing and other girls. She was a lovely girl, loyal and faithful, but it seemed unfair to expect her to stick around when the threat of another spell in jail was always hanging over me. I was slowly rising through the ranks of the Glasgow underworld, still carrying out jewel thefts but wanting to break into really big-time crime. I needed a serious think about what path I was going to take, whether I should take bigger risks for a bumper pay day.

I often pondered about the Thompsons, especially during my visits to the Provanmill Inn, where old Arthur appeared glued to the seat from which he could check out everyone who entered. His life seemed enmeshed in violence – as if death was attracted to him as moths are to light – even if on occasion the tragedy was none of his doing. That probably could not be said of what happened in 1966: as he flicked the indicator of his car on the street outside his home, it triggered an electric charge to a bomb planted beneath the vehicle, instantly killing his kindly pensioner mother-in-law, Margaret Johnstone. He survived but spent weeks in hospital. Three months earlier, Arthur's Jaguar car had forced a van carrying two long-standing rivals, including a member of the Welsh family, into a lamp post, killing both occupants. The skill of his lawyer, Joe Beltrami, convinced a jury that Arthur was not the driver. Nobody was ever convicted of planting the bomb. The Godfather was certainly not involved, however, in the brutal fatal stabbing in July 1973 of William McBride by George McEwan, although the bloody murder took place just a few yards from his house.

Arthur ran legitimate businesses but also had a reputation for operating murky enterprises, including moneylending, protection rackets and drug selling. For these, he needed a lieutenant, an enforcer, to make sure customers paid their dues. I liked young

Arty, but obviously his dad did not want to put his elder son in the firing line, so one night I was asked to meet the old man in the Provanmill Inn. Maybe it was more of a summons than a request.

I'd had one of these a while back when I was sitting in Ma's house and there was a knock at the door. Standing there was Arthur's younger son, Billy. 'My dad would like to see you,' he said, and I thought to myself, 'Fucking hell, what is it now?' At that time, I was knocking around with Fergie. 'OK, then, I'll come,' I told Billy.

It was just a couple of minutes around the corner to Arthur's house (or Mr Thompson, as he was to me then). He took you into the front room and was always courteous. This day was no exception, and after a couple of pleasantries he said, 'Right, son, I'll cut to the chase. What it is, son, is this. Your young brother Alan sold my daughter Tracey a couple of chains, and after about six weeks her neck went green.'

I looked at him and thought, 'For Christ's sake.'

He went on, 'They aren't genuine chains. Tracey hasn't got much cash. Can you see Alan and get the money back? She and one of her friends paid him about £150 each.'

Frankly, I was dying to get out of the place, so I said, 'All right, Mr Thompson, I'll see Alan,' and he said, 'Thanks, son.'

I went back and told my mother. Alan wasn't in, but I thought, 'That's the fucking Razzle Dazzle scam he's been doing.'

Razzle Dazzle was a shop in Argyle Street that sold these cheap chains. Alan used to put a nine-carat attachment on them and then sell the chains for £150 or £200. They were worth a fiver. But after a few weeks your neck turned green because they were made of copper. He'd also sold one to a neighbour.

After an hour or two, Alan came back to the house and I told him, 'Listen, I've just been summoned round to the Godfather.'

'What for?'

'You've sold those chains to Tracey Thompson. Her neck's gone green. He asked me if I'd get the cash for him, and I said I would.'

Alan said to me, 'Oh, fuck him.'

I said, 'Are you kidding? You can't fuck him. You better get this sorted.'

Alan just said, 'OK, no problem.' And that was that. But Tracey didn't get her money back and I was never summoned back by the Godfather over that. I did get summoned later on, but that was about something much more serious.

I didn't keep my date with Arthur at the Provy because I thought I knew why he wanted to meet me, and I was proved right the next day when Fergie came to see me. He told me he had met up with Arty and had been asked if he wanted to come on board the Thompson firm. I could understand why the Thompsons would be looking for Paul, because they shared with him a common hatred of the Welsh family. Old Arthur had told Fergie he could see the potential in the two of us and was always looking for up-and-coming Young Turks like ourselves who weren't afraid to get their hands covered in blood for him.

One of the tasks would be to collect outstanding debts. The long-term game plan was to get the money in other ways rather than putting up with the bother of the 'hurry up and pay' demand. Instead, the debtor would simply be slashed and, if necessary, shot in the leg to persuade him or her to stump up what was owed.

I didn't need much time to think it over because I could see that in the long run there would be too much trouble and hassle. So I said no to Paul, Arty and the Godfather.

'I want to make money,' I told Fergie, 'not get involved in violence full time.' I'd do a bit of both, of course, but 75 per cent of what I did was for the cash.

'We'll be earning good money,' Fergie told me. 'Old Arthur runs Glasgow.'

That left me wondering why, if the Godfather had the town sewn up, he needed us. 'Enjoy your new career, Fergie,' I said, 'but I'm off to do my own thing.'

Not many people turned down the Godfather in those days, but I did. And I don't regret my decision the tiniest bit. Admittedly, I would do the odd slashing, stabbing or shooting to earn money, but only if somebody crossed my path. I wasn't looking to go out day after day chasing people or confronting them as old Arthur sat back on his arse in the Ponderosa – the name the locals gave his house – sipping his brandy, smoking his cigars and watching *Minder* while I was out doing my bail bondsman act all over the city. Because Ma lived so close, I had visions of constantly being at his beck and call. I knew from now on my life wouldn't be as hectic as the one that awaited Fergie. When I shook hands with my old friend and wished him the best, I was sure he was going to need it.

In between carrying out jewel thefts, I began doing armed robberies with a friend I'll call 'Peter'. I was new to this work and he showed me the ropes. My first job was a post office in a housing scheme. With a shotgun each, we made off with £50,000. 'Not a bad day's work,' I thought. We pocketed £75,000 from another, but after a while Peter decided he wanted to call it a day. He was married with two kids. 'It's getting too dangerous now. I couldn't handle being away from the family if I copped a ten stretch,' he admitted. Peter was good on a job and I had total confidence in him. He was discreet and trustworthy, and, selfishly, I called him a shitebag and tried to get him to change his mind. A week later, I went back to see him and apologised, telling him I had been wrong not to understand his reasoning.

In a city-centre club, I was introduced to John Lynn and John Friel, the latter known as 'the Irishman'. They were suave, stylish and knew their way around town. After that, I would often join them in the Warehouse, in casinos such as the Regency and the Chevalier, and in a pub in Ingram Street called Sylvesters. John Friel reminded me of the Pied Piper. He was in his late 30s and led us young guns to all the best nightclubs, where we would be ushered to the front door, ahead of the queue, and walk in free of charge. It was a lot of fun to do this. All the nightclub owners had tremendous respect for John, waving him and his entourage inside regardless of whether there were two or twenty with him. John Lynn was originally from Parkhead, sophisticated, handsome and intelligent, and with businesses that included the Oasis Club, a sauna in Bath Street. I knew I should hang on to these guys' coattails. In later years, I'd become friends with John's cousin Rosina and her husband, Alex Manson, who stayed in the West End of Glasgow with their two daughters.

I met Ian McMillan, who had a boat at Duck Bay Marina, Loch Lomond, and his friend Pat McAdam, who had built up a successful business importing shoes from Italy and would go on to become a millionaire with Genoa Footwear in the city centre. Pat had a taste for the finer things in life. Unfortunately, things ultimately went belly up for Pat, and he lost the lot. In Chippendales in the Broomielaw, I met the owner John McQuade. He and Pat would both encounter trouble with the law in the years ahead. I got to know John Munro, Steph Osbourne and the Gemmells, Jim, Jack and Reggie, too. One night in the Diamond, a Chinese restaurant, I was introduced to Alex 'Hurricane' Higgins, the world champion snooker player, and shared a few drinks with this nice, down-to-earth superstar.

I could afford to visit these places and mix in good company because the money had rolled in through the robberies with Peter. I was reluctant to try these single-handed, so I went back to snatching trays of jewellery. Then my luck ran out. Driving through Springburn one day, I was suddenly halted by an unmarked car, from which jumped two men holding truncheons, obviously detectives. Ignoring their signals to stop, I drove at them, throwing one into the air. After a chase, I abandoned my motor and took to my heels. Remarkably, while running through flats in Galloway Street, I saw a door ajar, pushed inside and was confronted by a young woman of about my age holding a baby. She was clearly frightened, but when I explained why I was there she calmed down and even gave me a cup of tea and a biscuit while I watched the cops down below searching for me.

I knew I had to get out of Glasgow. It was possible then to get a passport lasting for one year, and I did so using the name and birth certificate of a good friend and my own photograph. Then I headed for Benidorm with a mate, Stewart Mulligan, who ran an ice-cream van around the housing schemes. In between relaxing in the sun and shoplifting, I got into a fight with a guy who had taken a dislike to Stewart. One of my opponent's friends joined in and I ended up with a black eye. 'When I get back to Glasgow, I'm going to take the face off you,' I promised. The group was from Glasgow and they left Benidorm the next day. 'I'm getting arrested when I go home,' I told Stewart, to his surprise. 'How?' he asked, and I told him, 'The guy who blacked my eye knows I've got that dodgy passport. I used the birth certificate of one of his mates. Now he'll be afraid I'm gonnae slash him. He knows I'll do it.' (And eventually I did, outside Panama Jack's club in Clyde Street.)

My prophecy came true. Somebody tipped off the cops, and six weeks later, when we flew back into Glasgow, the police were waiting. A detective I knew came on board the plane looking for me, but my pale face was now tanned and my dark hair lightened by the sun. I was also hiding behind a toy donkey and wearing a huge sunhat. After walking up and down the aisle, he left, but I knew there was no chance of getting away when we disembarked, although I did think of making a run for it. Sure enough, I was arrested at the customs desk.

'You nearly had us fooled,' a detective said. 'How are you doing, Ian?'

I told him, 'My name's not Ian, I'm Joseph. It says it on my passport.'

He laughed and simply said, 'Come on, Ian, let's go.'

They charged me with attempting to murder the police officer hit by my car. Worse was to follow after I was locked in a police cell. The detectives returned. 'We've got ten outstanding warrants for jewel raids all over Scotland and England,' one of them said. I told myself, 'I'm really in deep shit.'

Remanded to Barlinnie, in the exercise yard I recognised a few familiar faces. 'Fuckin' hell, Blink,' one of them said. 'Where the fuck have you been? You're as black as two in the morning.'

I told him, 'I got caught holding a donkey,' and went off without explaining further.

The prosecution did a deal, reducing the attempted murder to assault. The copper hadn't been badly hurt. When I appeared at Glasgow Sheriff Court, I got eighteen months for hitting him, three months for using the fake birth certificate to get a passport and another three months for what they called 'uttering' – another name for fraud – by using the passport. It was October 1983 and this all meant I'd be in jail until September the following year.

A girl in Carlisle claimed to have recognised the tall guy who'd robbed a jewellery shop and was being brought to Glasgow to see whether she could pick me out in an identity parade. Meanwhile, I was taken to Barlinnie, where I met my pal Brian Buchanan, who was wanted in London for fraud. We went off next day, me to Durham prison, Brian to Wormwood Scrubs. After a few months in custody, in February 1984, I appeared before a jury at Carlisle Crown Court charged with the theft of diamond rings worth £25,000. I pleaded innocence, but the girl witness had picked me out. She did her duty, and after a one-day trial I was found guilty and given another eighteen months backdated to start from December 1983, which meant my release date was now the beginning of December '84.

They packed me back off to Durham gaol. In April, I heard horrendous news from Glasgow about the so-called Ice Cream Wars and how a family of six had died in a fire at their flat in Ruchazie. What shocked me was discovering my friend Gary Moore was one of a number of men charged with murdering the six, one of whom was a baby. I knew there was no way Gary would have been involved. Joe Steele was another of the accused. He was a good friend and I was convinced of his innocence also.

A few weeks later, while lying in my cell one day, listening to my radio and reading a magazine, I heard something that made me sit bolt upright. Dennis Nilsen, from Fraserburgh in the north of Scotland, had been working as a civil servant in London when he committed a horrendous series of sexually motivated murders, strangling and cutting up his young male victims. He was caught when human remains blocked the drains in the block of flats where he lived. He was jailed for life and the news was that he had been slashed in Wormwood Scrubs. The announcer said that a Scot was on trial for causing Nilsen grievous bodily harm. It was my pal Brian. Nilsen had needed 89 stitches after he was slashed across the face and chest, but he refused to point the finger at Brian. He said he had been dragged to court against his wishes. 'I would prefer to be sunning myself in Parkhurst,' Nilsen said.

Brian's version was that Nilsen had come into the exercise yard with a knife. 'I knew the man was a murderer and I didn't want to give him a second chance,' Brian told the court. A couple of days later came more news when Brian was cleared. I was delighted for him.

8

The Ham War

WHEN MEN ARE locked up, squeezed together like sardines in a filthy tin and made to feel degraded, trouble is inevitable, violence certain. Often the cause is something that appears trivial, even silly, to an outsider. But prison creates strange tensions. Some of mine I relieved through exercise. In Durham, for instance, I paced up and down my freezing cell until I was dizzy and threw myself with enthusiasm onto the gym fitness machines. But there were times when I could not stop my anger from exploding. On one of these occasions, the trouble resulted from a piece of ham.

Gary wrote from Jessiefield to tell me he and Jack had become embroiled in a gang war with a mob from another area of Glasgow. These things happen when you've got particularly mad, bad and dangerous boys from No Mean City vying for supremacy. He and Jack had reacted by cutting and slashing their way through the rivals and were in the digger as a result. Gary told me that after one slashing he'd been lying dozing in his cell listening to a radio request show when he was astonished to hear someone had asked for Rod Stewart's version of the Cat Stevens song 'The First Cut Is the Deepest'. He wondered whether he should send in a similar request.

Durham's main claim to fame had long been that it was the prison from which the robber John McVicar had made a daring escape in 1968, an exploit that was vividly featured in a film about his life. *McVicar*, starring the Who vocalist Roger Daltrey. M꜄V꜀ ~ the reported to have once said, 'Being a crimin꜀᷉ only trouble is that they put you in prison for it.' I couldn't have put it better myself. The special security unit – E Wing – had been opened in 1967 to house some of the Great Train Robbers, who were joined by torture-gang brothers Eddie and Charlie Richardson and gangland personality 'Mad' Frankie Fraser, to name just a few. Now the old prison, shadowed by the beautiful cathedral on one side and the grim courthouse on the other, had been tarnished by the appearance there of the Moors murderess Myra Hindley, and the unit was tagged 'She Wing'. Hindley and her vile partner Ian Brady – he of Rottenrow origin – had been jailed for life in 1966 for abusing, torturing and killing children.

The wing held other women inmates, too, and I realised it seemed to be a ritual for the boys to shout across to the girls. Some would actually strike up a relationship with one of the females, ask for their prison number and they would send each other smuggled letters. Some inmates shouted declarations of love to each other, so in bed at night I would turn off the radio and listen to their efforts at non-touching courtship. Others, though, just screamed abuse and sexual innuendo. I noticed the women could be as vile with their tongues as the men. I joined others in shouting at Hindley, telling her she was the most evil woman on earth. She would never come to her window, and probably put on her radio to drown out the constant invective.

I was due to leave prison in December, but out of the blue came good news. I was told that the Home Office, in order to ease overcrowding, had announced the early release of any prisoner who had served eight months or more of a sentence less than two years. Luckily, I fell into that category, and in August I found myself walking through historic Durham, heading for the railway station and home. But happy as I was to get out, I was saddened just two days after my release when my granda Big Jocky died suddenly.

Like most of those who knew them, I was gutted when in butcher Joe Steele and T.C. Campbell were convicted of killing be two dec... ...in Gary Moore was acquitted, but it would ...nted that Tommy and Joe had been the victims of a terrible miscarriage of justice. Their loyal supporters never gave up fighting for the Glasgow Two.

I was really trying hard to stay out of trouble. However, if being unfaithful had been a crime, I'd never have been out of jail. Having a drink in a pub in Possil with my friend David 'Fitzy' Fitzsimmons, I met a really good-looking blonde named Linda Halldane, 'Hally' to her friends. I became a regular at the pub, where one of the barmaids was Betty Dempster. Betty was always pleasant and cheerful, and her son Bobby was making a name for himself on the streets and would eventually run a very successful security company.

Everybody was very friendly and I came to know members of another family of Moffats – no relation to Tam and his brothers – including Irene and her brothers Billy, Hugh, Alan and Jimmy. I met Billy and Linda Fraser and their ma – a nice woman – Big Billy Bates and his brother Joe, Big Calum, John Duggan, Bobby Bennett and Bobby Maxwell. I also got to know, and like, Rab and Marie O'Hara and Rab's brother Ronnie. Rab and Marie had a son, Robert, who developed a passion for looking after birds, and as a result was nicknamed 'the Birdman', a tag that has stuck with him to this day.

With Christmas approaching, Hally and I and two friends were sitting in the living room of her flat in Possil Park one day when there was an almighty bang, followed by shouts of 'Police, don't fucking move!' The door was literally ripped off at the hinges, and in they charged, shouting and bawling like maniacs. They were dressed like tramps and I knew right away who they were: the drug squad, known on the streets as 'the Manky Mob' because of their appearance. This wasn't Miami but Possil Park, and they certainly were no Don Johnsons of *Miami Vice* with designer suits and good looks. Without bothering about the niceties of introducing themselves, they demanded to know who we were, where we lived and why we were there. I had been warned by others to beware of these people. Someone had said, 'If they ever come to your home, film everything they do.' But there was no time for that. We were handcuffed and two officers stayed with us while the others disappeared. We heard the sound of the flat being ransacked, followed by a cry of 'Found something!' and we looked at one another in astonishment.

One member of the Manky Squad wanted to know if we knew the whereabouts of drugs in the flat, and we were honest in pleading ignorance. Then one of them suddenly produced a cellophane bag and asked who owned it.

'It's got a brown substance in it. Looks like heroin,' he said with an enormous grin.

I'd been smoking hash, which can make you feel happy and say daft things, and I said, 'Brown substance? It looks like shite to me,' and that admittedly angered them. When one walked over I thought he was going to take a swing at me. Instead, he put the bag in between my handcuffed palms and squeezed them together. Then he took back the bag, complete with my fingerprints. I was taken to Maryhill police station and charged with being concerned in the supply of diamorphine (the real name for heroin). They advised me to own up to possession, because if I didn't Hally was going to be arrested and charged as well. I was raging, but when I cooled down I decided to take the rap for something I had not done to keep Hally, who was also innocent, in the clear. So it was back to familiar territory: Barlinnie.

Out on exercise one day, someone said, 'I heard your wee pal's in reception,' and I asked who. 'Paul Ferris,' was the reply. Next day, I met Paul, who said he had been on the run from the police and had been lying low in Arthur Thompson's holiday flat in Rothesay on the Isle of Bute. Police had suddenly arrived and, surprise, said they'd found drugs. We were in serious trouble and convinced they were out to get us.

Later, while chatting to Pat McAdam and Mark Watt from Bailleston, I pointed Paul out to Mark, who said, 'Surely that's not him. He looks like a fucking choirboy.'

But I warned him, 'That choirboy is a dangerous wee fucker. He's no angel.'

Mark found out the hard way the next day that he ought to have listened to what I'd told him. He was on a different landing, and he went down to Fergie's cell to confront him over some previous incident in the city centre. Mark punched Fergie and thought that was the end of it. He didn't know Paul, who followed him outside carrying a metal bar and whacked him over his shaven head. That ended the dispute and both stayed silent when the governor asked what had happened the next day.

Just a few hours into my trial at the High Court in Glasgow in March 1985, the prosecution dropped a charge of 'being concerned in the supply of diamorphine'. And after listening to police and other witnesses, the jury cleared me of the lesser charge of 'intent to supply'. I was given 12 months' imprisonment after pleading guilty to possession, and the judge even backdated the sentence to December, which meant I would get out in August of that year. When his trial came up, Fergie was also found not guilty, but he was sentenced to 18 months' imprisonment for having an offensive weapon. We ended up doing our time in different halls in Barlinnie.

While doing that stretch, I met Grant Mackintosh from Paisley, where he was known as 'Mister P', and our friendship lasts to this day. Grant was serving seven years for supplying cannabis. His co-accused, Ned Kelly and Norrie Speirs, had also been jailed. Grant was easily good enough to have made a career as a professional footballer but chose crime instead. He always had me in his team during prison matches, not because of my skills, but just because he liked me. Playing football was one way of getting rid of pent-up energy. But now and again there was no way to release it, and that's when trouble would brew.

That June, with my release date just a few weeks away, disgruntlement over the standard of the food came to a head one Saturday lunchtime when we were served cold ham that was raw and smelled as though the time when it should have been dumped was long past. We complained and refused to leave the dining hall until something fresh was served. The normal response from the screws was to make an example of the guys at one table, scaring everyone else into behaving and leaving. That day, they picked my table. A screw pointed to Ted Cuddihy from Springburn and ordered him back to his cell.

'Don't move, Ted, we're with you,' we promised, and he held on to the table.

'Move!' a uniform shouted at him.

'Fuck off,' Ted responded.

A screw grabbed him, so I hit him over the head with our teapot and that kicked everything off, or at least I thought it would. At the start, everybody had pledged to stick together. Now, as I battled with the screw, I realised only myself and one other guy had the balls to see it through. I was on the verge of freedom while lifers and guys doing ten years left us to it. Reinforcements arrived and I mingled with the others as we were shepherded back to our cells. I knew what was coming. The governor of Barlinnie at the time was 'Slasher' Gallagher, known as that because he was said to have slashed an inmate who had crossed him. I always had a blade discreetly planked in the cell; it was soldered onto the end of a toothbrush. That was my favourite weapon whenever I was in Barlinnie.

On weekdays, we'd be locked up at eight o'clock, but at the weekends everyone in Barlinnie was banged up for the night at five. Clutching my razor, I listened and heard the doors at the bottom of the hall opening and closing repeatedly. I paced up and down my cell then climbed on the bed, wondering what to do. Shouts from other inmates told me screws were in my hall, and while I could slash one, it would just mean longer in prison. So when the door was opened and Slasher stood there looking sinister in a long dark coat, a trilby pulled down over his forehead, I dropped the blade and prepared to take what was coming.

Slasher said simply, 'Get him,' and half a dozen screws piled in, pulled me off the bed and dragged me outside. They'd waited until everybody was locked up and now the place was black with warders who, their charges safely banged up for the night, had come to join in the punishment. My cell was on the third landing. I saw a line of screws and was hauled between them as they kicked and punched. It was a gauntlet of agony. That was repeated on the second landing, then the bottom landing. The pain was excruciating. I spotted the Pie Man, who had just been transferred to the Bar-L from Longriggend. He punched me in the testicles.

Finally, thrown into another cell, I took another beating. All in all, it was the worst hammering of my entire life. The door was locked but opened later to admit the doctor, who asked what had happened. A screw answered for me, saying I had fallen down the stairs, and the examination was over.

The next morning, I looked in the mirror and saw the red, blue, swollen, discoloured mass that had been my face. I looked like the Elephant Man in the film starring John Hurt. It was grotesque. I wasn't the only one who had been given that treatment. The guy who had fought alongside me had been dragged along as well. 'I wish I'd gone first,' he told me later. 'I could see through the door and the whole place was polluted with black uniforms.'

Three days later, Ma came on a visit that had been arranged for some time. She was astonished at being told I had refused to see her and knew something was wrong. But it was only later that she was able to discover the truth. Of course, the explanation was simple: the staff didn't want her to see my injuries. To make sure none of the other prisoners would be able to write home with a description of how I looked, I was held in solitary, away from the other inmates, and only taken to the toilets or out to exercise when no one was about. To add insult to injury, the police turned up and charged me with assault. Rage built up inside me, but I took comfort in the fact that I was getting out soon.

Screws played games, trying to noise me up, hoping I'd react, lose my temper and my release date. Excrement was put in my food, urine in my tea. I don't know who did this – although I had my suspicions – but instead of taking the bait, I would ring my bell and when somebody came to the spyhole, show them an empty plate and cup and say, 'Any more leftovers? That was great.' I felt it was a victory to me.

Meanwhile, word filtered through that Arty Thompson and two pals, Tam Bagan and Jonah McKenzie, had been arrested for being concerned in the supply of heroin. It sounded familiar. On remand in the Big House, Arty began munching through Mars Bars as if they were being taken off the market. He was still eating when I finally got my freedom.

9

Showdown at the Bar-L

A FEW MONTHS AFTER I was born in 1961, Yorkshire housewife Viv Nicholson won more than £150,000 on the football pools – equivalent to £3 million nowadays – and famously announced she was going to 'spend, spend, spend'. Viv and I share the philosophy that if you have money you should enjoy it. And that's what I have done. The problem has been that getting it has led me into so much trouble. That wasn't always the case when I was younger, though.

For example, after my release from Barlinnie, I took a flat in Langside but then realised I had little money left after paying the rent. I needed cash. Some guys faced with a similar situation would have turned to drug dealing, but the risks involved in that were awful. Arty was about to get eleven years and his sidekick John 'Jonah' Mackenzie seven, after they'd allegedly been caught with heroin. So I went to see my friend Peter, to try to talk him out of retirement from the robbery game.

It came as a pleasant surprise to learn no persuasion would be needed. 'It's good to see you again, Blink. I heard about the doing you got in Bar-L,' he said, and I told him, 'Don't worry, I'll get those fucking animals back.' The small talk over, he admitted that his not bringing in money was causing rows with his wife. To add to their difficulties, they now had a third child. Peter and his missus still stayed in a council house, which was just as well, because if he'd had a mortgage they'd have been in arrears and evicted. So it was game on. Peter had kept our guns; we discussed a target and arranged to meet ten days later.

That night, I celebrated the likelihood of shortly having money falling out of my pockets. Hally and I had parted. Now I started frequenting Stripes bar in Springburn, owned by Charlie Madden, whose brother George I already knew. Once you got to know Charlie, he was one of the nicest guys you could meet. He had a smile for everyone, and when a customer came in he took time to say hello whether he knew them or not. He would mostly be standing at the bar with his girlfriend, Jean McGovern. I came to know her McGovern cousins Joe, Tony, Tommy, Steven and James. I'd see Russell Stirton, who I had met a couple of years earlier and who went on to marry the cousins' only sister, Jackie McGovern. I got on really well with Russell.

On the day of the robbery, I sensed Peter was nervous, but I was confident I could trust him to get things right. I knew he was worried about getting caught and jailed, but he was familiar with the three elements necessary in a robbery: the Intel, the Eyeball and the Plot. The Intel is the intelligence, the details of the robbery, who is taking part, what are their jobs, where is it to be, and so on; the Eyeball is the planning, noting times, who goes in and out; and the Plot is how to get in and out of the location quickly with no fuss. When it mattered, it all came together, and in we went, he with a double-barrelled shotgun hidden under his coat and me carrying a pistol and a cosh. Less than half an hour later, we left carrying more than £140,000 in ready cash. I stashed most of my share and shoved a couple of thousand into my pocket. I was going to have fun.

I met Annette Daniel through a friend, Alan Kerr, and we dated for a time. Annette was an expert shoplifter and I drove her and a couple of her friends to London, not to take in the sights but anything going from the shop shelves. She took me to Harrods, told me to pick out a suit or two then go outside and wait. And I did, but it was the next day before I saw her again. She and a friend were jumped on by store detectives, arrested, charged, held overnight in a police station and bailed. Undeterred, they continued shoplifting up and down Oxford Street as if nothing had happened.

Back in Glasgow, and very smartly dressed thanks to Annette, I would go to the Mayfair club in Sauchiehall Street, where on Thursday reggae nights customers slyly smoked hash. I knew Jim Sinclair and his two brothers Rab and Raymie from the Gorbals, Gerry Carbin and Tommy Kilmartin from the Calton, and Sammo and Caff from Cranhill. It was always a good night. Sometimes we'd see the band Scheme, who could have made it to the top but didn't, probably because their songs were too anti-establishment. They played in Maxwell Plum's on Clyde Street, Stringfellow's in Paisley and the San Mile bar – now the Fullarton Park Hotel – in Tollcross. I'd also visit Zanzibar on Sauchiehall Street and Rockefeller's in Keppochhil Road.

Near the end of that year, me, Ma, James and Fitzy went to Tenerife for two weeks. Billy Bates drove us to Newcastle Airport and we promised him a present. Annette joined us on the island and as a result we returned laden with leather jackets, aftershave and perfume courtesy of the shops in Playa de las Americas. Back home, I threw a couple of parties at Ma's and invited Jimbo Trainer, Alan Kerr, John Meanen, Danny Reid, Hiram Holliday, Fitzy and the boys from Springburn, Geo and Joe Madden and Tony McGurn. I was a social animal, with the result that my funds started to drop. It was time for them to be replenished.

Someone I knew had a cousin who worked for a security-van firm. He had drunk and gambled himself into debt and, for a cut of the take, was willing to be robbed. Peter and I preferred turns with nobody else involved, but this was an offer it was difficult to refuse. Peter agreed, on condition he didn't meet the informant or his cousin; that way, if something went wrong, they wouldn't be able to identify him. I'd take the whole rap, but I was willing to take that chance. It all went to plan and we copped a mind-boggling £230,000. To this day, the lips of the go-between and the van man remain sealed.

My friend Gerry Rae was in Peterhead prison, and, motoring up to visit him one day, I heard a radio flash that Charlie Madden had been knifed outside a club in Possil and was dead at just 27. It was the same Charlie I knew from Springburn, George and Joe's brother. I couldn't believe it. When I got back to Glasgow that day, I called on his ma in Springburn and saw the family. Charlie and Jean's son was not long born. They named him Mark and, many years later, I met him in Victoria's nightclub in Sauchiehall Street. It must have been a sorrow-filled Christmas for them that year.

In February 1986, I went back to Tenerife, knowing that I would be on trial the following month, accused of the Ham War assaults. My lawyer at the time didn't want to bring out in court the background of brutality at Barlinnie, so I said I would defend myself. It was my chance to publicly question some of those running the prison, but my forthright attitude did not go down well with the sheriff, who revoked my bail, and I was remanded to, of all places, Barlinnie.

On the bus to court next morning, I was given words of encouragement by John Jackson, who went on to become a trusted confidant of Stewart 'Specky' Boyd. As we were being separated, John called, 'Best of luck, Blink, you'll need it.' I didn't get any. The sheriff found me guilty and gave me the permitted maximum, a 'concrete mixer', otherwise known as six months.

It was back to Barlinnie, where I waited for repercussions. When nothing happened, the suspense worsened, but the next morning I was put out of my misery by being hauled in front of a governor, who was with a prison officer. The former told me, 'If I had my way, you'd have got six years,' while the latter added, 'You're getting one chance. Just don't dare look at any officer the wrong way.'

As the weeks passed, I met Gary 'Gonzo' Conway from Balornock. We shared many a pacing session up and down the joiners' work shed, chatting away. By now, Jack Woods was out for good. My brother Gary had written telling me he had been moved to Dungavel, where he was in a dormitory with Walter 'Wattie' Norval, leader of the XYY robbery gang. Wattie was serving 14 years and Gary said he was a top-rate guy who kept everyone enthralled with his stories. Dungavel was a semi-open nick, but not open enough for Gash, who did a runner while two screws taking him on a visit to Ma's were tucking into her sandwiches. On the run, he tucked a few women into bed with him but was caught in a car at Lockerbie and had three months added to his sentence.

At the beginning of May, two security guards were held at gunpoint and a substantial sum of cash taken from the Clydesdale Bank in Blantyre. Two weeks later, my old pal Ernie Barrie was arrested, charged and remanded to Barlinnie, where he vigorously protested his innocence. The next month, Sammo the Bear was sentenced to six years, along with his mate Jaimba from Cranhill, after attempting to rob a security van at the Easterhouse shopping centre. It was sad to think of them just starting their sentences as I was ending mine, but that was the game we played.

A couple of weeks after being freed, I went on a night out to Warehouse and met Marie Coyle, whose brother-in-law, Arthur Robertson from Govan, I got on well with. Marie and I started dating regularly and then flew off on holiday to Alcúdia in Majorca, where we stretched out on white, sandy beaches and admired the majestic yachts in Palma marina. On our return, I visited Ernie, who said he'd been picked out wrongly at an ID parade by two security guards, and that night I told Ma he was in deep shit. I was about to discover he wasn't the only one in trouble.

Fergie had been arrested along with a policeman after a gun had been found at the officer's home. I'd visited him in Barlinnie too.

'Listen, Blink, a pal of mine has a key to a lock-up. There's a stash. You want to go see him and sell it for me?' he asked.

'Aye, all right,' I said. 'Who am I giving the money to?'

He gave me a name. I never asked questions. He had drugs and wanted me to sell them. There was an earner in it for me.

A few days later came the trouble, when Billy Thompson knocked at Ma's door with a familiar message. 'My dad would like to see you,' he said. I followed him around the corner to the Ponderosa, dreading what was coming and wondering if it was connected with my knocking back the Godfather's job offer.

Courteous as ever, Arthur took me into the front room. It felt surreal.

'How are you, son?' he asked with a smile.

'I'm fine,' I said, still mystified.

Then it was down to business. 'Have you been up to see Paul and did he ask you to sell anything for him?' he enquired.

I was shocked. How did he know that? I was honest. There was no need to lie. 'Aye, he did,' I said.

'What did he tell you to do with the money when you sold it?'

I told him the name Fergie had given to me.

'Do you know, son, it doesn't belong to Paul? It's mine.'

'No,' I said, 'he just asked me to sell it. I just presumed it was his.'

'No, son, it's mine. Have you still got the stuff?'

This was serious. I told him, 'I've sold some of it. I've got the money in my flat.'

'Can you sell the rest?'

'Aye,' I replied, 'that's no problem.'

'Will you bring the money over tomorrow?' It wasn't a question, more an order, and then he added, ominously I thought, 'And come with me to see him in Barlinnie in a day or two.'

'Aye,' I replied.

'I'll see you tomorrow, then,' he said, and I took my cue to leave.

I walked away dazed and confused. In my flat that night, I thought about things. Why would Fergie put me in this position? Nobody could fuck with the Godfather. He was bound to find out. And what if I got in the shit for it? Why should I lie for him? He should have at least been honest with me. I always believed his run with the Godfather would come to a sticky end. I had told him that. Here it was, I thought, the beginning of the end.

I went to the Ponderosa the next day and gave the Godfather his money. To my relief, he seemed happy. He asked me to meet him the following morning in the Barlinnie jail car park for the showdown with Fergie. I was dreading the visit, because I felt I was caught in the middle, stuck between whatever their differences were. And I was sure it wouldn't end well. Everyone was staring at Arthur when we walked into the prison. He was dressed casually, a far cry from the dapper suit and tie that most people associated with him. We sat in the waiting room, making small talk, until we were called in.

Fergie's face was a sight when he saw us approach. Obviously, he hadn't expected to see his employer. At that time, you didn't need to give your name or any details beforehand for a visit, so you could just turn up and the inmate wouldn't know who was coming. We sat down and greeted one another.

'So, what've you done with that stuff?' Arthur asked.

Immediately, Fergie tried to find a way out of the situation. 'Blink, you know I gave it to someone else, don't you?' he said, looking at me hopefully. He was almost willing me to come up with the right answer.

I wasn't too sure what to say, but surprisingly it was Arthur who came to my rescue. 'On you go, son,' he said to me. 'I'll talk to Paul alone. I'll see you outside.'

I left the visit and waited, and Arthur came out after a few minutes. 'Son, that boy thinks I'm buttoned up the back,' he said. 'I can't understand it. He put himself where he is just now.' He wasn't a man of many words, but what he did say, you listened to.

Within a few weeks, I'd sold the stash and given Arthur his money. He asked if I wanted more to sell, and I took him up on his offer, regularly calling on one of his associates in a Glasgow bar to pick up a bag containing the next batch I was to deal. He was not a man you refused.

All of this made me a few pounds, but it was small stuff in comparison with the stakes that I knew were out there for the taking. I'd been keeping in touch by letter with a couple of guys I'd met in Durham prison. One of them – I'll call him 'Johnny' – rang me from his home near Liverpool.

'How you doing financially?' he asked me.

'Not bad, keeping my head above water,' I answered honestly.

'I've something that might interest you,' he told me. 'Come and see me.'

And that was it. We hung up. That weekend, I headed to Liverpool with Marie. She had no idea why we were going and was never involved in what transpired. Johnny checked us into a hotel and was waiting when we arrived. We had a drink and then a meal, but, with Marie there, nothing was discussed about the job I knew he was wanting to propose. The next day, she went shopping while Johnny and I got down to business.

'I've got a robbery lined up,' he said. 'I need two men for it. It's a bank down here, £300,000, possibly even more. Everything's sorted. It'll be in the next few weeks. You up for it?'

'Definitely,' I replied. 'And I've got a pal.' So the second man was sorted. I'd need to call on Peter.

Johnny and I shook hands and it was now simply a matter of waiting for him to call me.

I visited Ernie again. He was facing trial for three robberies and had a co-accused for two of them. The jury quickly cleared both men of those two alleged offences, but then convicted Ernie of the Blantyre robbery. I couldn't believe it. Nor could Ernie. He was innocent. There was worse to come, when the judge gave him 18 years. I went off to the Ship Bank bar to get drunk and was probably saved from doing something stupid by meeting my friend Brian Hislop, whose family had owned the pub for years. Brian was a very good boxer, so good in fact that he could have been a professional, but instead he turned his hand to car sales.

So there was Ernie starting that terrible sentence for a robbery he hadn't done as I was about to embark on another stick-up. If it went wrong, I'd be ending up in a cell too. I visited Peter, whose doubts were soon dispelled when I mentioned the anticipated haul, and we headed to Liverpool.

It was all so easy. Me, Peter, Johnny and another guy I'll call 'Martin' sat in a van watching security guards taking cash into a bank. Then three of us ran inside, the other two jumping over the counter and running for the vault while I guarded the front, ordering customers and staff to get down and not to move. After five minutes, Johnny and Peter emerged with two holdalls and Martin drove us away. We stopped in the countryside to switch to another car we had parked there earlier and drove to a safe house, where we opened the bags and counted £320,000. My share was £75,000.

It was going to be a good Christmas, which was more than Fergie could expect. After a trial at Glasgow High Court following the discovery of the gun, he was sentenced to three years.

In January, Sammo Ralston was battered in Barlinnie, sparking a riot. Inmates took three screws hostage, and two dozen prisoners, wearing masks and balaclavas, climbed onto the roof, displaying banners protesting against brutality. Ten officers had to lock themselves in cells for their own protection. The trouble made national news headlines and drew attention to the vicious treatment of inmates. I went along, holding a bed-sheet on which was written in black boot polish: 'Bar-L Brutality! Slasher Gallagher & Men Are Nothing But A Bunch Of Thugs! I Know, I'm A Victim!'

The riot lasted five days. The hostages were freed after the boys up on the roof had sung to their hearts' content. Fitzy led the choir, with a baton in his hand, a screw's hat on his head and a balaclava pulled over his face. They sang mostly songs by Scheme, like 'Innocent As Hell', 'Keep Your Head Up' and 'Growing Stronger'. They came down on the promise they wouldn't be beaten up. It was a victory for the prisoners, and I celebrated by taking Marie to Tenerife, where I lay in the sun as police in Liverpool hunted the gang with the odd accents.

10

Assassin in my Shoes

ALL OF MY life it had seemed as if I had to face the music in one way or another. Now, just like Ernie Barrie, I was going to discover how it felt to suffer because of something for which I wasn't to blame. It all began well enough, with Jack Woods and I going off to see Madonna when she dropped in on London on her Who's That Girl? world tour. After a couple of nights in Blackpool eyeing the girls, we headed for Wembley. We didn't have tickets, but we made it inside after paying one of the security guys £50 each. The music was superb, with an added bonus in that the Scottish duo Hue and Cry were one of the support acts. But we should have stayed in London instead of going back to Glasgow.

Four armed people had walked into a car sales garage in Dennistoun and opened fire, targeting a man in the office area. Before they ran off, four or five shots were fired, one of them hitting this guy in the shoulder, and although he wasn't badly hurt, the police announced they were treating the incident as attempted murder. A few days later, Gary, now finally released from prison, was lying in his bed at Ma's house when he was suddenly woken by a loud crashing noise and shouts from the hallway. Rushing to see what was happening, he found himself face to face with armed policemen, screaming at him to raise his hands in the air. Ma was ordered out of bed and told a warrant was in force for the arrest of Ian MacDonald. She explained who Gary was, but the police didn't believe her and hauled him off, only letting him go hours later when his identity was confirmed.

Word filtered through that the police were hunting Jack and me for the garage shooting. I wasn't about to present myself at a cop station to face the music for something that was nothing to do with me, so I made myself scarce, kicking my heels in Edinburgh for a week then going to Liverpool to meet Johnny. While I was there, I saw on the television news a report about the riot in Peterhead that was ended by the SAS.

After a month, I decided to head home, but it was not a wise move, because while I was driving to Stripes bar soon afterwards, I was spotted by the local CID. They did a U-turn and came after me, but, confident I'd shaken them off, I parked in a side street and went into Stripes. However, I was just taking my first drink when a customer ran in to say the police were outside. George and Joe Madden came rushing over to me. 'Quick, Blink,' George said, 'down here,' and he led me to the cellar below the bar. I hid down there for more than 20 minutes and was thinking the coast was clear when the door opened and a voice shouted, 'Ian MacDonald, if you're down there, come up now!' I knew it was the cops and held my breath, but when two of them entered, shining torches, I realised the game was up and came out. 'Nice try, Ian,' one of the CID said as we walked outside, 'but it's not your lucky night.'

So it was back on remand to Barlinnie, where the screws were still demoralised from the riot and trying to ease their tensions by strictly enforcing every petty regulation. By November, I'd had enough. One afternoon, before the teatime lock-up, a pal gave me five 'yellow eggs', very powerful sleeping pills, telling me to keep them for that night. Pacing up and down my cell, I took them all, but, instead of becoming drowsy and tired, I felt wide awake, buzzing with energy and on an intense high. When the doors opened for association and I came bursting out of my cell, a young screw tried to stop me visiting pals on another landing, so I tipped my plastic cup over his head and then hit him. Suddenly, other inmates were throwing furniture, shouting and screaming. It was pandemonium. When it had calmed down, I found myself in the segregation unit – known to staff and prisoners as 'the Wendy House' because it had the appearance of a giant dolls' house – and I was still there when the police turned up and charged me with three assaults and causing a breach of the peace. And all of this while the trials of nine men – including Ernie Barrie – accused of instigating the earlier riots were going on at the High Court in Glasgow.

When the hearings ended, three had been found guilty and Allan 'Bongo' McLeish, who had only been doing six months when the trouble kicked off, got ten years, William 'Moose' Marshall was given eight and Hughie Twigg four. The result of it all was that the Wendy House was packed with hostile and pissed-off prisoners ready to explode at any time. And that's just what happened, when, following a protest about food and conditions, we smashed up our cells. Sinks and toilets newly installed in the Wendy House cells were ripped from the walls, causing a flood. They would not be replaced and we went back to slopping out.

In January 1988, my trial started at the High Court. Jack and I were accused of attempted murder at the garage. It didn't last long, because our QCs pointed out that none of the early witnesses had been able to identify us as the gunmen, and the judge directed the jury to acquit us. They formally found us not guilty, and he said we could go.

I quietly followed Jack out of the dock. 'Where'd you think you're going?' asked one of the policemen who had been guarding us.

'You heard the judge. I'm free to go,' I said, chancing my luck.

'No you're not, you're still remanded for assaulting prison officers in Barlinnie,' he pointed out, and it was back to the Big House and the remand hall, where I passed the time chatting with good guys like Bernie McQueen from Castlemilk and Gerry Carbin. We'd be joined by Mick Healy. Mick had been accused of an armed robbery and was facing a heavy sentence if he was convicted. The screws, meanwhile, were on a knife-edge, knowing the slightest hint of a threat could spark new mayhem.

One night we heard them running around, shouting, 'Numbers check! Numbers check!' They entered each cell, looking under beds and refusing to say why. I guessed somebody had escaped and was proved right the next morning when I woke up to be told that my wee pal Danny Graham from Govan had vanished. Somehow he had managed to mingle with visitors and walk out of the gym, which was being used as a temporary visiting room.

This good news was followed by more, about the assault. My lawyer, Joe Shields, came to Barlinnie to tell me the procurator fiscal had been in touch and was willing to drop the indictment to a summary complaint if I pleaded guilty. 'What're you waiting for?' I told him. I'd been expecting 18 months, but in February the sheriff listened to excellent mitigation from Joe and admonished me. It meant I was free again, and I celebrated by spending two weeks in Tenerife with Marie. However, our love was cooling and I sensed the cracks in our affair were widening. I liked Marie a lot, but the ups and downs in my life didn't make for a stable relationship. It wasn't fair on her, and so we parted.

Back to being single and fancy free, I resumed my forays into the city clubs and bars with the troops. After my long break in prison, I revisited old favourites like Warehouse, Mardi Gras, Videodrome (owned by Colin Robertson, who was a good pal of John Lynn and John Friel), Tin Pan Alley, Henry Africa's and the Savoy in Sauchiehall Street.

I was able to repay John Friel for some of the many kindnesses he had shown me. While in Maxwell Plum's watching Scheme one night, I was told someone was outside asking to see me and went out to find one of my friends – I'll call him 'Barry' – wearing one of my suits and even my shoes. He opened the jacket to reveal a pistol. I was horrified.

'What the fuck are you doing with that and my suit?' I asked.

He said, 'Pay my taxi fare and I'll tell you.'

I was already annoyed at finding him in my clothes and now I had to pay a £20 taxi bill. 'OK, what's it all about?'

He told me, 'I've been promised £20,000 to shoot John Friel. I needed your suit to get in to see him.'

I asked who was behind it and he mentioned a couple of names, one of them Arty Thompson's. This was appalling. I knew John would be in the nearby Chippendales club.

While we were talking, some guys wandered past and saw Barry waving the pistol. One said, 'That's probably a pea shooter,' at which Barry blasted the door of Maxwell Plum's to prove it was the real thing, and they took to their heels. The sound of Scheme drowned out the noise of gunfire.

I took Barry into Maxwell Plum's to calm him down, and after an hour I said I'd take him to meet John Friel. At Chippendales, I told Barry to wait outside the club office while I went inside to warn John his life was in danger.

I told him, 'Mr Friel, if you'll talk to the guy, I promise you nothing will happen.' John went along with this and, while talking to my pal, discovered one of his best friends was a close relative of Barry. That broke the ice, and John went on to take my friend under his wing, treating him almost like a son for months afterwards.

However, Arty wasn't prepared to let Barry off for failing to shoot the Irishman. One day, Barry had been meeting me at Ma's home and was driving away when a car pulled up and a gunman fired. The bullet passed through the door of the car in which Barry was sitting, fortunately only grazing his body.

The Savoy took on a very special significance because I was in there one night when a friend, Marie Martin, introduced me to a good-looking, tall, leggy blonde who told me her name was Sheila McGourlay, that she was from Bishopbriggs and that she was not long back from the Costa del Sol, where she had been living for two years. Right away, I felt at ease with her, and we spent most of the evening together chatting. I told Sheila I hoped we'd meet again and, by chance, on my next trip into the city, I visited the floating nightclub the *Tuxedo Princess* and there she was. She invited me to stay the night with her at her home. It was to be a turning point in my life. I told Sheila I was a partner in a heating engineering business and she seemed to accept that. As the days passed and we saw more and more of each other, I knew I was falling in love, and within a couple of weeks we went on holiday to Greece. It kept running through my mind that I needed to come clean about myself – face the music, so to speak – but then something happened that took the timing of my planned confession out of my hands.

Rumour spread like wildfire that Jack and I had chased a so-called gangster known as 'Mr Versace' along a street and had slashed and stabbed him in front of all his pals. This had supposedly happened near the Ropeworks pub around the corner from the Warehouse. The gangland rumour factory was in full production and, inevitably, Sheila got to hear and asked if the story was true. I said nothing at first, then tried to dismiss it as just tittle-tattle. Next, I heard on the underworld grapevine that I was to be the target of a hit by rivals. Because of who these people were, I took this seriously and began carrying a loaded firearm whenever I went out. I heard another rumour that I would be shot at Ma's home but had this down as pure fantasy. None of the talk or threats stopped me continuing to go into the city bars and clubs, and part of the reason for that was that I was prepared to make myself an easier target away from Provanmill rather than risk some idiot having a go at me when I was at Ma's and she was there. Of course, we might have been criminals – bad men, maybe – but there was a strict code that you never put non-players, especially women and children, at risk. That was totally taboo.

But there are always those who break our rules. One night, Sheila, me, Ma, James, Gary, Alco, Tracy and a couple of pals were drinking in the Ranza Club in Royston when Alan had a drink spilled on his shirt and went to Ma's to change it. He told us he'd be back right away, but that stained shirt nearly cost him his life.

Ten minutes later, a man dashed into the club to say Alan was outside. 'He's in a state, saying something about gunmen and shooting at your ma's house.' We rushed outside to find Alan in shock. 'I think I've been shot,' he gasped, but there were no signs of blood.

He was disorientated but eventually we managed to get out of him that he had only been in the house a couple of minutes when someone had chapped the door. I had previously warned him to always stay behind the door, never in front, when he opened it, and fortunately he had followed this advice. When the door opened, there were two loud bangs. He ran into the back of the house, climbed out through a window and headed for the club.

When Gary, our pals and I went to Ma's, we found the door wide open and plaster and wood splinters peppered with shotgun pellets all over the floor. I knew somebody was sure to have called the police, so I got out the vacuum cleaner and sucked up all the debris, the evidence of the shooting. By the time the police arrived, there was nothing to see and nobody, including our neighbours, was saying anything. The police took me in for questioning and said I was the intended victim, probably in retaliation for the shooting at the garage or the attack on Mr Versace, but I kept mum.

Back at Ma's, I found Sheila waiting with the rest of the family. I was enraged and, backed by my pals, ready to go to war. Whoever had blasted shots through Ma's door was totally out of order. What if she had opened it? A neighbour described seeing a car circling the area, then going up and down our street before pulling up outside the house. Two men wearing balaclavas had climbed out. One was carrying what appeared to be a double-barrelled shotgun. There was the sound of shots and he saw them run to the car and speed away.

Fergie had completed his three-year sentence and came to see if he could help. Tam Bagan and Billy Reid were with him. Paul never blamed me for what had happened about the confrontation with Arthur Thompson in Barlinnie. Peter arrived, too, wanting to know the names of those responsible. I was everywhere asking questions, but the police were all over me like a rash, waiting to pounce the moment I found my prey. As for Sheila, she had worked out the truth about me, and while her head told her to walk away, her heart forced her to stay. She confided that she had fallen for me big time, but she had found herself in a world that was totally alien to her.

While I switched between leading a normal existence with her and using my gangland contacts to track down the gunmen, I heard good news from Ernie Barrie. The television programme *Rough Justice* had taken up the case of his wrongful conviction, ensuring nationwide publicity. Ernie had magnificent support, too, from his partner, Mary, a tower of strength who never weakened even when he was transferred to the Alcatraz of Scotland, Peterhead, and its brutal regime.

Mick Healy, meanwhile, was found guilty of armed robbery, sentenced to ten years and sent to Shotts jail in Lanarkshire. He had told me, 'I have a plan B if I get a guilty. Watch this space.' I waited and watched.

Sammo had been convicted, after a trial, of taking part in the Peterhead riot that was ended by the SAS. Seven years were added to his six-year robbery stretch. Savage sentences were also meted out to his friends Malky Leggat and Jake Devine. Jake, who was badly hurt when the SAS threw him downstairs, later unsuccessfully sued for damages.

Sheila, ignoring the worst and hoping for better, took me to meet her mum, also Sheila, who had run the Lion Hotel at Colston in the north of Glasgow for many years, and her dad, Frank, who was retired from his job with an oil company. They were kind and put me at ease, but Sheila was trying to steer me towards a more settled life and asked if I would work with her if she took on a pub. I was all for this, but I was surprised when she returned from a meeting with brewery executives and told me she was taking over Thomson's Bar. I knew it. It was in Springburn and previous landlords had quit because it had a reputation for trouble. Ma agreed to work with Sheila. The bar was at the time a favourite haunt of my friends the McGovern family.

I was excited, not just because I was sure Sheila could succeed where others had failed but also because she had told me she was pregnant. I was to become a father.

And there had been good news, too, for Ernie. The authorities had finally seen sense and realised he should not have been charged, never mind convicted. He was released in August 1988 on interim liberation pending a formal appeal hearing, at which he would be cleared. He telephoned me from a luxury hotel in the

Lake District, where a newspaper had taken him after a dramatic release from Peterhead that could have come straight out of the pages of a James Bond novel. A car sped out of the prison gates, carrying Ernie to freedom, pursued by a pack of press vehicles. Ernie hung on for dear life through winding country roads until the driver suddenly pulled into a field and he was rushed over to a waiting helicopter and airlifted to Cumbria.

Now things began moving fast. Sheila quickly made a success of Thomson's Bar. Everybody knew I was her boyfriend, which was probably the reason why the troublemakers had disappeared. Gary became friendly with one of the McGovern brothers, Steven, as well as his wife, Nora, and they'd socialise at the bar. I had a soft spot for another of the McGovern brothers, James, and would sneak him into the Ultrateque disco in the city centre even though, at 14, he was legally too young.

After six months, Sheila told the brewers she was leaving to take on another pub in Springburn, the Talisman. They begged her to stay on, but her mind was made up. Around the same time, Tracy met a guy who became her boyfriend, Pat McCulloch from Barlanark. Their daughter Cheryl was born on 1 January 1990.

It was a time for leavings and arrivals. Sheila left Thomson's Bar, and on 15 February 1989 our son Daryl arrived, born two weeks early in Stobhill Hospital, Springburn. By then, Mick Healy had left Shotts, hidden in a butcher's van. He went on the run, but our paths were destined to cross again.

11

My Famous Alibi

I KEPT A SHOTGUN stowed out of sight beneath the bar of the Talisman after it opened in March 1989, reasoning there was no point in taking chances. Most of our customers were welcomed, including many familiar names. Tam Bagan, Paul Ferris and Joe Hanlon would pop in for a chat, as would the McGoverns, Frank Ward, George 'Goofy' Docherty and my good friends the Shannon brothers, Pawny, Tam and (during brief leaves from the Army) Alex, who always had something of an air of mystery about him. People wondered what he did and assumed he would be skilled in the use of weapons, a highly sought-after quality in the underworld. We were pals with Davie and Agnes Hutton, who drank in Thomson's Bar, so Sheila offered Agnes a job in the Talisman, which was handy for Agnes since they lived close by. Davie worked as a brickie and was a good wee guy to have a drink and a laugh with. Paul Kelly, sometimes called Kelso, whom I'd known for years, was a regular as well. From the opening night, when the well-known Glasgow band Jamie Barnes and Cochise did a super gig, all seemed to be going well. I was especially happy for Gary, who had settled down with Lorraine Shields, whose dad owned the Ranza Club and who was from Provanmill.

This was the year of rave culture. Everyone was going about the Warehouse dancing, hugging, kissing and even talking to one another, not usually as a result of drink but from taking the new drug of choice, Ecstasy, dubbed 'the love drug'. Whereas before, the same people were enemies and wouldn't look twice at each other, now they were spilling their innermost secrets back at parties.

But not everyone was inclined to be friendly. One day I walked into the Talisman and immediately sensed something was wrong. Tracy was having a drink with a man. At first glance, I thought it was Da, and then when he turned I knew it was him. As soon as she saw me, Ma gestured me to one side.

'He's been here about half an hour,' she said. 'I'm not happy, but Tracy said we should give him a chance. I just know he's going to start something.'

'Let's see what happens,' I told her.

I had a drink with Da, but then heard him making a cheeky remark about Ma. I let that one go, but then the unpleasant comments about Ma became more frequent and I lost it. I grabbed him, threw him against the fruit machine, then ran him out of the doors at the front of the pub. He fell down the stairs and looked a pathetic sight lying on the pavement. 'Don't come back to this pub,' I told him. I felt sorry for him, but he was out of order. 'That was my da,' I told curious customers.

That apart, life was good. We bought a caravan at Anstruther in Fife, and Sheila and I would go there with Daryl. It was great taking walks with him in his pram, the sea air filling our lungs, away from the smog of Glasgow. Fatherhood agreed with me, and all my family remarked how I seemed content and happy.

Around this time, I called in at the Caravel pub in Barlanark, owned by Tam and Margaret McGraw, and met Tam for the first time. There were other visits to the Caravel, but there was something about Tam that left you with a feeling that he wasn't to be trusted. I'd been hearing street gossip about him at the time that wasn't very complimentary. Joe Hanlon, a very handy amateur boxer, worked on the door of the Caravel. Joe was a happy wee guy with a great sense of humour, and a joke from him was generally enough to sort out any trouble if it started.

When she needed a night out, I'd take Sheila to the *Tuxedo Princess*. It had two huge dance floors and several bars, and in one we would see our friend big Sam Bowman buying champagne for the girls who always seemed to flock around him. I called them his angels. And we'd often bump into my friend Chas Tinney, his pal Harky and all the boys from Shettleston.

It wasn't always plain sailing on the *Tux*. One night, after Sheila and I had had a row, I spotted her with her pal Marie, who had originally introduced us, talking to the Celtic footballer Derek Whyte and the football agent John Viola. At the time, Derek was recovering from an injury sustained on the pitch. One thing led to another, and I ended up giving him a slap. It was one of those heat-of-the-moment flare-ups over nothing and had been settled amicably by the time the bouncers came over. But it shouldn't have happened, especially as it turned out that John Viola was pals with Chas Tinney.

Another footballer caused even more of a furore at this time. Mo Johnston had gone from Celtic to the French side Nantes but wanted to come back to Scotland. Everybody expected him to return to the East End of Glasgow, to Parkhead, but instead he shocked the football world by signing for Rangers. The move led to Mo getting death threats, with disgruntled Celtic fans being blamed.

We worked hard at making the Talisman a success. I was taking a real interest, organising a pool tournament every Thursday and even buying a trophy for the winner to keep. So the months seemed to shoot by. Early in 1990, Gary moved to Lennoxtown with Lorraine, whose parents had bought a pub there called the Piggery. From time to time, a busload of locals from Blackhill and Provanmill would visit them.

But trouble seemed to follow me. In June 1990, I went to an open-air concert on Glasgow Green in aid of the Glasgow Council for the Single Homeless with Sheila and our friend Terry Curran. It featured Sheena Easton, who was originally from Bellshill. She had achieved huge successes with a number of songs, including '9 to 5' and the Oscar-nominated James Bond theme 'For Your Eyes Only'. Sheena had settled in America but her semi-American accent did not go down well with the Glasgow Green audience, who threw empty plastic bottles and cans at the stage and told her in no uncertain terms to clear off back across the Atlantic.

As we were leaving the concert, three rivals approached. I immediately put my hand in my inside jacket pocket to suggest I was pulling a gun out, and the ruse seemed to work, because they backed off and we got into my car to drive away. But then I saw what appeared to be a double-barrelled shotgun pointed directly at the windscreen. It turned out to be a spear gun, and when it was fired the short spear bounced off the glass. As I was frantically trying to reverse and get away, the other car windows were being smashed. Sheila was screaming hysterically, but I managed to drive off, cursing, angry about what had happened.

I had to stop at traffic lights in London Road and spotted, in my rear-view mirror, a car approaching at speed. It made no effort to stop but smashed into my motor, sending it spinning around. Before we knew it, we had been surrounded by the same trio of rivals. One produced a handgun and aimed at me through the offside driver's window, but before he could pull the trigger I managed to drive away, black smoke belching from the rear of my car and pieces of glass and metal falling off. Sheila was badly shaken and we decided to get out of Glasgow for a wee while. A friend had a holiday flat in Rothesay – the same town where Fergie had been hiding out when the police turned up – and we set off for the ferry to the Isle of Bute with Daryl, Ma and James.

A couple of days later, over breakfast, James raised his head from his morning paper and asked, 'Does Tony McVey have a brother called Paul?'

I knew who he was talking about. Tony McVey, whose nickname was 'Scarface', was well known in the underworld.

'Aye,' I said, adding, 'Why?'

James told me, 'Paul was shot in the city centre last night and it says here he's in a bad way, fighting for his life.'

I reached over and took the newspaper, which said that McVey had been shot in the chest at point-blank range in the Merchant City. I thought nothing more about this, because it didn't concern me.

But the next day, after I'd taken the ferry home, my lawyer Joe

Shields arrived to say that he understood the police were looking for me in connection with McVey's shooting. Joe rang Stewart Street police station to find out what the situation was and was told that although there was no warrant in force for my arrest, the police would like to interview me. Because I had nothing to hide, I agreed to speak to them and told Sheila, 'I'll be back in time for dinner.' Joe and I drove there, but as I was walking towards the main entrance, police suddenly surrounded me. I was forced to the ground, handcuffed and told I was under arrest for the attempted murder of Paul McVey in Ingram Street.

The police had lied, but I had come to expect that sort of treatment. So we went off to an interview room for a formal question-and-answer session on tape and in Joe's presence. It began with the usual stuff: name, age, address. When I was asked where I had been and answered, 'Rothesay,' I noticed a few eyebrows go up. Who was with me? 'Sheila, my son Daryl, my ma and her man, James.' Doubts were beginning to creep into the interrogators' minds.

They gave the time of the shooting, around 7.30 in the evening, and asked where I had been then. 'Driving around the island with the others,' I replied. Hope appeared in the eyes of the police. My witnesses were family; it was expected they'd go along with whatever story I told.

'Anybody see you?' was the next question.

'Yes,' I told them. I knew what was coming next and waited to provide the punchline.

'Who?'

Now came my bombshell. 'Sir Richard Attenborough.'

The tape was switched off. A hand slammed onto the table. 'Think you're funny? You a comedian or something?'

'No,' I said. 'We met him and his wife when we were driving. They were walking their dogs.' Even Joe didn't know I'd be coming out with this, but then I had no reason to tell him. I wondered if even he was having doubts and said, 'He and his wife have a holiday home on Rothesay. We saw them walking the dogs and stopped for a chat.'

The interview ended soon after, the cops saying they would need to speak to Sheila, my ma and James. There was no mention of Sir Richard or his wife. I was remanded, and before I was led off, I asked Joe, 'Would you ring Sheila? I won't be needing my dinner. I'll be getting the Barlinnie stew tomorrow.'

I lay in my police station cell wondering if Sir Richard and his wife were taking another stroll around their 1,700-acre Rhubodach Forest estate on Bute's east coast. I knew there was no way they'd be stuck in a dingy, stinking hole like I was that night.

What had happened to me was shocking. I had done nothing wrong, had provided an unshakeable and easily confirmed alibi, yet I was being denied my freedom. I knew how Ernie Barrie felt. The next morning, I was remanded to Barlinnie for a week. Sheila, Ma and James were summoned to Stewart Street and grilled for hours. The police suggested I might have left the island earlier than them, hinting that they were covering up for me. But my alibi was rock solid. James, a big film buff, said it was he who had spotted Sir Richard and insisted that I stop the car. On the fourth day, I was taken back to Stewart Street and put in an ID parade, but nobody picked me out as the shooter, and bail was not opposed when I next appeared in court.

So I felt as though I had at last been given a decent break. But not everybody was getting a square – or fair – deal. On 30 November, a gang battered down the door of Gerald Rae's home in Langside, Glasgow, and proceeded to set about him with baseball bats and pickaxe handles. He was given a dreadful beating, kicked, punched and dragged almost unconscious out into the tenement close. Half a dozen terrified and appalled local residents rang the police, telling of a man screaming and shouting in pain, surrounded by a crowd of dark figures pummelling him. The callers warned that unless help appeared soon, the man might die. Sirens screaming, blue lights flashing, Strathclyde's finest raced into action. Surprisingly, the attackers seemed indifferent to the sound of approaching police. One of the locals shook her head in disbelief and told the neighbours why. The attackers were police: the Manky Mob.

Gerry was no angel. He had a criminal record and had served a few long prison sentences for being involved in the drug trade. Some extreme observers suggested he deserved a beating. But what he suffered that night was way beyond reason or the law. Yet that was not the worst part of it, because more would come. He was taken off to hospital for emergency treatment. When he recovered, he was hauled off to a police station and charged with heroin dealing. He was shown a package.

'Where did that come from?' asked Gerry and was told, 'We found it in your hall.'

'I've never seen that before,' he protested, demanding, 'Where in the hall?'

The answer was: 'In the electricity meter box.'

It would be nine years before the saga finally came to an end.

A month later, Gary was arrested following a fight outside a Lennoxtown bar. He was accused of cutting his victim on the hand with a knife but said that it was in retaliation for being hit over the head with a wooden plank. So much for trying to lead a quiet life in the country. He was remanded to Barlinnie, where he spent Christmas and saw in 1991 in a grim cell.

There wasn't much festive cheer for Rangers legend Ally McCoist, either. The striker wasn't having a good time of it. As a result of the arrival of Mo Johnston, Ally was left on the bench so often that he was given the nickname 'the Judge'. Sadly, I never got the chance to appear before him.

12

Return of the Fugitive

A FEW DAYS AFTER Daryl's second birthday in February, a familiar but unexpected face walked into the Talisman. I had to look twice to make sure I wasn't seeing things, but, sure enough, there stood Mick Healy. I hurried him through to the back room, because, while none of the customers I knew would be spilling the beans if they recognised him, you could never be certain about strangers. Mick had been on the run for 26 months since his dramatic escape had made headlines. He had watched for the butcher who supplied Shotts with meat to make his daily delivery, and just as the van was about to head off he hid in the back. The driver, wholly unaware that he had been joined by a live carcass, headed into the centre of Glasgow, and when he stopped at traffic lights Mick leapt out and took to his heels. Some believed Mick's distinctive appearance and the prominent newspaper and television appeals for information about him would be enough to guarantee he wouldn't be at large for long. He was six feet tall, fair-haired and tattooed. Police who knew him were more sceptical, warning that he could easily dye his hair and grow a beard. And there was more. The police suspected that he sometimes went about in women's clothing to conceal his identity. In fact, Mick was a master of disguise.

Over a drink, he told me that his travels as a fugitive had taken him to London and even France and then to Torquay, the seaside holiday resort in Devon, famous as the home of the crime writer

Agatha Christie. As he talked, I knew Mick had called to see me for some specific reason; he wasn't risking his freedom just for a chat about the old days. And then he cut to the chase. He had a bank job lined up. Would I be interested? It would set me up for life. He had all the details worked out, had done his homework, but he said, 'Don't give me an answer now, Blink. Have a think about it and I'll come back in a few months when everything is ready. This is so good I'm not rushing anything.' I asked if he needed anybody else, thinking of Peter, and he told me he would let me know. Before he left, I asked what sort of money he was talking about. 'Millions, not even hundreds of thousands,' he said, and disappeared.

I knew Mick would keep his word and be back, but until he returned there was nothing to do but wait and think. I obviously needed to know more, but even at that stage my gut reaction was to say, 'I'm in.'

Meantime, life had to go on. We had a busy bar to run, I was still watching my back and I had Gary to worry about. He had been remanded to Barlinnie, where I visited him. Jack and I went to see an old friend, William Ballantyne from Haghill, known as 'Bally', who was in the special unit at the Big House. This had opened in 1973 as an experiment to offer some of the hardest troublemakers in the prison system the chance to pass their sentences in a less restrictive atmosphere. Jimmy Boyle had been its most celebrated inmate; Hugh Collins was another. Both would go on to become famous in the world of art and sculpture. T.C. Campbell was also in there, still fighting as hard as ever to prove his innocence and Joe Steele's. And Joe's brother Johnnyboy was there too.

Bally had stabbed a screw in Peterhead and had been involved in an incident where another was taken hostage, and as a consequence he'd spent a load of time in solitary. Then he was moved to the unit. He cooked us mince and tatties, which went down well with the vodka we'd smuggled in. The unit was a relaxed place; inmates were allowed their own televisions – unheard of in mainstream prisons at this time – and there were no limitations on visiting hours.

RETURN OF THE FUGITIVE

One of the guys in the unit with Bally at the time was Londoner Alan Brown, who knew the Kray twins. Alan had been sentenced to life after a payroll snatch at Springburn railway depot in 1973 during which a gateman was shot dead. Little did I know that Alan and the Krays would become a part of my future.

To celebrate my 30th birthday on 2 March, we had a party at the Talisman with our families and friends. It was a great night. But shortly afterwards two young plain-clothes detectives turned up at the bar.

'You Ian MacDonald?' one asked.

'Aye.'

'Our boss wants to see you. Would you come with us?'

'What for?'

'Look, if you don't come down, we'll come to your house.'

This was starting to get nasty. 'Am I going to be arrested or charged with anything?' I asked.

'If you were,' said the one who appeared to be running this show, 'you'd have had the cuffs put on you already.'

His colleague, sensing this conversation was going nowhere, decided to chip in. He said, 'It's to do with your brother and needs to be sorted. You'll only be ten, fifteen minutes, then we'll bring you right back.'

I was wary, remembering the last time I'd been told something along those lines, when half an hour had turned into seven days in Barlinnie. But I needed to find out what this was all about, so I told Sheila I'd be right back, hoping this time I'd be right. She agreed it was best I go and get whatever it was over with.

At Baird Street police station, their boss, a detective inspector, introduced himself and repeated the promise that I'd be home in a few minutes. No messing about here. 'I know you've been trying to persuade your brother's victim to change his statement,' he said. As I opened my mouth to protest, he went on, 'No, hear me through, Ian. I'm not stupid. If anything happens to that witness before your brother goes to court, I'll come down on you like a ton of bricks. Even if you're in Spain and something happens to the victim, I'll be coming for you. Understand?' I told him I didn't know what he was talking about. 'You get the message,' he said. 'We're clear on that. You can go now.'

I walked out, stunned. Sheila was surprised to see me this time and could tell I was angry. 'Your dinner is ready,' she joked to break the tension.

A few weeks later, Gary went on trial at the High Court in Glasgow, where the alleged victim and his wife were escorted by police. But Gary walked free. One worry less.

At the start of April, Mick reappeared. His homework was completed, he said, the final details worked out. Everything was in place and we were good to go. He had recruited the rest of the team, a bunch of capable and reliable guys. That was shorthand for telling me Peter would not be required.

All that was needed to complete the line-up was a nod from me that I was in. I trusted Mick completely and knew I would be in safe hands. He assured me that what he had planned was a 100 per cent goer.

The target was the National Westminster Bank on the Strand, the Torquay seafront, next to the department store Debenhams. It was one of the largest banks in the Devon and Cornwall area and was a holding bank, which meant its vault held lots of money for distribution to the other, smaller banks. At our first meeting, Mick had mentioned millions. Now he put a number to that: six, six million pounds, at least six million pounds. The team would be six-handed. The sums were simple. Six into six million worked out at a million pounds each.

I had thought long and hard about this since Mick had first come to me with the proposition. On the one hand, my life was going well; I was mostly keeping out of trouble and had a great family. Looking back now, I suppose I was being greedy. I saw the bank job as an opportunity to start a new life abroad with Sheila and Daryl. I'd often hankered to open a nightclub in Spain and, with the kind of money I would make, that dream could become a reality. But we were playing for high stakes here. This wasn't walking into Woolies with a water gun. We would be taking on a large bank with shotguns and balaclavas. Innocent people could be hurt, and if it went wrong, not only would my dream of a new life with my family be destroyed but any hope I had of spending time with those I loved at all would be gone. It was a big gamble. If we are honest, we all wonder what it would be like to be a millionaire, but I suppose most people wouldn't dream of sticking a gun in someone's face to become one. Granted, I was trying to settle down with Sheila and Daryl, but at the back of my mind I was always waiting for the big one, the one that only comes around once.

I had weighed up the pros and cons, and the pros had won. By the time Mick came back, my mind was already made up. He had only to cross the 't's and dot the 'i's to convince me. I had thought long and hard about the consequences. That old adage 'Don't do the crime if you can't do the time' never really crossed my mind at the time. When you set off to commit a crime, you have to maintain a positive frame of mind, confident you won't be caught, otherwise pressure and nerves build up, draining confidence. Think too much about what you are going to do and you'll probably end up too scared to walk out your front door. 'Count me in, Mick,' I said. We discussed more details, shook hands and he left.

I told him I'd travel with his younger brother James and bring the guns with us. It would be safer that way. Mick was heading to Torquay by car with two of the others, Rab Harper and Tam Carrigan. The sixth member of the team, Mick Carroll, already stayed in Torquay with his girlfriend Christine. We were all from Glasgow. Occasionally, I'd told Sheila I was going away for a week. I never said where or why, and she never asked, because at the end of the day she understood there was always food on the table for the family and a wee bit more just for fun. Now I simply said I'd be going away shortly for a few days, and she left it at that.

Two weeks before the day we had fixed for the raid, Thursday, 9 May, the time came for me to leave and head south. I kissed Sheila and said goodbye. Now there was no turning back. I was either going to be sipping champagne in Marbella or cold tea behind grim prison walls. James Healy picked me up at the

Provanmill Inn in a private taxi. I had two holdalls stuffed with clothes, a sawn-off double-barrelled shotgun, a pistol, plenty of ammunition and other tools needed for our plan.

Glasgow Central Station is usually busy. So instead of boarding the London train there, we decided to join it at Motherwell, where there was less chance of us being recognised. Disaster almost struck before we reached Motherwell when our taxi driver decided to take a short cut through Strathclyde Country Park. Two motorcycle policemen pulled us over. 'Fuckin' hell,' I said to James, 'we're going to get the jail before we even leave Scotland.' Our driver rolled down his window and was told to slow down as he was driving too fast. He was let off with a warning and the cops fortunately didn't recognise us. So off we went again, wondering if this was a lucky omen. In London, we took another train to Newton Abbot, where Mick Healy and Rab Harper met us in a BMW. They had booked two caravans in Grange Court Holiday Centre at Paignton, four miles from Torquay on the English Riviera. Mick had assumed the identity of John Weir and had hired one caravan and a car under that alias. Rab, who was with his girlfriend Maureen, had booked the other under the name Mr R. Sloan.

While we were waiting to carry out the raid, some of us made trips into Torquay to watch the bank early in the morning before it opened, checking the movements of more than 20 staff as they arrived for work and went in. While he'd been on the run in London in 1989, Mick had met a French student called Nathalie. They'd lost touch but he'd contacted her through her college in Montpellier and suggested a trip to Devon. She came over with her sister, Sandrine. Mick and Tam went to meet them at the airport and arrived back at the caravans about one in the morning.

It was a tense time, and each of us tried to ease the pressure by making it feel like a holiday. Grange Court was idyllic, really peaceful. Just a mile away was a leisure centre. We'd often go there to relax, using the sauna and badminton court frequently. Just days before the robbery, I decided to bring Sheila down with Daryl, asking if she fancied a sunshine break, and we booked into a flat along the Paignton seafront. Now that we were with our families, some of whom knew what was going to happen while others did not, there was an easing of the feeling that some sort of crisis was approaching. We blended in well as a group of tourist friends, managing to mask what was really on our minds: the contents of the bank vault and a passport to a better life. We'd visit the local pub, Cockfosters, near the entrance to the holiday centre, while Sheila and I took Daryl to the zoo. James Healy joined us.

All seemed to be going well. Too well. We were enjoying our stay, having fun with our families and the final preparations were in place. But three days before the plan was due to swing into operation, Rab Harper and Tam Carrigan pulled out because of a packet of crisps. I had been with them on reconnaissance in a hired car, registered to Mick's alias John Weir, when we were pulled over by a traffic cop who stopped us for littering because he had seen an empty crisp packet float out of one of the windows. A crisp packet. It would cost us dear. And I didn't even like crisps. We all gave false names. Tam was driving and gave the details of John Weir. The cop checked it out and let us go, but the incident made Rab and Tam uncomfortable. They talked it over and announced they were leaving to try to make their fortune elsewhere. There was no dispute. The rest of us agreed with their wishes, albeit reluctantly. It meant we were two men down and our plan was in disarray.

The original idea had been for Mick Carroll not to take part in the actual raid. Now Mick Healy asked him to join in, since it would take more than three of us to complete the job. And he asked me to take over as driver. Mick Healy needed to be in the bank to supervise the raid, Mick Carroll was needed alongside him and James couldn't drive. It was too late to bring in anybody else, and I agreed, but I wasn't happy. On reflection, however, I saw it as a lesser risk, although I'd still be taking part.

Just after midnight on the 9th, we made preparations to get into the bank, silently going down a back lane at the side of the building, climbing a wall and heading towards a fire escape that was hidden from view. We drilled through this and went inside. There was no CCTV, no floor alarms, no security beams, nothing. That sort of sophisticated security would come later. Only the vault was alarmed from a security panel. We could have tried to burn through the vault, but we had a simpler plan. The bank staff would open it for us. All we had to do was get inside, hide and wait for them to turn up.

The staff had a straightforward routine. Whoever was first inside opened the door for the next person, who opened it for the third and so on. Before Rab and Tam had left, we had decided to let the first member in, then when the second came grab them as soon as they opened the door. We would then seize the others as they turned up and force them to lie on the floor beside the vault. That needed a full crew and, being two men short, we had to have a rethink. It was decided that we would act once we were confident most of the staff were inside the bank. But first we needed a hideaway.

On the ground floor, in the main office suite at the rear of the bank, we cut a large hole in a partition wall underneath a staircase with a cordless saw and then fashioned a section of plasterboard to fit the hole. We would hide behind it, watching the vault through spyholes drilled through the partition wall. Not wanting to cause suspicion by leaving signs of disturbance, we carefully swept up the debris from our building job in a bank dustpan. Any artisan would have been proud of our work.

To pass the time, we played pool in the staff recreation room, and at three in the morning I left, carrying the bags with the power tools inside. Sheila and Daryl had moved out of the flat into the caravan that had been occupied by Rab Harper, and I rejoined them there for a few hours. The plan was to use one car to drive with the bags of loot to where a second would already be parked and switch to it to return to the caravans before our getaway from Paignton. While Sheila slept, I sat in the living room and watched a rerun of an episode of *The Sweeney*, with John Thaw and Dennis Waterman.

I'll never forget that night. It was one of the longest of my life.

RETURN OF THE FUGITIVE

I went back out just after eight, parked up the back street from where we had entered the bank and hung around waiting for my friends and watching. The first member of staff arrived at a quarter past eight. All seemed in order. A second rang the bell and the door opened to admit them. Others followed until there were fifteen people in there, including seven females. Inside, the three lads lay cautious and silent, waiting for the staff to begin their day. They had entered the hiding hole just after seven and watched for the moment when the vault would be opened. Then they saw a member of staff emerge from it pushing a trolley laden with cash.

13

The Torquay Job

IT WAS TIME to go, the moment they had been waiting for, mentally building up to the peak of the drama. Nobody was more hyped up than Mick Healy, who had devoted four months to carefully nurturing and fine-tuning the project. He planned to vanish to the south of France, and suddenly its vineyards and the warm blue waters of the Mediterranean had never seemed closer. With a whoop of 'Showtime!', the three guys burst from their hiding place, guns raised and shouting orders to the bank staff not to move. Shocked and scared, the workers were ordered to lie on the ground. But at the very moment of triumph, it began to go wrong.

To the guys' horror, they discovered that what filled the trolley was not money but worthless credit cards and paperwork. Shit. Well, there was still the jackpot, the strongroom vault. Mick Healy ran in and came face to face with a heavily grilled gate, blocking him from going further. The money, all our hopes and dreams, lay on the other side, just a few feet away. All it needed was a key.

'Who's the fucking manager?' Mick demanded. He was furious, raging. A man rose and identified himself as Brian Thomas, the senior manager, but before he could say anything further he was grabbed by Mick, who hauled him to the strongroom, forced his face to the grille, put a gun to his neck and bellowed, 'Open that fucking gate!' Thomas explained that he didn't have the key and, repeating his claims in the face of threats from a volatile Mick, was believed. So who had it? He was taken back and thrown to the ground with the other members of staff, whom the guys suspected of playing a highly risky form of Pass the Parcel, only in this case it was Pass the Key. Each in turn was questioned and each denied having the key to open the grille and give access into the vault. Our fortune might as well have been on the dark side of the moon. It was unattainable. For Mick now, the south of France had never seemed so far away.

The tension that had been swiftly building up suddenly exploded with the crack of a gun going off. It was fired into the ceiling, causing debris to fall onto 20-year-old clerk Nina Lowley. Blood began to drip from her head into her hands convincing her colleagues she had been shot. Screams and shouts filled the bank as the rest of the staff panicked, drowning the sound of someone ringing at the doorbell. For a tick of time there was silence and suddenly the only sound was that of the doorbell. 'They'll get suspicious if you don't answer it,' Thomas told the raiders. He was ignored. The bell continued ringing. It was time to leave, and they fled through the rear. Thomas led his staff out through the front door and then called the police.

I had been sitting patiently in the BMW, but I was apprehensive, not knowing what was going on inside the bank. The sun had come up and it looked like being a fine day. I told myself, 'They'll be slow if they're carrying six million pounds.' And then, in a flash, everything changed. 'They've fucked up,' I muttered as Mick came running out clutching only a holdall big enough to carry a weapon, his arms otherwise empty. No bundles of money, bags of banknotes. He was running very fast, followed by Mick Carroll and James, equally unhindered. My heart sank.

As they climbed sweating and grim-faced into the car, I barked, 'Did you even fucking do it?' and without waiting for an answer drove away. It was Mick Healy who answered as we headed for safety. 'Bastards. We didn't get the fucking key for the gate,' he spat, and nobody tried to disguise their dejection. All the planning and preparation for nothing. No money anyway. The accounting was yet to come.

BLINK

It was much later that we learned through a friend who knew one of the bank workers what had gone wrong. The chief cashier's name was Roy. Maybe he had a dream that hardnosed Jocks were about to rob Roy, but whatever the reason, for the first time in years he had failed to turn up for work on time. Somebody suggested he must have slept in, but we never discovered the truth. His job was to open that grille, and he had the key. The key that had come close to getting his senior manager killed, the key that led to the staff being terrorised, the key that held all of our dreams.

After switching to the second car, we arrived at the caravans not jubilant millionaires but broken men. James Healy sat with me while I confessed to Sheila the real reason why we were in Torquay and saw the panic build inside her. She insisted we leave immediately. I was nonchalant, however, confident we could not be caught. In fact, we were already on the police radar. Word was spreading about an armed raid on the bank. That sort of news travels fast. A local painter and decorator had watched as we'd switched from the BMW, thinking it was suspicious when the car was abandoned and noting what he believed was the registration number. He telephoned the police to pass on his information. A computer check initially showed that the number he gave did not exist, but when two of the letters were transposed it revealed a vehicle registered to a car hire firm in Devon. And that company said it was hired to a John Weir, who had given the caravan site address.

Unaware that the net was closing, I asked Sheila to make a late breakfast while I sulked with James. Around one o'clock, Mick Healy arrived with the two French girls, on his way to book their flights home. He took James aside, admitted he had forgotten to dispose of the holdalls containing the tools and other incriminating evidence and had left them in the caravan he and the girls had just vacated. He asked him to throw them into one of the ponds around the site. James was annoyed that Mick had forgotten a vital part of the plan and asked me to help. I was furious, but I agreed, and we crossed to the other side of the site and into Mick's caravan to collect them. As we set off, I sensed James was nervous, continually looking about and telling me, 'I think we're being followed.' I looked but saw nobody. 'It's OK,' I assured him. We reached a large pond and were opening the holdalls when a shout rang out: 'Armed police! Get down!'

A few minutes earlier, armed officers had arrived at the site seeking 'Mr Weir' and had hidden in an empty caravan to watch the one hired to the mystery man. They saw two guys enter it and leave immediately carrying two bags. One cop had followed us alone, a colleague running for help because their radios had broken, and had drawn his pistol.

I told James, 'Don't make a move. He might shoot us,' and we lay face down on the ground. The policeman approached. I knew he was nervous because I could feel him shaking as the cold handcuffs slapped against my wrist. For all he knew, we might have had easily accessible firearms tucked into our waistbands. 'Get up and walk back in the direction you've just come from,' he ordered. I turned and saw him for the first time.

He was tall, about six feet four, well built, wearing a black leather jacket and jeans. His gun looked like a Magnum or a .45 Colt. 'If you try and run, I will shoot you,' he told us. We walked back to the caravan, devastated and cursing Mick Healy, wondering whether if he'd got rid of the holdalls earlier we might not be in this situation. The policeman ordered us into the caravan they had been using, telling us to close the curtains and sit down. We were then handcuffed together.

Until this point, he had gone by the rule book. Now he began making mistakes. Instead of staying with us inside, he stood outside, his gun holstered. Then he turned his back to the door. But it was his fourth error that gave me five extra weeks of freedom. My cuff was slack, allowing me to get a hand free. James, aware of what was about to happen, warned me, 'He'll shoot you if you run,' but my mind was made up. When we heard voices, James peeked out and saw the officer distracted. 'Go,' he said. I crawled into a bedroom, opened the window, climbed out and ran like a hare, expecting at any second a shout or shot that would warn me I had been spotted, across the site to the caravan where Sheila and Daryl were waiting.

Gasping out what had just happened, I urged, 'Make your way home. I need to go, right now.'

She burst into tears, but I had no time to comfort her. Stopping only to change from the jacket I knew the searchers would be looking to see me wearing, I was in and out of that caravan in two minutes. Then I was bounding across fields, never stopping for breath until I reached the leisure centre. From there, I made my way to the main road along the seafront, knowing I had to get away in double-quick time. The area would soon be swarming with police. Should I make for London or Glasgow, I wondered. Then a dreadful realisation hit me. My money was in my other jacket. Searching the pockets of the replacement, I found a lone pound coin. Matters worsened when I heard a whir and looked up to see a police helicopter. Crawling, creeping, crouching and walking, I managed to make it to the neighbouring town of Brixham and, from a telephone kiosk at the harbour there, used the pound coin to call a friend in London. Having quickly told him what had happened, I listened as he told me to lie low until he could reach me.

It was midnight before we met up. By then, the tension had even got to him. He was sweating and wary. Expecting roadblocks, I hid under a blanket on the back seat. Once we were well away, I climbed into the front and breathed a sigh of relief. He took me to his home in Kensington, where he chain-smoked joints. I couldn't blame him. It must have been a nerve-racking drive for him to Devon, not knowing whether we might be ambushed by the police and then having to motor back slowly, desperate to avoid speeding and giving the police a reason to pull him over. His wife, he told me before showing me to a bed in a spare room, was eight months pregnant, and that only added to his fears.

I fell into an uneasy, broken sleep, but during the morning I felt myself being roughly shaken awake and heard a voice shouting, 'Drug squad. What's your name?' My friend was a suspected drug dealer operating around the west of London. I knew he had recently dealt with a Turkish gang only to discover that they were being monitored by the police. But my mind was hazy and I wondered if he had persuaded some pals to wind me up.

'You're fucking joking,' I protested.

'What's your name?' I was asked again.

'Gary MacDonald,' I said automatically, then wondered what name my friend would give when he was asked who his visitor was.

'What brings you here, Gary? How do you know him downstairs?' asked the police.

'I went to school with him,' I said. 'I'm down here looking for work.'

By now, four or five officers were in the room. I was still in bed. I could hear more of them harassing my friend downstairs. It later turned out he had been sitting smoking a joint when the police smashed in his door and stormed into his home. I was finding it hard to believe that this was happening.

'You ever been in trouble, Gary?' the officer asked.

'Yes,' I said sheepishly. 'I done my borstal. Then I got eight years just before I turned nineteen.'

I was suddenly aware that the cops were moving closer. A couple in particular were taking an increased interest. 'And what did you get your eight years for, Gary?'

'Slashed a guy's throat,' I said, then added, 'But that was years ago.'

'Typical Scot, eh?' the officer said, and followed up with the question every Englishman seemed to ask anyone from Scotland who had a criminal record. 'You from the Gorbals?' I said nothing.

I could hear voices on police radios checking Gary's record but was still sweating over what my friend would tell them when he was asked for my name. Then, suddenly, I was told that my details had been confirmed and the police would be leaving – but they would be taking my friend with them.

After they left, I climbed out of bed and went downstairs to meet his wife. She said he had been asked for my name but was so furious at the way they had stormed into his house that he had answered simply, 'Fuck off and ask him yourself. I'm not saying anything about anything. You kicked in my fucking door, you cunts. So fuck off.'

I rang Gary, who said Sheila and Daryl had also made it to

London and were staying with another of my friends. He passed on their telephone number and when I called it Sheila answered and described how armed police had swarmed over the caravan site. They didn't know about the caravan we had been using and she was able to leave the site, pushing Daryl in a buggy. As she left, she saw James Healy being driven off in the back of a police car.

Her host gave me directions to the Charlie Chaplin, a pub in Elephant and Castle where he suggested we meet. My friend's pregnant wife handed me a hundred-pound note, walked me to the nearest Underground station and wished me luck. From the Charlie Chaplin bar, I was taken to a high-rise flat a few streets away, where I was reunited with Sheila and Daryl and told we could stay for a week until the heat died down. But I had unfinished business to take care of in Glasgow. I knew it wasn't the wisest thing to do, but I had to go back. It was only a matter of time before I was caught. My fingerprints were on the window of the caravan, so I would be easily identified from police records.

Later in the day Sheila, Daryl and I boarded a train for Glasgow at Euston. It was a terrible, sad journey. I knew I couldn't stay on the run for ever and that when I was arrested I would be going away to prison for a long, long time. I would miss my son growing up, would be without Sheila for years. But it was no use spilling tears. I'd known the risks and now it had all gone wrong I had to accept that prison was inevitable. I left the train at Motherwell, aware the police might be watching arrivals in Glasgow, and Sheila and Daryl went on to the city after a tearful farewell. A mate took me to a safe house in Lanarkshire, and the next day I acquired a gun, a .22 revolver with dumdum bullets for maximum damage.

Now I was armed and dangerous, resolved to take out my enemies before I was caught and locked up. But they were lying low too. Over the next five weeks, though, I did bump into Mick Healy and Mick Carroll, who were both on the run and back in Glasgow. And my brief spell of freedom would cause a breakdown in my relations with an old friend.

14

Cooked in China

I HAD BEEN ON the run for a month, continuing to visit many of my old haunts in the city. News that a Glasgow gang was suspected of a failed bank raid hundreds of miles away in Devon had not made the Scottish papers. I was well known on the club scene, and to have suddenly disappeared might have caused people to wonder why, sparking curiosity. So I thought there was safety in not hiding away. In fact, very few people knew I was on the run. But you can't keep a secret in Glasgow; rumours persisted and these led to problems with Fergie, my old partner in crime.

One Saturday night in June 1991, I went to Gloss, a nightclub in Hamilton that is now called the Hamilton Palace. It was a favourite venue for a lot of Glaswegians, and I was with Willie Lyle and other friends including Jim Hynds, Jack Woods and my brother Gary when Paul arrived with William 'Wid' O'Neill and Wid's brother Kevin. Paul wandered over and said, 'I heard you were on the run.' I didn't want to tell anybody that was the case, especially in a nightclub, where tongues can run loose by accident. In addition, I was carrying a gun after the shooting at Ma's house. Paul was a good friend, we'd been through a lot together, but those close to me had warned me to say nothing to anybody. The fewer who knew, the better, they advised. So I said, 'No, I'm not on the run,' and he told me, 'Well, Blink, I've heard differently.' I was simply non-committal, and Paul said, 'Listen, I want to help you.' Credit to Paul for saying that, but I insisted I was not on the

119

run. He was, though, a long-time pal, and so I began laughing and admitted, 'OK, then, I'm on the run, Paul.' He asked, 'Well, what is it you're on the run for?' and I said, 'Driving while disqualified,' and he went, 'Ach, fucking no talking to you.' I think he was hurt and aggrieved because I wouldn't open up to him. But I had decided to play it that way with everybody. It was clear Fergie felt I no longer trusted him and there was a frostiness between us that would not melt for many years.

At this time, Mick Healy and Michael Carroll were still at large and staying in a flat where I visited them now and again. Later on that night, I called and told them about meeting Paul. They asked, 'What was he saying? What did he want?' and I told them, 'He seemed to know I'm on the run.' They asked what I had said. 'I never told him and I don't think he's too happy' was my reply. Mick wanted to know why and I replied, 'Because I told him I was on the run for driving while disqualified.' Michael went, 'Fucking hell, what did he say to that?' I answered, 'Well, Paul was saying he could help me, but I don't think he's too happy.'

Because both of us knew there was a possibility the police were secretly watching Sheila, hoping she might lead them to me, I'd begun knocking about with another girl from Barmulloch. I don't want to mention her name because she's now a successful businesswoman. On the Friday following the Fergie meeting, I had arranged to take her to a bar in the West End of Glasgow. Realising bouncers were searching guys as they went in, I said to her, 'Open your handbag.' She wanted to know what for, but I insisted, 'Open your bag,' and when she did I dropped in my gun without her seeing it. Inside the bar, she asked what was in her bag and I told her. She was stunned, but later on that night when we went to Cleopatra's club – known to regulars as Clatty Pat's – she was still carrying my gun in her bag. Those were the days when security staff rarely checked a woman's handbag.

The gun was back in my pocket four days later when I decided to risk it and meet Sheila. So far, I had managed to stay clear of the police, but I was realistic enough to know that unless I got right away from Britain my freedom was running out. I knew I had been identified, because the coppers had stormed over Ma's house, telling her they were looking for drugs. Nobody was fooled by that; they were looking for signs I had been staying there. In fact, it was Sheila who used to go there, to take telephone calls from me. How to escape the country and where to go had been occupying my thoughts more and more. Now I had determined to make a new life in Spain, if I could get away. On 11 June, exactly 30 days after the robbery, Sheila went to Ma's and I rang telling her to get a taxi to Poa San, a Chinese restaurant on Alexandra Parade.

I got there just before eight o'clock and waited. I was wearing a black shell suit with the gun tucked into a pocket. Mick Healy would be joining us later, around 9.30. It was a Tuesday and there weren't many diners, although five guys seemed to be helping one of their number celebrate his having passed his driving test. It was quiet enough for me to be able to notice anyone suspicious entering.

'Did you get followed?' I asked Sheila as soon as she came to my table.

'Stop being so paranoid,' she said.

'I've every reason to be paranoid, Sheila,' I told her.

Five minutes into the meal, I noticed a couple walking through the door and immediately told Sheila, 'Undercover coppers.' They were dressed from head to toe in denim and I had a gut feeling about them.

She thought my paranoia was still there and said, 'They're probably a lovely couple. If you keep going on like this, I'm leaving.' So I decided to keep my mouth shut and concentrate on the meal and our drinks instead. Maybe she was right.

I knew that if they were police, then I was trapped. They'd have the front and rear covered. When nine o'clock came and went with nobody announcing 'Police!', I began wondering if maybe they really were just a lovely couple. By ten o'clock my worry had returned. There was no sign of Mick. Where was he? Had something happened? I began to notice a large number of people coming in to order takeaways, which was unusual for a Tuesday,

normally a quiet night in any restaurant. I started knocking back
drinks, thinking, 'If I'm going to jail, I'm going to get drunk first.'
Then I spotted something on the lovely couple's table: a large
silver pen. Why was it pointing directly at where we were sitting?
'Listen,' I said to Sheila, 'I need to get abroad. As soon as possible.
It's getting too hot for me here.' It was a quarter to eleven and our
meal was about to be ended.

Suddenly, a crowd of men and women rushed in. I heard Sheila
ask, 'What's that?' and put my hand into my pocket. The lovely
couple were the first to jump on me, followed by the party
celebrating the driving licence, who were pointing guns at my
face. More appeared. Sheila had been wrestled to the floor and
the crowd who'd rushed in lifted me into the air. They had me by
the arms and were squeezing my neck and throat. One of them
pulled the gun from my pocket. 'He's got a gun!' I heard one of
them shout. I was turning blue. They had the gun, so why were
they choking me? Sheila was already handcuffed. This was
overkill. I thought I was about to pass out, feeling myself drifting
amid all the yelling and chaos. Then I noticed the restaurant
owner rushing over shouting and I thought that at last somebody
had come to my rescue. He could see I was gasping for breath.
Was that a call of 'Leave him alone, you're going to kill him'? But
he was demanding to know: 'Who's paying his bill?' I emptied my
dinner and drinks over a man and two women from the Scottish
serious crime squad. It was one of the most momentous moments
in my criminal career – and one of the saddest.

In the back of the squad car taking me to London Road police
station, a young detective was having his five minutes of glory,
squeezing the handcuffs tighter while shouting, 'Come on, Blink!
Get out of these cuffs!' I said nothing, because I'd had the last
laugh. The cops would have to pay the little Chinaman his bill.

After I was charged with being in possession of a loaded firearm,
one of the senior detectives told me they had debated letting me
go at the end of the night, then following me in the hope I would
lead them to 'the Shotts Runner', Mick Healy. That was why they
let me sit in the restaurant so long. But, after weighing everything

up, they decided they couldn't take a chance on losing me and having their balls chewed off by the top brass. The intention had been to arrest me and send me to Devon, where I was wanted over the bank raid, but the discovery of the gun changed everything. What had made up their minds to take me in the restaurant had been hearing me discuss fleeing to Spain. How had they heard that? Because of the pen. Only it wasn't a pen; it was a directional microphone picking up our conversation.

In the police cell that night, I remembered Gary and my pals getting long prison stretches. Now, finally, at thirty, it was my turn for the big one, to be beckoned into the cold, unwelcoming walls of a top-security jail.

The next morning, I was remanded at Glasgow Sheriff Court. The ever-reliable Joe Shields was there. He must have been sick of the sight of me. It didn't take him long to tell me that this time I was going away for years, not months. I was also facing the dreaded Bar-L – Bar-Hell that should read – and the wrath of the screws after my last stint in there when they had lost control of the place in 1988.

I expected to be messed about and hardly had I been locked alone in a cell to try to digest the all-too-familiar Barlinnie stew when the door was unlocked and two warders blocked it, telling me, 'Cell search.' The rest of the hall was deathly quiet. Nobody else was being opened up so I knew something out of the ordinary was about to happen. I was told to take off my shirt, standard routine in a cell search, but then I realised what they were looking for, and it wasn't anything I might have hidden. As the cell filled up somebody shouted, 'Payback!', and I was punched and kicked, dragged out by my hair, handcuffed with my thumbs twisted back and slung naked into a padded cell. Through the humiliation and pain, I vowed to slash one of my antagonists. It would be worth it even if it meant an extra seven years.

The next morning, a screw I knew who had been brought up in the East End warned me I was facing another beating. Trying to be helpful, he advised, 'When you see the governor this morning, tell him you want to stay in the Wendy House.' He said it would be safer for me there. I was baffled why the governor would want to see me and the answer amazed me: 'You've been put on report for attempting to assault prison officers.' As I waited for the interview, I began talking to Carey Carbin, brother of Gerry. He had been shouting, 'Leave him alone,' and kicking his door as I was being dragged out of my cell the previous night. His support for me earned him a beating and an appearance before the prison hierarchy. 'Wish there were more like you, mate,' I said. The governor duly ordered me to be held in the Wendy House.

Sheila and Gary visited me and were shocked by my bruised face and blackened eyes. But she was even more alarmed by my threats to slash someone and the prospect of an even longer sentence. 'Think about Daryl and me. Make me a promise you won't hurt anybody and I promise I'll stand by you for the next ten years.'

And I did promise, but when the visit ended and I thought about her words, the horror of them struck home. She had said ten years. Ten fucking years. I was looking at ten years in prison. Ten years of my life taken away and ten years at the mercy of people I knew would want to make my life a misery.

A few days later, Gary came back to see me and said that the girl who had unwittingly carried my gun in her bag had called at Ma's asking about me. I said to Gary, 'Tell her to forget about me. I'm going away for years.' But she never forgot, because 11 years later I was in a bar in the West End of Glasgow when somebody tapped me on the shoulder and I turned to see her. I didn't recognise her, but after she introduced herself she told me, 'You should remember me, you slept with me.' I took her to another bar and after a few drinks thought I could pick up where we left off, but she said, 'Ian, I've moved on with my life,' and she walked on up the street alone.

I had tagged the Barlinnie screws 'the Chewing Gum Gang', as they swaggered about with gelled hair, chewing their gum, talking about their prowess in the gym and the women they pulled. But I never heard any of them mention a nightclub in Glasgow city centre. The reason was that such places were out of bounds for them – too dangerous with too great a likelihood of meeting men with scores to settle. So they were left to play petty games with their charges.

For instance, one Saturday they opened my door at three in the afternoon and told me to put on pyjamas and get into bed. That would mean my having to put my clothes on a chair outside, routine practice when somebody was deemed an escape risk. But this was two hours earlier than normal. It was silly and I wasn't biting. I knew the rules. I pointed to my window and the wall outside. 'What's over there?' I asked, and one of the screws brought roars of laughter from his colleagues with a sparkling snippet of wit, saying, 'The social club, but you won't be in it tonight.' I told him, 'Aye, but out there are kids five years of age and none of them are being told to put on their pyjamas, so you can fuck off.' Off they went like schoolkids, wondering if the joke was on them.

Not long after this, I began noticing that when I had to leave my clothes outside the cell, they would be wet when I retrieved them the following morning. There were no holes in the roof above and the shower room was far away. Some sicko had been urinating on my clothes, so I complained to the Chewing Gum Gang.

'It must be the cats,' they said.

'No, it's you fucking dogs,' I shouted, before slamming the door.

I heard giggles as they walked off.

15

Gangster Wing

ALTHOUGH I HAD promised Sheila I wouldn't slash a prison officer, that didn't apply to a shooting. After a couple of weeks, I'd had enough of the Chewing Gum Gang and made my feelings known to mates on the outside, who said they would shoot some of them in the legs outside their social club at Barlinnie. This would send a direct message to all prison officers that brutality would bring retribution. I listened to bulletins on Radio Clyde for news of an attack but heard nothing. Then I discovered that one of the prospective gunmen had been arrested in England after an armed robbery and the plan had had to be called off.

Further disappointment followed. While visiting me in the Wendy House one day, Willie Lyle warned the Chewing Gum Gang that anybody assaulting me would be in deep trouble. A week later, someone pushed a newspaper under my door and a voice said, 'Your pal isn't so hard now.' Inside was a report of a machete attack on Willie in a Duke Street pub. Happily, he recovered after a stay in hospital.

On 18 July, I presented myself at reception to be taken to the High Court at Edinburgh, where I would plead guilty to the gun offence. I thought my luck was in, because I knew the screw going with me. Before joining the prison service, he'd been an unemployed tradesman who drank in the Talisman. He got a real ribbing when his mum revealed his career move, but he promised not to forget his old pals and would do us favours if we were ever under his charge. Now I was looking for one of those favours, hoping he would at least take off my handcuffs during the journey – and not just to make me more comfortable but to give me the chance to run off when we arrived at the court building. But he spent the time boasting about how much money he was making, his new house, his girlfriend and an expensive foreign holiday. The only favour I received was a solitary Polo mint. At court, I was given 30 months, and the return journey passed in silence. As if to demonstrate how quickly he had distanced himself from his old friends, when Ma and Sheila said hello after spotting him during a visit, he ignored them totally.

In August, I was taken to Durham jail, where five armed officers from Devon were waiting to drive me to Plymouth to be questioned about the bank raid. The following day, I had to stand in an identity parade, and I was picked out by the cop who'd guarded the caravan from which I'd escaped. I was interviewed but simply said 'No comment' to the questions and was then formally charged with conspiring to rob the bank.

From Plymouth, I was taken to Dartmoor prison in Princeton, Devon. It was an old, bleak jail on the moors, perpetually surrounded in mists and steeped in history. I'd read about Dartmoor, how Frank Mitchell, known as 'the Mad Axeman', had escaped from there in December 1966 with the help of the Kray twins, who were later cleared of murdering him. The week I spent there was a week too long. After that, I was taken back to Scotland and Barlinnie.

That same month in Barlinnie, word filtered through one Sunday of a shooting in Provanmill the night before. On the Monday, the name of the victim was splashed all over the newspapers. Arty Thompson, son of the Godfather and my friend from Army Cadet days, had been shot three times outside his dad's house. He had been freed from Noranside open prison near Forfar on the Friday to spend a weekend at home as part of the run-up to completing his long sentence. After the shooting, Arty was taken to the Royal Infirmary, where doctors confirmed he was dead. Gossip was rife in the jail; everybody wanted to know who had murdered Arty. Lots of names were mentioned, but the one most talked about was that of Paul Ferris. I thought, 'Old Arthur is going to go off his nut. This is where he's going to demonstrate just what he is capable of.' I had been close at one time to Paul, Tam Bagan and the others they knocked about with. At least the fact that I was locked up meant the Godfather couldn't suspect me of being involved. For the only time in my life, I told myself, 'Thank God I'm in the nick.'

The rumours continued for a month, with the whole of Barlinnie buzzing. This was no ordinary murder; the victim was the son of the Godfather, and Arthur had loved his boy. I'd gone to school with Arty, he was one of our neighbours and I had liked him. Everybody waited for something to happen, and when it did the message was clear. A month later, on the day of Arty's funeral, I was chatting to a couple of the physical education instructors when one of them said, 'There have been another couple of murders. Two bodies have been found in a car in Shettleston.' Rumour was they were those of Bobby Glover and Tam Bagan. An hour later, I was told it wasn't Tam Bagan but Joe Hanlon whose body had been left beside that of Bobby in a car abandoned outside the Cottage Bar in Shettleston. Then it emerged that Bobby and Joe had been seen last driving off after William Lobban rang asking for a meeting. The many friends of the dead men began talking of betrayal and of Lobban as a despised Judas figure.

Here I should put right a popular myth. Nearly all the reports of the killings say the car was left on the route of Arty's funeral cortège. That's simply not true. Arty's body was taken from the family home and buried in Riddrie Cemetery, which backs onto Provanmill Road. It was a short journey and went nowhere near Shettleston. The significance of the killings was that the bodies were meant to be found on the same day as the burial and were deliberately left outside a bar with which both were associated. The word that went around the streets and into the darkest corners of Barlinnie was that Arthur had taken his revenge in a very spectacular fashion. He had sent out a message that nobody messed with his family.

128

And there was more. Fergie would have ended up dead as well, but, like me, he was in Barlinnie facing a number of charges. These were unrelated to the Arty hit, but he would later be charged with the murder (and acquitted of it). Mick Healy, still on the run, heard his name was being bandied about in connection with the shooting of Bobby and Joe and wrote to newspapers angrily denying these accusations. As for me, shortly afterwards I was transferred to England.

Horfield was the prison at Bristol, and when I arrived I met up with Michael Carroll, who had been in there a couple of months. I was to appear before Torquay magistrates and be remanded to await trial. I expected a quick trip there and back. Michael warned me I was in for a shock, however, and he was right. The police and prison service did it in style. I was shackled in a prison van sandwiched between Range Rovers carrying armed police. A helicopter whirred overhead and I saw marksmen on the courthouse roof. Formalities over, I wrongly assumed I'd be rejoining Michael. Instead, I was taken to Long Lartin, near Evesham in Worcestershire. This was a dispersal prison, made to house men categorised as the most dangerous and highest security risks.

At reception, I was told I would be housed in E Wing. That meant nothing to me.

An officer said, 'You're serving two and a half years? You're lucky to be here, then.'

'Lucky, what do you mean lucky? I don't want to be here. I don't know anybody.'

He said, 'This is a relaxed prison. Come on, get your bed pack.' Then he laughed and added, 'You're going to the gangster wing.'

He wasn't joking. No sooner had I got there than a wee guy with a Liverpool accent was beside me, telling me his name was Tony and he was doing six years and asking what I was doing. 'Two and a half years,' I told him. He looked puzzled. 'Two and a half years? Don't you mean twenty-two and a half years?' and I answered, 'No, I'm doing two and a half years.' I later found out that a guy called Peter Mitchell, from London, had arrived that day and he was doing twenty-two and a half years. He was sent to another wing while his co-accused, John Reid, had been put into E Wing with me.

Then it hit me. A dispersal jail was for long-termers, not somebody doing a piddling two and a half years. The other inmates would think I was a grass, planted there to spy on them. I needed to do something, and fast, but I was taken to a cell and no sooner had I put down my bed pack than my next-door neighbour appeared at the door. His name turned out to be John Haase.

Without waiting for introductions, he asked, 'How are you doing, mate?' I told him, 'Not bad.' But that wasn't really the case, so I said, 'Look, mate, I have the feeling you all think I'm a grass because I'm only doing two and a half years. I've been brought here from Barlinnie in an armed convoy.' His look suggested he didn't believe me. Then I remembered I had my depositions with me, giving details of the allegations against me. I told him to read my paperwork, which he did, and his attitude changed from suspicion to friendliness. He told me doubts about me had arisen because I had the lowest sentence of anybody in the jail, but now he would make a point of telling the other inmates, 'The guy's all right.'

I explained, 'I'm only here because a couple of my co-accused are on the run. Mick Healy has escaped from a top-security nick and is being blamed for two murders. The coppers think he's going to organise an escape to get me out. I don't want to be here.'

Haase looked surprised at that. 'Take it from me, you do want to be here. This place is brilliant.' I asked what he meant and he said, 'Here, you can do anything you want. This is a really good nick.'

It turned out he was right, although there were nights when I lay awake listening to the radio and heard Rozalla singing 'Everybody's Free' and thought, 'I wish I was, but I won't be free for years.' Then I thought, 'At least I'm alive,' which was not the case with Wee Bally. One of my friends wrote to say he had been found dead in his cell in the special unit. Johnny Haase was freed in December, and it was evident he was going to become the top man in Liverpool. He was somebody whose progress I followed with interest in the newspapers.

From time to time, there were visits from Sheila and Gary, but one in early 1992 from him ended in near disaster. I used to enjoy smoking hash and, because at that time there were no cameras in the visiting room, it was easy to smuggle stuff in. Visitors were only given a quick, cursory frisking. Gary used to bring an ounce of hash as well as booze, and one day turned up with half a bottle of Smirnoff vodka. Lots of people did this, pouring the booze into plastic cups under the table when the screws weren't looking. Sheila did the same when she came to see me. Gary had brought a girlfriend that day and all was going well, especially the vodka, so that by halfway through the visit we had finished the bottle. A few of the London boys had sent me some of their booze, while I had given them a share of my vodka. 'Got any more drink?' I asked Gary, and he said, 'I've another half-bottle. Do you want it?' I told him I did, so off he went, leaving me sitting with this strange girl. He seemed to be away for ages and when he didn't reappear I asked one of the screws if something had happened to my brother. He just stood there, at first playing dumb then saying, 'I don't know.' All I could do was go back to my seat and struggle to continue the conversation with his girlfriend. Finally, prison officers came over and said, 'Your brother's been caught trying to bring in alcohol. We're waiting for the police.'

I couldn't believe it. Here was a jail filled with men in for murder and shotgun robberies and they were locking Gary up over half a bottle of vodka. His girlfriend went off, not knowing what to do, and when the police came they took Gary to the station. When I returned to the wing and told the others what had happened, they went to the principal officer's office and kicked up fuck, pointing out that normally when someone was found with drink it was simply taken from them and handed back when the visit ended. Realising things were threatening to brew into trouble, the PO intervened with the police and as a result Gary was released on bail, but he was told he couldn't have a planned visit with me the next day.

My pals had a motive for taking action. Gary had been bringing in hash that I would pass to them, including my very good friend Sati, a lifer from Birmingham. I had to admit I'd forgotten to get it from him. That pissed them off, but when I told them his next-day visit had been banned they stormed back to the PO and demanded he be allowed in, warning of trouble if the ban stood. The visit was restored, and as soon as Gary came in I told him, 'Give me that fucking hash.' My pals ended up happy after all, which was more than could be said of Gary. He later copped a £400 fine.

There was no need to risk trying to take booze back to your cell, because we had our own home-made hooch waiting there, and it was stronger than Smirnoff. As for hash smoking, which was prevalent, the screws turned a blind eye provided we behaved and in particular made no efforts at escaping. They might come into your cell after you'd been having a joint, sniff the air and say, 'Open the window,' but that was it. At that time, there were actually people having sex in the visiting room. You were allowed to wear your own clothes, but the prison issued big coats for keeping warm out on the football pitch. Some guys kept the coats on in the visiting room. They'd sit in a corner with their girlfriend or wife straddling them and the inmate would wrap the big coat around her. You would look over and see them bouncing up and down.

Throughout my time there, I wondered about Mick, and finally, in April 1992, he was arrested in Glasgow and given an extra two years for escaping, on top of the ten he'd been serving when he'd gone on the run. Two months later, after a lengthy trial at the High Court, Paul Ferris was found not guilty of murdering Arty Thompson. Old Arthur was among the Crown witnesses.

Mick arrived at Long Lartin in August, and now we were all in custody. Mick's brother James was in Brixton, south London, Michael Carroll still at Horfield, and Rab Harper and Thomas Carrigan in the high-security unit of Belmarsh, London. After breaking from us in Devon, they'd gone to Norwich and rented a farmhouse for a base. They obtained .357 Magnum guns and pump-action shotguns by reversing a stolen jeep into a gun shop and then carried out three bank robberies in the area, first confusing staff by throwing in flares. After their arrests, some of the weapons were discovered buried under the farmhouse.

Mick clearly hadn't lost his desire for freedom. The cell doors at Long Lartin operated electronically. There were keys, but the screws simply needed to press a switch to open or close them. One Friday night, Mick and I had been drinking and somehow his door clicked open. Next moment, mine did the same. Mick reckoned he had used a piece of tinfoil to break the electromagnetic circuit that kept the doors locked, but I think it was just a freak fault in the system. We were steaming drunk, going to other doors and waking up inmates for fun. There was no chance of us getting out of the prison. When the screws spotted us, we were ordered back to our cells. When we continued our antics, they threatened to come for us in riot gear. That would have meant them leaving their club, where they were having a drink, and probably putting them in a bad mood. We decided it was time to return to our cells and the doors clicked shut.

Now, another time approached: that of our trial on 5 October at Bristol Crown Court.

16

Florida Phil

THE WHEELS OF justice are said to grind slowly. They certainly did in our case. We pleaded not guilty when all six of us first sat in the dock at Bristol Crown Court on 5 October 1992, but four trials, ten months and one hundred and twenty miles would pass before we learned our fate.

By the time it all started, Mick Healy was already doing ten years for robbery plus two for escaping; Thomas and Rab had been warned by their legal teams to expect around seventeen years each for the Norwich robberies, predictions that were unfortunately accurate; and I was serving my two and a half years. The jury were not to know any of that, of course.

Transferred back to Horfield for the trial, we had caused mayhem, continually arguing with screws and constantly complaining. But if there were problems at the prison, they were nothing compared with the farcical proceedings at court. A couple of weeks after the first trial got under way, it was announced that one of the dozen jurors was suffering from depression. One short. Then another told court officials her husband had suffered a severe heart attack and she needed to look after him. Two short. Trial one was abandoned.

The second got under way on 27 October but didn't last long. During the lunch break, one of the female jurors was spotted having a nibble with a local barrister. It was innocent enough but shouldn't have happened, especially as the prosecuting solicitor in our trial often dealt with this barrister. Red faces all round. Trial two abandoned. One of our barristers suggested we should be given bail. When everybody stopped laughing, the judge knocked that back.

A couple of days later, the Crown was hoping it was a case of third trial lucky. Just as well nobody was taking bets on that. The prosecution was reaching the end of its case when during the lunch break our frustration at having had to put up with day after day of nothing but corned-beef sandwiches blew up. We hadn't minded the trial delays because none of us was looking forward to hearing our inevitably long sentences and the hold-ups were putting off the day of reckoning. But we weren't prepared for the corned-beef diet to continue, and while the jury were tucking into their three-course meals, we started chucking soup and sandwiches about. The date this happened? Friday, 13 November!

The trouble continued back at the jail, and, hoping to get some of the tension out of us, they put us in the exercise yard. Maybe they were thinking the mad Jocks would start battling among themselves. Fat chance. But things were about to get very serious.

The next morning, fighting broke out in our wing. Chairs were chucked about and six screws ended up in hospital, one with a broken arm. Others had facial and bodily wounds. The disturbance received considerable publicity, and a newspaper referred to 'two prisoners who are currently remanded in custody while standing trial'. It didn't take a genius to work out that that meant some of our crew, but if the jury still hadn't put two and two together by the time they turned up on the Monday morning, the prison service filled in the answer for them by refusing to produce us, while suddenly security at court was hugely increased. When we did appear the next day, we were handcuffed in the dock, police marksmen were fiddling with their weapons on buildings overlooking the court, and inside armed officers patrolled the corridors.

Why were the authorities taking no risks? The answer was this. Mick Healy and I in particular didn't want to do long stretches and reckoned escape was the only way of avoiding them. We had been all over the prison looking for breaches in the defences. There were none there, but the old court at Bristol was a different matter, and we'd come up with a plan to get away. Each day at court, all six of us were put into a room together. The toilet was downstairs. From its window, we could see a fence and realised that an outsider could get access to the window just by climbing over it. Then they could leave something on the window ledge, a gun maybe. We had written a letter with a diagram showing the position of the fence and window and given it to one of the girlfriends. She delivered it to a pal, who arranged for a Colt .45 handgun wrapped in a towel to be left on the window ledge. The plot was for one of us to go to the toilet, collect the gun and, when we rejoined the others, grab the screw accompanying us, handcuff him and lock him in our room. We would take our revenge on the screws who had given us a bad time by battering them. Then it was to be everybody for himself. Mick and I would go into the city centre, drag drivers from their cars and vanish. We were all ready to go. Sadly, so were the police. Somebody – we found out who – had given us away to a member of the Scottish serious crime squad, who warned Avon and Somerset police.

At court, nobody was saying why gun-toting cops were all over the building, but Mick and I knew. I told myself, 'They've found a gun. That's us doing 20 years. We'll be old men when we get out.' The judge was told about the discovery of the plot. One of the defence barristers was called in to be given a brief but not full explanation, and, astonishingly, he was ordered to give a formal and binding undertaking not to tell anybody else. Not even the other defence briefs. Just what did the police reveal? That answer only emerged many months later, in a letter from the prosecution barristers to the Bar Council, their professional body. It said the police information was 'precise and extremely detailed'. It included how a gun was to be smuggled into the building and how it was to be used. The police even suspected we already had it. Further, the coppers were claiming that if we found out all they knew, we would easily be able to work out who had grassed on us and the informer 'would be dead within a week'. But we'd known the name of the betrayer from the minute our plan was uncovered.

For a couple of days, the authorities scurried about wondering what to do next. Finally, the judge, aware that people's lives were at risk, including those of barristers and court staff, announced his decision. Guess what it was? The trial was being abandoned. They'd have another go, but for security reasons this time it would be at the Old Bailey. That day, none of us went back to Horfield. Instead, we were moved to jails all over the country, with me and Mick heading to Long Lartin. So, once again, the only bars I saw that Christmas and New Year were those on the cell windows.

March saw me reunited with James Healy when I was transferred to the special unit in Brixton prison, from where, in July 1991, two IRA activists, Nessan Quinlivan and Pearse McAuley, had escaped after a pair of training shoes concealing a loaded gun was smuggled in to them. The normal thing was to use training shoes for smuggling in hash. As if to rub salt into the wound, they even hijacked a prison officer's car. Screws were still talking about the pair and were touchy about the subject. One of the stories in circulation was that MI5 had let the terrorists escape, hoping to follow them and be led to a cache of weapons and explosives hidden in a safe house, and that the plan had gone wrong when they lost the runaways.

Not long after I got to Brixton, word came from Glasgow of the death of the Godfather. I was sorry to hear the news, because I'd always respected Arthur. While the official cause of death was a heart attack, I wondered if he had really died of a broken heart, never recovering from the murder of young Arty. As the years rolled by, I would come to learn just how far-reaching was the esteem in which he was held.

Meanwhile, Brixton had a bad feeling about it, and I didn't get on with the screws. I'd only been there a couple of weeks when I had a run-in with one of them. He was playing chess with an inmate and I wanted to be escorted to the canteen to buy Mars Bars, sweets and tea bags. I kept telling him, 'I want my canteen,' and when he made it obvious the only move he was going to make was another on the chessboard, I picked up some snooker balls and potted them through the television set. Instead of my canteen, I got a cell in solitary. I told James, 'I don't like this place. It's a fucking dump.' The next day, I was told I was being transferred out.

One of the screws who had been giving me a hard time was a black guy. He came along with other officers, one of them an older man, to take me to Wormwood Scrubs. My belongings were in two black plastic bags, and when the black guy ordered me, 'Come on, move,' I told him, 'Get my bags, Benson.' Benson was the name of a sarcastic black butler played by Robert Guillaume in an American television series called *Soap*. He also played the title role in another series, *Benson*. The screw was taken aback. 'What?' he said, and the others burst out laughing, but the older screw brought a halt to the fun and told me if I didn't pick up my bags I would not get my move. So I did, and off we went.

I was at the Scrubs until July 1993. Not long after I got there, back in Brixton, Benson and the others must have been laughing again, because at the start of April Nessan Quinlivan was recaptured at a remote farmhouse in Tipperary.

In May, the police arrested Phil Wells and he was remanded to the Scrubs, where I took him under my wing and acted as a sort of unofficial bodyguard to him. Phil was accused of taking nearly a million pounds in foreign currency from Heathrow Airport in July 1989, when he had been working there as a security guard. He had immediately gone on the run. London gangsters were supposed to have taken the money from him and financed him. He first hid out in Essex, while police thought he was in Florida, his favourite holiday destination, but when the heat died down 'Florida Phil', as he became known, visited 20 different countries. In Texas, he married a six-foot-tall waitress, and in a bar in Croatia he met Olga, a Russian gymnast, and married her in Uzbekistan. He had finally been caught when he flew to Britain to try to sell his story to a newspaper.

Phil and I got on tremendously well. He told me he'd stashed the money in his wee Fiesta van but couldn't fasten the doors because the locks were broken. He was waved past airport security and shouted, 'See you later,' as he drove off into the sunset.

FLORIDA PHIL

One day, he was playing table tennis with me even though he had a bad heart. He had been telling me, 'The gangsters took the money off me,' but I suspected he'd kept the money. Anyway, this day he went on and on about Olga, how she'd fallen for him after he'd told her he was a wealthy greengrocer, how he'd gone to Russia to buy her penniless family a television set, how much she loved him and how she was standing by him. In the middle of the game, he was called away to take a telephone call from Olga. He came back, said, 'Olga's left me,' and went off. Suddenly, the alarm bell went, screws were rushing everywhere and I thought, 'Fucking hell, Phil's not kicked off has he? He doesn't seem the type of guy who would cause any trouble.' But then medics arrived. I ran into his cell and asked what the matter was. He said, 'Oh, my heart. Olga's told me it's finished.' I had to force myself not to burst out laughing. A week later, a newspaper ran a story telling how Olga was a go-go dancer, flashing her tits and going with punters for a bottle of vodka. Guys can be cruel in prison and made fun of Phil after that, but I felt sorry for him. Like me, he knew he was looking at a long sentence.

I made friends, too, with a couple of really good, dependable guys from Manchester, Mal Murphy and big Wesley from Moss Side, and I am glad to say that these are friendships that still exist. They were keen Manchester United supporters, and this was the year Alex Ferguson, who had played for my team, Rangers, captured his first league title with the Reds. I used to rib them that it took a guy from Glasgow to win anything for them.

In May, Joe Steele slipped away from accompanying screws while on a home visit. He made it to London and superglued himself to the railings of Buckingham Palace to draw attention to his and T.C. Campbell's plight. Joe later wrote a letter of apology to the Queen.

Our trial was set to start in July. John Haase was back in custody that month after he and his nephew Paul Bennett were arrested in London and charged with serious drug offences. What happened to them would lead to a political sensation. Meanwhile, I left the Scrubs and rejoined the rest of Glasgow's version of the Jesse James Gang in Belmarsh prison. It was time to pay the piper.

17

Judas, the Bible and the Bailey

THE OLD BAILEY is the most famous criminal court in the world. Over the centuries, it has been the scene of tens of thousands of trials, many ending with the accused heading to the gallows. In more recent times, it had attracted packed galleries for sensational gangland cases. A Scot from Coatbridge, Victor 'Scarface' Russo, was a prime witness in 1956, claiming he had been offered £500 by then London underworld supremo Billy Hill if he would slash himself and put the blame on Hill's rival Jack 'Spot' Comer. Then, in the late 1960s, the Richardson brothers, Charlie and Eddie, were given long sentences after their infamous 'torture trial', with victims telling of being nailed to floors, having toes cut off with bolt cutters and teeth ripped out with pliers. They were followed into prison by the Kray twins, Ronnie and Reggie, convicted of murdering George Cornell and Jack 'The Hat' McVitie. But even the Bailey was taken aback when it staged a performance of the Glasgow gangland show.

From the outset, Sir Lawrence Verney made it plain he would not be messed about, warning us to be on our best behaviour or else we would be sent to the cells with the hearing proceeding in our absence. But even he struggled to prevent the case of bank robbery turning into a public airing of Glasgow underworld rivalries. While the other five of us had QCs to represent us, Mick Healy sacked his counsel and announced he would defend himself. This is always a risky manoeuvre, but often defendants get the

140

feeling their wishes are being pushed to one side by legal representatives who are too willing to let the judge or prosecution determine what course to take. I have to say that my QC, Colin Hart-Leverton, who often acted in major organised-crime cases, never ceased telling me he'd get me off. He had more confidence than me. My problem was that my fingerprints had been found at the caravan.

Mick's defence was that Paul Ferris had organised the plan to raid the bank with Joe Hanlon and Bobby Glover as the robbers. This was where it began to get complicated. Joe and Bobby were dead, of course. It was said that they were killed because of the shooting of Arty Thompson. He was dead too. So was his dad, who was suspected of having paid for the killings of Joe and Bobby. The judge must have been struggling to keep up with who was still alive. Then Mick threw a spanner into the works. He'd told me, 'I have an ace in the hole. I'm bringing down Lobban as a witness.' Astonished, I'd asked him, 'Fucking hell, Mick, why are you calling Judas?' His answer was that Lobban would back up his version of who had been behind the bank job. Lobban, 'Gibby' to his few cronies, had been Mick's co-accused in the robbery for which he had been serving the ten-year sentence from which he'd gone on the run. But what baffled me about Mick's decision was this.

Not long after I'd been nicked in the Chinese diner, I was in the Barlinnie Wendy House expecting a visit from Sheila when, instead, Ernie Barrie turned up. It had been me who had once introduced him to Fergie, and the two of them got on well. 'Christ, I'm surprised to see you, Ernie,' I said, and he told me, 'I called on Sheila to ask if I could come instead of her. Paul came to the Gorbals looking for me. He saw me in the street, took me into a pub and said he wanted to talk about you.' Ernie had then asked why and Paul had told him, 'Don't you know what happened with Mick Healy a few days ago?' When Ernie said he had heard nothing, Paul told him he had pointed a gun at Mick's head. When I told Ernie this was news to me, he went on, 'It gets worse. Mick's so-called friend Billy Lobban set him up.'

I said I had always understood Mick and Lobban to be good friends. I knew Lobban was on the run from prison at the time, as was Mick from the Torquay robbery. Then Ernie told me the full story. 'Billy Lobban went over to Mick's mother's house and asked her if she could tell him where Mick was staying. She told him to come back in an hour or two and in the meantime she'd ask her son if she could pass on his address. She said she thought there wouldn't be a problem because she knew they were pals but wanted to make sure.' Ernie said Lobban went back and by that time Mrs Healy had been in touch with Mick, who had a flat in Rutherglen. She told Lobban what he wanted to know and he called on Mick.

Ernie told me Mick didn't know that Lobban had been jumping about with Fergie, Bobby Glover and Joe Hanlon, and Lobban never mentioned this fact to him. Instead, Lobban was chatting away when he suddenly slipped in a question Paul had apparently primed him to ask. 'I heard Blink met Paul and has been badmouthing Paul. Paul wasn't too happy about him. You heard anything?' I realised that this referred to the time when I'd been in the club at Hamilton and Fergie had been asking if it was true I was on the run. When Mick asked how Lobban knew Paul was unhappy, his visitor admitted, 'Oh, I've been to see Paul and he told me.'

Mick had replied, 'No, Blink just came back to the flat and said Paul was asking him if he was on the run and that he'd said he was but it was for driving while disqualified.' At that, Lobban told Mick, 'Well, Paul's not too happy.' Ernie said Lobban had then told Mick he needed to leave to see somebody and would be back in a couple of hours. He had asked, 'Is that all right, Mick?' and was told, 'Of course it is. You're my pal.'

But Lobban had treachery in mind. When he returned, he was only there two minutes and said he was going to the toilet. He went out of the room, but not to the toilet. Instead, he opened Mick's door and Paul came in.

Ernie told me, 'Paul came in and produced a .22 with a silencer, shot into Mick's stereo and told him to put his hands on his head.

Then he started to interrogate him.' I was amazed at all of this and asked Ernie what it was all about. He said Mick and I were being targeted because we'd been involved together in the robbery. 'Paul thinks you've been badmouthing him,' Ernie said. 'Lobban was telling Paul to put one in Mick's nut. Mick's so-called friend is standing there saying, "Look, Paul, you need to finish him off."'

By this time, it was all getting a bit too much for me and I asked Ernie, 'Why was he saying all this?' Ernie said, 'Because Paul was affronted by the way you'd spoken to him at the dance. He sent Lobban in because Mick didn't know Lobban was hanging about with all of them.'

I asked what happened next and Ernie said they'd been interrupted by somebody knocking at the door. The caller, Basher from Castlemilk, refused to go away and Paul ignored Lobban's urging him to shoot Mick. Instead, he asked if Mick had a gun in the flat and when he admitted having a shotgun Paul took it and left with Lobban. Ernie told me, 'While I was in the pub with Paul, he said, "In my mind, Ian is trying to badmouth me and call me a grass." I stuck up for you and told him there was no way you would do that. But Paul said, "Well, me and Ian are like brothers. But that's it finished, Ernie. I know myself, that's it finished. I want you to do me a favour. Go to Barlinnie tomorrow, see Blink and tell him we are finished. I'd have looked after him in prison, but he's tried to badmouth me, saying I'm this and I'm that." So that's why I'm here instead of Sheila.'

'Well, fuck him. If that's the way he wants to go, fuck it,' I said to Ernie. 'That's it. I'm going to be inside for the next ten years anyway. I don't need him to look after me. I'll need to look after my fucking self, because I know I'll be in for a long time. He's the least of my worries, to be perfectly fucking frank.' My thoughts were on getting through whatever sentence I was given and coping with losing Sheila and my son.

When I went to prison in England, Mick eventually came down after he was recaptured and I asked him for the full story. He confirmed what Ernie had told me and admitted he had been hurt and shocked by what Lobban had done, not just to him but to his mother.

I told Mick, 'I can't understand then why you're going to cite him as a witness. If he comes down, I'm going to attack him because of what he did to Joe and Bobby.'

Mick pleaded, 'Don't do that. He could be doing us a turn. He'll badmouth Paul Ferris.'

I told him, 'Doing us a turn? You shouldn't be calling a rat like that.'

I realised Mick could have been killed that night because of me, and that always left me with a sense of guilt. But it had never occurred to me that Paul would take our conversation in Hamilton the way he did.

So Lobban, who had been caught and jailed for robbing a bar in Glasgow, came to the trial. To me, he was a rat, a Judas, a prick, a complete bastard, because there was no doubt in my mind that he had set up Joe and Bobby. It was hard to believe he would do that after Bobby's wife, Eileen, had taken him into their home when he needed help.

At the trial, he insisted on not having his name mentioned and was referred to only as 'Mr X'. He came into court clutching a Bible and at one point complained that some of the jury weren't taking notice of his evidence. He backed up Mick by accusing Fergie of being the brains behind the plot to rob the bank.

Throughout all of this, the judge had continued asking who was alive, but eventually it was clear he'd had enough of hearing about Glasgow's gangland. He told Mick to stick to the facts about the Torquay robbery.

I asked the others as Lobban was in the witness box, 'What's this bastard doing? He's making it worse for us.' He was slagging Fergie, talking about him setting people up with leggy blondes, and I had to stop myself jumping up and shouting, 'You're a liar!' One of my big regrets was that I was never able to get to Lobban and slash him. I wasn't alone in being disgusted by Lobban's citing; Rab Harper was equally appalled by the presence of such a despised figure.

The MacDonald boys with their mum at Butlins in Ayr, around 1970. Left to right: Ian, Gary and Alan.

Royal Marine Charlie Muir, Ian's uncle, who was killed in Malta in 1975.

A smartly suited Ian at a wedding in 1982.

Ian and attractive Annette Daniel during a holiday in Tenerife in 1985.

Paul Ferris, a close friend of Ian in their youth. (© Brian Anderson)

Ian turned down an offer of work from near neighbour Arthur Thompson, the Glasgow Godfather. (© Brian Anderson)

Police at the National Westminster Bank
in Torquay minutes after the robbers fled.

The caravan site where the gang hid out before and after the
raid. Bottom right is the area where Ian's caravan was situated.
The pond where he was arrested by armed police as he was
about to dump the guns is top left.

Ian at Long Lartin prison in 1992, with his mum and Sheila Gourlay.

A police photo of Mick Healy at the time of the 1993 bank-robbery trial.

Sheila in 1994, the year after Ian was jailed over the failed bank raid.

Torture-gang boss Eddie Richardson had some odd advice for Ian about life after prison. (© Brian Anderson)

Tam McGraw in Tenerife where he met secretly with Ian.

Ian's friend Gordon Ross.

Tam McGraw at the funeral of Gordon Ross, who was murdered in 2002. (© Brian Anderson)

Ian and Steff McVey in 2002 with television star Ford Kiernan, who said he hoped they weren't gangsters.

Ian in Benidorm, shortly before a wild night out led to a fight with Spanish police.

Ian in London, where he met gangsters to discuss plans for a £3-million robbery before holidaying in Thailand.

Ian, flanked by Alan (left) and Gary, helps James McGill and sister Tracy celebrate his mum's 68th birthday.

Ian in 2007 outside the Old Bailey, where he was jailed in 1993.

London gangster Vic Dark has remained in contact with Ian since they have been freed from prison.
(© Brian Anderson)

Ian and his good friend David Fitzsimmons on
holiday in Portugal in 2007.

Great Train Robber Ronnie Biggs invited Ian to meet him
in the north London care home where he now lives.
(© Brian Anderson)

So, after five weeks, the jury retired. While we sweated it out, wondering how it would end, they took so long to make up their minds that they were sent off to a plush hotel. I think all of us had tried putting off the verdict day, but in my heart of hearts I just wanted to get it over with, find out the length of my sentence and start serving it.

Eventually, we were all found guilty and sentenced to a total of 101 years between us. Mick's 19 years consecutive meant he would have to serve 31 years. 'You got a bigger sentence than the Great Train Robbers,' I told him as we walked, handcuffed together, from the Old Bailey. 'They got three million pounds. We got nothing.'

Although we took our punishments on the chin, I would be lying if I said I wasn't devastated and struggling to cope with my emotions. I had been secretly expecting around ten years. The longest I'd done before all of this was 18 months, and now I'd got a total of almost 18 years.

In Belmarsh the next morning, as the six of us wandered around the exercise yard, a cloud of depression covering us, I told Mick, 'I can't see an end to this black tunnel,' and he agreed: 'How are we going to get through this?'

Now we were about to plunge head first into the depths of the very worst England had to offer in high-security prisons. What lay ahead, I knew, was not going to be easy.

After I had been in the system for a while, I met loads of other guys who told me their briefs had been giving them the same optimistic messages as I had had from Colin Hart-Leverton – that either they would get off or, at worst, get light sentences. Invariably, these words of hope had turned out to be a load of bollocks. It was just the same at appeal hearings.

We'd been in Belmarsh throughout our trial. It had a bad feeling about it, and we wanted out of there as soon as possible. I thought I would try cheering up the Healy brothers by doing them a favour, so I requested a meeting with one of the assistant governors. 'Can I have a word?' I asked, and when he gave me the nod I told him, 'It's about Michael and James Healy. It would be a tragedy to put one up in Durham to Frankland and the other to, say, Whitemoor in Cambridgeshire, because that would be a real hardship for their families. People in Glasgow don't have a lot of money and travelling is expensive. Could you try and see that the two go to the same prison?' He listened and told me, 'I'll see what I can do, but I'm making no promises.' I'd been reasoning that their folks would want the two close together. 'They won't want them at opposite ends of the country,' I told myself.

Later that night, after my chat with the assistant governor, James asked what we'd been discussing, so I told him. He stormed, 'I don't want to go beside him.'

'Whaat?! I've put my neck out here for you.'

'Look, I want to be split up from Michael,' he told me.

'James, you're brothers. I thought brothers wanted to stick together.'

'I want us to be separated. I want to get on with doing my time on my own.'

So I said, 'Well, OK. What I've asked for probably won't happen anyway.'

But it did. A couple of days later, they were moved up to Frankland together.

Two days after they'd gone, I was shifted up to HMP Full Sutton in the East Riding of Yorkshire. It's close to the village of Stamford Bridge, which was the scene of a famous battle in 1066 between an English army and invading Norwegians. That's also the name of Chelsea Football Club's ground, and when a screw said I was going to Stamford Bridge I told him, 'I wish I was serving my time in there.'

At Full Sutton, one of the first people I hooked up with was a guy from Walworth, near the Elephant and Castle, called Dessie Cunningham. Dessie, quiet and bespectacled, was highly respected by everybody, a man who would never let his friends down. He was serving 17 years and was reputed to have stabbed Charlie Bronson in the exercise yard at Parkhurst. Charlie was said to be the most violent man in the prison system. I would come across him in a hilarious episode years later. Dessie took me under his wing and showed me aspects of prison life that, had I not experienced them for myself, had somebody only told me about them, would have had me suggesting my informant was living in a fantasy land. I enjoyed cordon bleu cooking, exotic oriental meals better than the finest restaurants could offer, drinking sessions that left my best nights in the clubs and bars of Glasgow dismissed as mere children's parties and friendships worth more than the riches that any bank robbery could have brought. But throughout I would fight a bleakness that only the truly lonely know.

18

Secret in the Cereal

THE SENIOR CIVIL servants who run the prison system dislike inmates rioting, causing damage, killing themselves or murdering others. But what they really hate is the thought of one of their charges escaping. Escapes make them answerable to politicians and set back their chances of promotion. Everybody entering prison is given a number – mine was CK1536 – and a category, which is worked out by what you are in for, the length of your sentence and how determined you are to escape and then commit mayhem while on the run. Mostly, the categories are covered by the first four letters of the alphabet, with the lowest rating (D) given to those wanting to get their heads down and serve out their sentences without causing any bother. Category A prisoners are looked on as menaces to society who will take advantage of any chance to escape. They are normally held in dispersal prisons, those jails classed as having the highest levels of security and specially built so as to make escape virtually impossible.

The theory is that ideally everybody wants to behave and work towards a D category and early release. Probably because of my escape from the caravan following the bank raid, being copped carrying a gun in the Chinese restaurant and my involvement in the murderous escape plot during the trial, I was given the highest security classification, AA. Having that rating gave me something in common with the likes of Eddie Richardson. A special category A review team based in London periodically decided whether I had minded my p's and q's sufficiently to merit my being reduced in the danger stakes to an A or even a B, improving my chances when it came to applying for parole. But I never managed to convince these faceless, nameless men and women to give me a break.

After my arrest and remand to prison in England, I had quickly discovered that dispersal jails could have their advantages. For instance, instead of having to dress every day in drab standard prison-issue clothing, some allowed you to wear tracksuits or denims and walk about in trainers. And, as time passed, I would learn of major bonuses when it came to food and drink. But all of these relaxations of the regulations came with an unwritten but unbreakable condition, which was that you agreed that the wall and barbed or razor wire fence surrounding you would not be breached. In other words, you promised not to try to escape. Staying within the walls meant you could exist in a relaxed atmosphere, while the governor had no awkward and career-threatening questions to answer about security. Of course, from time to time there were flare-ups, but these were dealt with internally, with loss of privileges, spells in the digger or beatings – rather like the manager of a football team fining one of his stars for misbehaviour but keeping the whole business out of the glare of publicity. The prison system existed to make sure nobody got away, that you only went free after you had served your sentence and not before. If nobody breached the walls, everybody was happy, or that was the theory. And so those thought most likely to break that golden rule came under the A or AA category.

By the time I was sentenced, I already knew of some of the consequences of being branded AA. In 1992, while I was at Long Lartin doing the two and a half years for possession of the gun and on remand awaiting trial, my family had got in touch to tell me that Ma's mother, Granny Muir, was dead. It was a shattering blow, because we had been very close and I remembered so many really happy childhood memories of going on holiday with her. As soon as I heard the news, I went into the wing office, where a senior officer was sitting behind a desk, his head in a newspaper. I waited for him to acknowledge that I was there and when he carried on reading told him, 'Listen, my granny has died.' There was a pause before he looked up and said, 'Yes?'

It was obvious he was totally indifferent and utterly uninterested in what I was talking about. But I carried on, saying, 'I want to go to her funeral.' Finally, he put down his newspaper, looked up and said, 'It has got to be close family.' I thought he might at least have said he was sorry that my gran was dead, shown some sort of willingness to help, but his attitude was frankly rude, that of somebody bored by what he was being told, and this irritated me. I knew from my experience of prisons in Scotland that the dead person didn't have to be a close relative, or even a blood relative, for an inmate there to be given permission to be present at the funeral. Shotts, regarded as the most secure jail in the country, even allowed inmates out for the funeral of a brother-in-law. I told this guy, 'Close family? My granny practically brought me up. She didn't raise me, but she was really close. That's close family.' When there was no response, I grabbed him by the throat and, within seconds, his shouts brought in other screws, who hustled me off to the segregation area, where I was locked into solitary.

I stayed there for a couple of days, but at least one of the assistant governors had the decency to enquire what the trouble was about. He was patient and courteous and heard me out when I gave him my reasons for believing I was entitled to be allowed to go to Gran's funeral. But, sympathetic though he might have seemed, his answer brought no comfort. 'Listen, Ian, I know this might sound callous, but you are double-A category. We couldn't take you to Scotland with all the security that would involve.' I protested, 'But it's my granny who's died. If I was in Scotland, I would be allowed out to her funeral.' His answer was final: 'I'm sorry, but the rules are clear and we cannot change them.' At least he had me returned to my normal cell.

Maybe it was partly because of the loss of Gran, who had been so kind to me, but the weeks and months seemed to drag after that. Nights were the worst. Anybody who has been in prison will tell you that your sentence begins each evening at nine o'clock, the time when inmates are normally dubbed up in their cells until morning. I was no exception. Days were bearable, because there were lots of other guys around to chat to, there were meals to prepare, work to go to, the gym in which to work off tensions, exercise periods with the chance to stretch your legs and recreation periods when you could meet up with friends. But at nine, when the door was slammed and the key turned, the nightmares started. Everybody goes through this, and even today – when inmates have computers in their cells, PlayStations, satellite television channels to watch, smuggled mobile telephones with which to keep in touch with family and friends – the ghosts of life on the outside remain. You might think about your wife or girlfriend. What is she doing? Where is she? Has she really stayed at home or is she out drinking with pals or another man? And the worst of it is that you can't go outside to find out the truth for yourself.

I'd worry about Sheila and Daryl, Ma, the rest of the family. But during those long hours in the dark there was nobody to talk to about your fears. Friends who have never tasted prison life have asked why I didn't ask to be dubbed up with another guy. Maybe they've watched *Porridge*, which paints a cosy, friendly picture of life behind bars. In that show, Ronnie Barker is dubbed up with fellow inmate Richard Beckinsale, and the pair frequently indulge in banter with the prison officers. In reality, it's nothing like that. The rule in the high-security prisons in which I was held was that inmates were confined in single cells. That meant I was on my own, with just a radio, a book and a piss pot for company – and the smell of my own body, something not improved by being allowed, in Barlinnie for instance, just one shower a week. Alone, then, with thoughts, fears and knowing that the next night and the one after that, and the year after that, will be just the same.

I was an avid reader of books, magazines, newspapers, anything that came to hand. In January 1994, I spotted a newspaper article telling how Phil Wells, Florida Phil, had got six years. It emerged that on the day of the theft Phil had made a sort of Robin Hood gesture by deliberately leaving behind the wages of his colleagues and other Heathrow staff so they would not lose out. Phil had lived the high life for years before he'd been caught. He'd got away with a fortune. I'd got a Chinese meal and the bank had lost nothing as a result of our efforts. Yet we'd been given sentences nearly three times the length of that handed down to Phil. Still, good luck to him. I'd always enjoyed Phil's company and his stories of Olga and life on the run.

Like me, my legal team believed 16 years was harsh, especially as I wasn't even in the bank when the gun went off by accident and because nothing was stolen. So they lodged an appeal against both my conviction and the length of the sentence. While we waited for a hearing, I saved up my visits to allow them to be taken close together, and then successfully applied to be moved to Frankland in County Durham to make it easier for Sheila, Daryl, Ma and the others to travel.

I arrived at Frankland in May 1994 and linked up with John Lynn. In better times, he and I had spent many a happy night trawling through Glasgow clubland. Now John was serving 17 years after being accused of attempting to murder a man by shooting him at a hotel in Blackpool in 1988. He worked in the prison gym and did me a big favour by getting me a tiny Casio pocket-size battery-operated television, which I hid in my box of Alpen breakfast cereal and took with me when I moved back to Full Sutton. I also had a new friend for the journey south: a little budgerigar that a friend of James Healy had asked me to carry to James.

I was looking forward to watching Christmas television when the prison was locked down after a rumour that Semtex explosives had been smuggled inside. It was announced that 50 prisoners would be randomly picked for especially intensive searches, and I was among them. A male and female screw began emptying spice jars and looking inside envelopes, and then they came to the Alpen box. They tipped the contents into a plastic bag and there was the tiny TV set.

'What's this?' they asked.

'It must have come as a free gift in the cereal,' I told them. 'I've never seen it before.'

'Tell that to the governor,' they said.

And I did, but I was put off air.

It was January 1995 before my appeal was heard and, in case I was needed in court, I was transferred to Wormwood Scrubs for a couple of nights. My lawyers suggested we drop the appeal against conviction to give a better chance of getting the sentence reduced. I had anxieties about going to the Scrubs because rumours abounded about inmates being beaten up by screws there. The Chief Inspector of Prisons, Sir Stephen Tumim, had already said that brutality against inmates needed to be curbed, and in 1996 his words were echoed by his successor, Sir David Ramsbotham.

When I arrived, I was surprised to be sent immediately to the segregation unit, because this was unusual, as I had come from a normal wing at Full Sutton and had done nothing wrong. The explanation given was that there wasn't enough room for me in the mainstream prison, but being in segregation sent a tremor through me, because it was there that most of the brutality was said to occur. Rab Harper had been one of the victims. For no reason, he'd been attacked one morning as he went for his breakfast, and now the incident and a claim for compensation was in the hands of his lawyers. It would turn out that Rab wasn't the only inmate claiming damages.

No sooner had I entered my cell than a few screws walked in and read the riot act, warning me to behave. I'd had no intention of causing bother and told them, 'I'm not here for punishment. I'm only here for my appeal.' Nobody actually touched me. Their reply was sufficient to drive home their message: 'Ian, make even the slightest noise and we'll be in here and kick shite out of you.' And that was it. Welcome to Wormwood Scrubs.

I was glad two days later to see the screws from Full Sutton who arrived to return me there. They were astounded when I told them I had been put into the segregation unit, but the word was that finally something was about to be done about the brutes who terrorised the Scrubs. And it was, because, following a police investigation, twenty-seven officers were suspended and six found guilty of assault, although three later successfully appealed against their convictions. The Home Office had to pay out more than £3 million in compensation to ex-prisoners who had been victims of attacks.

Back in Yorkshire, I received a formal letter telling me that the Court of Appeal had knocked a year off my sentence, meaning that I would now be doing 15 years for a bank robbery in which nothing was stolen. The same appeal judges gave better news to Mick Healy. Instead of the brutal total of 31 years, his 19-year sentence was to run concurrently with his 12, meaning he would be released much earlier. Michael Carroll's sentence was reduced from 18 years to 15 and James Healy's lowered by 18 months.

I never complained about being jailed; prison was a risk for anybody who chose to commit crime. Eventually, I was able to come to terms with the prospect of losing nearly two decades of freedom, but at the start I found it difficult to settle and accept what had happened. However, I knew that at the end of the day there was no alternative to simply facing up to the consequences of my decisions. Others, though, took solace in a form of escape that was not for me. They became hooked on drugs.

I have to admit to smoking hash from time to time and lots of boys used cannabis, traces of which stayed in your body for up to a month. That was OK so long as there was no strict testing regime. But after Michael Howard became Home Secretary in 1993, he announced that the time had come to get tough with prisoners. Many voters seemed to think cons had it too easy, regimes were too relaxed, and one of the measures he introduced was drug testing. It was just about the worst thing anybody could have done. Fail a drugs test and it went down on your record, probably resulting in loss of remission and reducing your chances of parole. Then guys who were smoking hash discovered that heroin stayed in your system for just three days, greatly lessening the chances of your drug-taking being discovered. So they switched to heroin, and, in my eyes, this was a terrible thing, because heroin not only completely changed a person's personality but it was much more expensive.

Guys would be phoning their mothers, sisters, aunties, pals asking them to send all sorts of amounts of money to somebody on the outside who was smuggling heroin into prison. The money would be used to buy more to be secreted to the dealer operating inside. I would hear men desperately pleading on the telephone to their families, 'Send a hundred pounds.' Or it might be £200, £300, £500 or even £1,000. Such became the strength of the addiction that guys would sell their granny or their best friend simply to get a bag of smack. It reached the stage where you simply couldn't trust anybody in prison. It was sad to see genuinely hard men, major gangsters from London, Manchester or Liverpool, humiliated by coming along the landing carrying £20 bags of groceries – chickens and rice and mince and steaks and tins of tomatoes – and going into a heroin dealer's cell pleading, 'There's the £20 I owe. Give me my smack.' I saw men who were feared on the outside in tears because they lacked four or five pounds to buy a half-bag of heroin. The drug had broken their spirits, and they would slink away to their cells accepting rejection by slimeballs who in the past would have begged for the opportunity to lick their boots.

I watched men I had looked up to when I first entered prison change into cowed, pathetic specimens. Among these was a top figure in the London underworld. For the sake of his family and out of respect for the individual he once was, I won't embarrass him by naming this guy. It turned out he had become hooked on heroin and had arranged to have his own supply smuggled in, but once his supplier deserted him he was reduced to begging from the prison dealers. One day, he admitted to me, 'Yes, I'm on it. Fuck you, so what?' It was so sad to see somebody like that crumbling and begging from low lifes.

The heroin trade made Godfathers out of human detritus and reduced underworld kingpins to beggars. That was a road I promised myself I would never take. Even the screws had turned a blind eye to hash. It made everybody relaxed and happy. But by targeting it, Howard's reforms funnelled inmates down the heroin tunnel, causing increased tension within prisons and shame and poverty to the families of those who became addicts. It helped the prison dealers become richer. After nine o'clock lock-up, they'd recover their supply from hiding places, sometimes from within their own bodies, chop it up, perhaps mix in additives like baking soda or talcum powder, to make the raw drug go further and add to the profit, then pour it into scraps of paper, which they sold to hapless victims. They might have gone into prison as penniless failures, but they walked out to sit in luxury cars and live in newly bought mansions. Considering how much money they were making, it was no wonder some of them were reluctant to leave.

19

Charlie Bubbles

JAMES HEALY WAS a passionate Celtic supporter. He wasn't interested in books or reading, but he was a great animal lover. During my brief stay at Frankland, one of his pals there, a fellow Hoops follower from Maryhill, said James had been in touch asking if he could get him a budgerigar. A friend had brought him the bird from Glasgow, and he'd been given permission by the bosses at Frankland for me to take it with me to Full Sutton. It meant that, unlike my tiny television set, I didn't have to try to smuggle it. When I asked if the bird had a name, the guy in Frankland told me, 'Charlie Bubbles.' I never managed to find out whether he took that from the title of the 1967 film in which Albert Finney played a working-class man who became rich and drove about in a Rolls-Royce or if he'd heard it mentioned in the Kinks song 'Where Are They Now?'

On the trip south, the budgie perched in his cage beside me in the prison service van, both of us guarded by screws. Someone had suggested covering the cage with a towel to help Charlie relax. About half an hour into the journey, a distinct cry of 'Celtic! Sack the board! Celtic! Sack the board!' broke the silence.

'Where the fuck did that come from?' asked one of the screws. I lifted the towel and there was Charlie chirping away merrily.

'The budgie,' I said, and the screw told me, 'Fuck, that was as clear as anything.'

Around this time, most Celtic followers had been loudly and

publicly protesting their annoyance over the inability of the club's directors to halt the continuing domination of Rangers and had been demanding they stand down. But it had needed the appearance on the scene of the wealthy entrepreneur Fergus McCann, strongly supported by wealthy local businessman Brian Dempsey, to rescue the club from bankruptcy.

It was appropriate, for a follower of the Hoops, that the bird was green and white, and James was over the moon to see it. 'I'll have the wee fellow talking in no time,' he told me. Charlie pitched in with another rendering of 'Celtic! Sack the board,' and James promised, 'I'm going to teach you more words.'

Most lunchtimes we ate our meals in our cells, and whenever I looked in on James he'd open the cage door to let Charlie stretch his wings or walk about on the bed. Hour after hour, James would talk to the bird. It was very tame and sometimes would jump onto my finger. Because I'm a Rangers supporter, when James was out of his cell, I used to tell it, 'Ally McCoist, Ally McCoist,' and one day James caught me and said, 'Don't you fucking do that again.' He wagged his finger at the budgie and told it, 'You cheeky wee monkey.'

After about six weeks, I wandered into James's cell to find him smiling, and he told me, 'You're never going to believe what the budgie just said. Listen to this.' As if on cue, Charlie chirped, 'James Healy, I love you.' I was astonished. 'Jesus, no way!' I said, but the bird hopped onto James's finger and repeated, 'James Healy, I love you.' He beckoned a few others to join us and they stood around in silence, waiting. 'James Healy, I love you,' they heard.

A few weeks later, I was in James's cell and asked him, 'What's it saying now?' Charlie had been flying around. He alighted on my finger, looked up and said, as clear as could be, 'Gie's a wee whisky.' From then on, I took every chance I had to sit and talk to Charlie, telling him over and over, 'You cheeky wee monkey. You cheeky wee monkey.' I thought my words were falling on deaf ears, until one day James called me in and said, 'It's saying something that you've been teaching it.' I went, 'You're joking,' but a few minutes afterwards Charlie said, 'You cheeky wee monkey.'

The prison was filled with men who had committed every conceivable crime. There were murderers, drug barons, gang leaders and hardened IRA terrorists, but as word about the amazing talking budgie spread, they pleaded to be allowed to listen. James was happy to oblige. He was proud of his bird and extremely patient, teaching it more words. In time, the budgie had quite a repertoire and would chirp merrily away for hours, 'Celtic! Sack the Board. One, two, three, four, five, six, seven. James Healy, I love you. Gie's a wee whisky, you cheeky wee monkey.'

This was extremely impressive. 'I'm going to get a budgie,' I told myself. I phoned home that night to tell Ma, 'I want a budgie.'

She sounded astonished. 'A budgie! Where am I going to get a budgie?'

'There's a pet shop at Glasgow Cross where I used to go when I was a wee boy. Go down there and get me a blue and white one.'

I wanted my bird to sport the Rangers colours. Ma did just what I'd asked and put in a request to give me the bird, but we didn't think to get a cage. The result was that on her next visit Ma brought my bird down in a wee box that she'd kept beside her on the train. When she arrived in the visiting room, I asked, 'Did you get my budgie?'

Ma said, 'Your budgie! See my finger?'

I looked at one of her fingers, which was badly cut and still oozing blood. 'What happened?' I asked and she said, 'I was worried when it hadn't moved or made a sound and I even wondered if it might be dead. So I put my finger in the box and the bugger bit it. I told it, "You bastard, you!"'

I asked her, 'Where's the budgie now?' and she said, 'I brought it to the gate, but I was told that because it wasn't in a cage it wouldn't be allowed into the prison.'

'What did you say to them?'

'Well, I pointed out that we had been told it was OK and that in any case your friend James already has a cage with his bird in it.

The guy at the gate was still insisting the budgie wasn't allowed in, so I said, "I tell you what then, it's already bitten me once, I'm not taking that back on the train up to Glasgow. It's a three-and-a-half-hour journey." So I just left it on the waiting-room steps and walked in.'

Half an hour later, a couple of screws came over to us. 'Look,' they said, 'we've got the budgie. James Healy has agreed to take it and put it in his cell in his cage.'

I christened my bird Rob Roy. We thought we only had to put him into James's cage and Charlie Bubbles would teach him to talk. But after three days James complained, 'Charlie's clammed up. He won't say a word.'

One of the other guys reckoned he knew about cage birds and told us, 'Of course it won't talk. Do you honestly think one budgie is going to teach the other how to talk? It won't say a thing.'

A few days later, I went into James's cell on the lookout for Rob Roy. 'Where's Rob fucking Roy?' I asked, and James, clearly unhappy, pointed to a corner of the cage where my bird was perched, looking smug. 'Where's Rob fucking Roy?' he repeated. 'He's only eaten one of my fucking posters. Ian, I'm getting sick of this. You better get rid of it. I'm not keeping it any longer.' I pleaded, 'Wait until I get a cage.' But James was adamant: 'You know you don't want it because it'll fly about your cell and shit all over the place. If you don't get it out of here, I'm going to put it out of the window.' I said, 'James, don't be so fucking cruel.' He would not be swayed.

I went out into the middle of the landing, announcing, 'Budgie for sale, budgie for sale.' Jimmy Mullen, a double murderer from Liverpool, emerged from his cell and asked how much I wanted for Rob Roy. 'Five phone cards,' I told him. He said, 'I'll give you four,' and we shook hands. It turned out he already had a bird cage but no bird. So I gave him Rob Roy, disappointed that instead of being a Rangers supporter he'd be a Scouser. Almost from that moment, Charlie Bubbles started talking again.

One of our neighbours was the Londoner Ronnie O'Sullivan, dad of the sensational young snooker player also named Ronnie.

The two were really close. He was incredibly proud of his son. The elder Ronnie was jailed for life in 1992 after Bruce Bryan, a driver to Charlie Kray, died from stab wounds in a Chelsea nightclub. Ronnie junior had just started making his mark in the snooker world but took every chance he had to visit his father. Ronnie and I were good friends, and often at night after we'd been dubbed up we would talk to each other through the tiny gaps in the walls on the sides of the central heating pipes. We'd also have an occasional joint.

Both of us were fans of a radio show hosted by a character named 'Caesar the Geezer', in reality Chris Ryder, a friend of Kenny Everett. Caesar the Geezer ran a sort of problem page in which listeners were encouraged to call in and talk about their difficulties. Some of the advice given was hilarious. Someone suffering from depression might be told, 'Take a bath.' Ronnie and I used to be in stitches listening to this, roaring with laughter so that other cons would shout at us to be quiet.

One night, long after ten o'clock, James came to his window, something he never normally did, and shouted, 'Ian! Ian!'

Ronnie said, 'That's fucking James at the window, what's the matter with him?', so I called out, 'Aye, James, what is it?'

The reply was 'Charlie's not well.'

'What's the matter with him?'

'He just keeps shaking his head.'

'I hope he's going to be all right,' I said.

At that, Ronnie opened his window. 'James,' he called, and a voice answered, 'Aye.'

James must have expected to hear words of advice or sympathy. Instead, Ronnie told him, 'Phone Caesar the Geezer – he'll get on it.'

James shouted, 'I'm going to fucking kill you, you prick, O'Sullivan,' and slammed his window shut.

James was seriously worried about Charlie, and I told Ronnie, 'He loves that budgie. I hope nothing happens to it.'

'It's only a fucking budgie,' answered Ronnie.

'I know, Ronnie, but look at the way it talks. Even the IRA guys have said they've never heard a budgie talk like that.'

I fell into a really deep sleep because I'd been smoking hash, and in the morning I felt myself being woken up. I looked up to find James Healy shaking me.

'What is it, James?' I asked, and he said, 'It's Charlie.'

I thought, 'That fucking budgie,' but I asked him, 'What's the matter?'

'He's dead.'

I didn't know whether to laugh or cry, but I said, 'Oh, sorry, James.'

To be honest, I was just dying to get back to sleep. So James returned to his cell, and he wouldn't come out for most of that day.

Ronnie was forever winding up other guys and could be very funny. For that reason, I was worried when he told me he was going into James's cell.

'Don't you fucking start anything. He's really serious about this budgie,' I said.

'It's only a fucking budgie. Anyway, James probably poisoned it. He let it eat used matches.'

'I know that,' I told him, 'but James was really fond of it.'

So into his cell we went and found our friend lying on his bed.

'Are you all right, James?' I asked. 'I'm sorry to hear about the budgie.'

James was trying to put a brave face on his loss. 'Aye, it's all right,' he said.

Sympathetic as ever, Ronnie chipped in with, 'It's only a budgie.'

I said, 'James, he's only kidding you.'

James took the bird's death really badly. If you're locked up for a long time, a budgie can become your closest companion. Later on, I said to him, 'Get another budgie,' but he replied, 'No, never.'

The cage was still there, but it was empty. There was no sign of the late Charlie Bubbles. James had buried his pet in a wee soil-covered yard where inmates could grow vegetables. One of the other guys had even made a tiny cross with 'God Rest Charlie Bubbles' inscribed on it. When word spread about the budgie graveyard, everybody in the prison was saying, 'For fuck's sake, what next?'

But that wasn't the end of the story of the budgie, and Charlie Bubbles would have a sort of peculiar revenge on the prison service, probably for keeping James in for so long.

A couple of months after Charlie died, James was transferred to Frankland and soon afterwards the jail bosses decided to concrete over the little garden yard. It was suspected that blades and home-made weapons had been hidden there. Before the cement mixers arrived, a thorough check was to be made of the area. This job was given to a security team of specially trained officers known as a dedicated search team – a DST. We called them 'the Don't Stop Trying mob'.

When a cell was being checked out, this crew would move in, whip you off to another cell and go through everything with a fine-tooth comb, even photocopying documents. This led to a lot of bad feeling, because it meant that, at least in theory, they could pass to the Crown details of defence arguments at appeal hearings. Previously, you were entitled to stand outside the door and watch what they were doing. Now, you had no idea whether anything was being taken. Eventually, a couple of guys made a successful legal challenge, arguing that they had a right to witness searches.

Anyway, the DST got to work, digging and sifting through the soil. To make sure nobody could retrieve anything, they had closed the gates leading into the yard and ordered everyone to stay indoors. I was sitting in my cell smoking hash with another friend, Perry Wharrie, and told him, 'Fucking hell, Perry, James's budgie's buried in there. They're going to dig up Charlie Bubbles.'

Almost at that moment, we heard a shout from one of the searchers: 'Hoi, what's this underneath here?' They hadn't just unearthed the bones of the budgie. From underneath Charlie's grave emerged knives, bags of speed and blades. They had been put there by other cons, but it was obvious suspicion was about to fall on James.

'Who owned this budgie?' one of the DST members demanded,

and a chorus of voices shouted back, 'He's in Frankland.' Everybody was roaring with laughter, in my case probably because of the hash, which always made me feel happy and relaxed.

I wrote to James and told him, 'I'm sorry to be the bearer of bad news, but they've desecrated your budgie's grave.'

20

The Krays

AS A YOUNGSTER growing up in Provanmill, I often heard tales about Arthur Thompson being pals with the Krays, especially the twins, Ronnie and Reggie, and with other gangsters of that status. Like most others, I dismissed these stories as just myths. In prison in England, I discovered how wrong we had all been.

In just about every high-security jail, strangers would approach, say they'd heard I was from Glasgow and ask, 'Do you know Arthur Thompson?'

I'd answer, 'Aye, but you mean Mr Thompson.'

His death made no difference to his reputation. Arthur's name still opened doors, was still treated with respect; it was clear he'd known more people than I'd ever imagined he had. And it was because I'd been a neighbour of Arthur that I came to know Charlie Kray and, through him, the twins.

Quiet, likeable Charlie had been a promising welterweight boxer in his younger days. He was the oldest of the three Kray boys and was jailed with his brothers in 1968 following the murders of George Cornell and Jack 'The Hat' McVitie, the twins getting life and Charlie ten years for being an accessory. He was released in 1975 and played a crucial part in bringing to the cinema screen the 1990 movie *The Krays*, the twins' life story, starring former Spandau Ballet bassist and future *EastEnders* actor Martin Kemp.

Ronnie had died in 1995, and two years later Charlie was jailed again, this time for 12 years for allegedly plotting to smuggle cocaine worth £39 million, an accusation he always denied, saying he had been fitted up by the police. I met him when he was moved into the cell next to me at Long Lartin in Worcestershire and liked him from the start. Although he was fit and went to the gym most mornings, he smoked a lot and I had the feeling he would never live out his sentence. Often, he'd invite me into his cell and we'd chat, and inevitably Arthur's name cropped up.

According to Charlie, if they had any trouble that needed sorted in England they would get in touch with Arthur, who either took care of it himself or arranged for others to deal with the problem. He described Arthur as a gentleman, and said he was on really good terms with the twins. It was fascinating to sit and listen to Charlie, especially because it was said that the twins went to him for advice when they had difficulties. The young prisoners in particular were in awe of him and looked up to me when they realised Charlie and I were friends. They'd ask for his autograph and he would politely refuse.

'Ian, I get embarrassed by this,' he'd tell me. 'After I was released in 1975, I used to cruise on the *QE2*. There were always film stars and pop stars there who made a beeline for me. It was Mr Kray this and Mr Kray that, and they'd beg me to tell them about Reg and Ronnie. I'd even be invited to the captain's table. On cruises or dry land, I was treated like a celebrity.'

I told him I'd read books about the twins, and he said to me one day, 'Ian, you are going to meet Reg.' Like Ronnie, Reg had been ordered to stay in prison for 30 years, but the time was fast approaching when he would be able to apply for parole. His health, like Charlie's, was not good, so Reg had been given permission to visit his brother. I was a bit surprised by this, because the Krays' arch-enemies had been the Richardsons, and Eddie Richardson was just along our landing. Probably the fact that there had been no problems between him and Charlie had swayed the outcome of the visit application. There was a real buzz about the place when word went around that Reg was there.

So, Charlie brought Reg to see me. He was always polite and

chapped on my door. But I got the shock of my life to look up and see Reg Kray standing there. 'Come on in,' I said, and Charlie said, 'Reg, I would like you to meet Ian MacDonald from Glasgow. He knew Arthur Thompson.' As we shook hands, Reg said simply, 'Nice to meet you.'

Other meetings would follow, and during one Reggie asked my age. When I told him, he said, 'Ian, I came in at 35, and I'm probably never going to get out again.' He was wrong, of course, but when they did release him it was so he could spend a few pain-racked weeks in a hotel, dying of inoperable bladder cancer. It wasn't really what freedom was all about.

One day, he asked, 'Ian, what are you going to do when you get out?' and I told him, 'I don't really know, but I don't think I'm going to get into trouble again.' I really meant that. 'Let me give you a bit of advice,' said Reg. 'Crime? It's not worth it. I've spent nearly 30 years in prison. On the outside, I lived the life of Reilly. Prison is no place in which a young man should waste his best years.' He would often offer advice.

Once I told him, 'Reg, we have something in common.'

'What's that?' he asked, looking puzzled.

'We're mammy's boys,' I said, knowing how the boys loved their mother, Violet, and always treated her with the utmost respect.

He burst out laughing, then told me, 'Our friends would come around and we'd all go upstairs and mother would make the tea. She meant everything to us.'

I actually introduced my ma to Charlie once when she was visiting. He was extremely courteous.

During one conversation, the subject turned to Arthur Thompson. 'We had a lot of time and regard for Arthur,' said Reg. 'He sometimes came down to London and did a bit of work for us.' He didn't elaborate, and there was no way I was going to ask him to tell me secrets of the family business. After talking with him and Charlie, I knew for certain that Arthur was the real thing. I know people slag him off, but I knew from them he was the real deal.

One morning, I watched in amazement as Reg, Charlie and

Eddie Richardson walked together around the football pitch, old rivalries forgotten as they chatted like long-lost friends. 'A newspaper would pay a fortune for a photograph of them,' somebody told me, but nobody had a camera. The Krays never mentioned Eddie to me, nor he them. Like the other major London guys, they didn't want trouble, just to finish their sentences and get out. If the big London players had issues, they waited until they were back on the outside to resolve them.

It was my experience of most major criminals, especially the Londoners, that they were respectful to the vast majority of others, including somebody like me, who I thought of as just a wee guy from Glasgow. They might be crooks on an international scale, drug dealers and robbers, but they always showed good manners. Without losing face, they made it clear they wanted to avoid trouble, but if anybody was silly enough to start bother with them, then that person would get trouble back in spades. The troublemaker would be given one warning, and if that was ignored, he'd have a visit from a masked man carrying a sock filled with snooker balls, followed by a trip to the hospital. These top guys just wanted to serve out their time. They tried to make the days and months as comfortable as possible by doing their exercises in the gym and eating healthily. And they were generally respectful to the prison officers as well, knowing these were the men who could make their lives bearable or a nightmare.

That was another lesson I learned from them. I came to realise that trouble got you nowhere; the more respect you showed screws, the more they'd let you get away with. In the end, though, no matter how much they conformed to the system, prison destroyed Reg and Ron, men once thought of as virtually indestructible.

Over the years, I met hundreds of high-profile criminals. Tommy Bourke was one. In 1993, two MOT inspectors were shot dead at a garage owned by Tommy in Stockport, Lancashire. He was accused of their murders and vehemently rejected the allegation. Then, at Strangeways prison, where he was awaiting trial, a gun was discovered. I sympathised with Tommy, because the next day armed police appeared in court, a situation not unlike that which we had faced after the gun plot was discovered, although it at least got us a fresh hearing. Friends of Tommy argue that the sight of gun-toting cops around the dock must have swayed the jury to feel he was somehow involved. Even though the case against him was flimsy, he was found guilty and given two life sentences.

I met Tommy at Full Sutton. He was a wee, bespectacled guy nicknamed 'the Milky Bar Kid'. You'd think he couldn't harm a fly. In fact, when he was down at the kitchen one day, he couldn't even boil an egg. I said, 'You can't boil an egg. How the fuck could you manage to shoot the two MOT guys?' I hope some day Tommy gets justice.

Malcolm O'Halloran was another Londoner with whom I became great pals. I first met him in Wormwood Scrubs, but through the years we also found ourselves banged up together in Full Sutton and Long Lartin. Malcolm was a member of a gang of prolific armed robbers that operated for 15 years before a supergrass did the dirty on them. They were blamed for 101 raids, but Malcolm eventually admitted doing about 10 of them. He was initially jailed for 24 years, but this was later reduced to 18. We tagged him 'Skip', and together we'd clamber into the prison gym rowing machine and rocket through 10,000 metres in about 40 minutes – pretty good going by anybody's standards. He was a really good guy.

I got on really well with Vic Dark. He was a remarkable character who had been caught hiding in the mud in a potato field by police after an armed robbery went wrong and a copper was taken hostage. Typical of the Londoners, Vic was really into training and would take us to self-defence classes. He would hand me a plastic knife and say, 'Ian, try and attack me with this,' and a moment later I'd find myself flying through the air.

Mickey McAvoy was grassed up to the police and as a result found himself doing 25 years for heading up the armed gang that stole £26 million in gold bullion, diamonds and cash from the Brinks Mat depot at Heathrow airport in 1983. He was a pal, too, along with Michael Papamichel, an associate of the very powerful London-based Adams family. Michael was doing a stretch after a long police surveillance operation smashed a cannabis-trafficking network.

Occasionally, I'd come across a Scottish accent and make a point of finding out to whom it belonged. That led me to meet up in Long Lartin with Martin Brown, who originally came from Castlemilk but who, following his release, settled in Torquay, of all places. Martin's brothers, Tony and Paul, sometimes arrived from other prisons for visits.

Andy Rodger had moved from Glasgow to London, where in 1987 he had been sentenced to life for killing a nightwatchman during a robbery. Andy hit the headlines in 1995 during a dramatic escape from Parkhurst on the Isle of Wight. He and two others secretly made a copy of the prison master key and got hold of a 25-ft-long ladder. They used these to get over the perimeter wall. The plan was to fly to the mainland, but after reaching an airfield they discovered the battery of the light aircraft they were going to use was flat. They were recaptured after three days on the run.

I also met John Kendall and Sydney Draper, who got away from Gartree in Leicestershire in 1987 in a helicopter. John was doing eight years for burglary and Syd life for his part in an armed robbery on a British Rail depot in Springburn, Glasgow, in which a watchman was shot dead. A pal hired the chopper, saying he was doing an aerial survey, but pulled a gun on the pilot and forced him to land in the exercise yard. John was waiting and ran, followed by Syd and watched by cheering inmates and astonished screws. Syd was on the run for thirteen months, but John was recaptured after ten days. It was probably the most daring escape in British criminal history. In Frankland, Syd used to tell me, 'Ian, it was great. Everybody was waving and we waved back.'

Speaking of escapers, I met three great brothers from Islington, the Pewters, Ronnie, Terry and Stan. Ronnie was the first inmate to escape from Parkhurst. Another southerner I liked was Peter Pacitto from Essex. He and I had many great battles in the gym – playing soft tennis. Jason Vella came from Essex too. I liked

Jason, who was doing 17 years for a drugs offence. He was good company and got on well with the Scots, a hard man, not to be messed about with, who was so well off that in 1999 he made it onto a newspaper's list of rich young businessmen.

Friendship was a food of which the more you had the easier it was to survive. I was fortunate to have made so many friends, like Phil Brown, Ted Avis and Davey Holt from Liverpool, Jamie Batel, who knew the Pewters and, like them, was from Islington, and Mick Gillett from Preston in Lancashire, who had been caught up in a police drug operation and worked as a passman in the Long Lartin gym while he served out his 12 years. He and I sometimes had battles royal, but only on the badminton court.

Everybody had a story to tell, some of them so bizarre they were hard to believe. One guy from Birmingham had been a keen angler who took the sport seriously, using the weather forecasts to dictate when and where he fished. One day, a wrong prediction ruined his plans with the result that he went along to the local meteorological centre and shot dead one of the workers. He was known in prison as 'Peter the Weatherman'.

In Long Lartin, I met Colin Ireland, who was given five life sentences in 1993 for killing five gay men. At the start of that year, he had made a New Year's resolution to become a serial killer. He picked up his victims from a gay pub in west London. He told me, 'I just hated gays. I'd get off with one of them, go back to their flat, and before they knew it they were tied up and thinking they were into a kinky sex game. Then I'd just kill them.' It may sound strange, but I actually felt sorry for him. He said his life had fallen apart, his wife had left him and he had had nothing to live for.

Colin insisted he was not gay. Archie Hall, on the other hand, never denied he was bisexual. Born in Anderston, Glasgow, Archie ended up in London, where he became a butler to, and occasionally lover of, wealthy celebrities both male and female. He ended up killing five people, including his occasional mistress 'Irish' Mary Coggle, and was given life in 1978. I'd sit in his cell and ask him about the details of his murders, and he'd say, 'Ian, for Christ's sake, you're sick.' But he couldn't resist telling me about them and described how he'd battered Irish Mary just because she wanted to keep a fur coat belonging to another victim. Even though he was in his 70s, Archie was still held in top-security nicks. He never lost the courteousness you'd expect from a butler, but he loved taking speed and drinking prison-brewed hooch.

While I was at Full Sutton, the authorities tried to put Michael Sams into our wing instead of sticking him with the other sex offenders. This one-legged rat kidnapped and murdered Julie Dart, a teenage prostitute from Leeds, and then kidnapped estate agent Stephanie Slater, keeping her in a wooden box for seven days while demanding a ransom from her employers before this brave woman was rescued by police. Immediately we discovered Sams was among us, we were at his cell door threatening him and shouting, 'As soon as you come out we're going to kill you, you cunt.' So the screws were forced to move him.

Somebody we ignored, on the other hand, was Donald Neilson, 'the Black Panther'. He murdered three sub-postmasters during robberies, then kidnapped teenager Lesley Whittle, kept her hidden down a drainage shaft with a wire around her neck and pushed her to her death when ransom demands failed. Like Sams, Neilson was told he would die in prison. At Full Sutton, he was forever eating raw carrots and doing press-ups. Nobody ever spoke to him. The prediction came true when he died in December 2011.

At Long Lartin, however, the inmates managed to burn the cell of Paul Bostock, a devil-worshipping karate fanatic who murdered two young women and then told a girlfriend, 'I am an animal that should be prevented from walking the streets again.' Somebody did their best to make sure he got his wish. Shortly after a screw made an illegal search of my cell and confiscated some drink, leaving me feeling cheated and angry, Bostock's cell went up in flames. I was blamed for the fire and thrown into solitary, but they never managed to pin anything on me.

I was in there five months and met Alan Condon, a Chelsea fanatic who never gave up believing the Blues would one day hit the heights of success again. It took a Russian billionaire to make Alan's wish come true.

Warren Slaney was a really nice guy who took a shine to me. Boy, could he box, but he was a dangerous fucker. We had some good times together. He and a pal had been given two life sentences in 1992 for allegedly shooting dead two guys who ran hot-dog stalls in the Leicester area and stealing the takings. One night, when we were at Frankland, where Warren shared food and cooking duties with James Healy, Mick Carroll and me, a few of us were sitting in James's cell. As I walked past Warren, I flicked his ear playfully with my finger. He went ballistic, shouting, 'I'll fucking kill you!' He chased me, but he couldn't catch me. He was in a bad, black mood after that and kept warning me, 'Ian, you'll have to get your punishment.'

This went on and on, until I told him one day, 'Right, Warren, what is it you want to do?' and he says, 'I want to break something.' I thought, 'Oh, fuck.' He asked, 'Where do you want me to hit you?' I thought it over and told him, 'OK, one of my shoulders.' Next thing, I felt a bang and thought my shoulder was broken.

My friend Perry Wharrie had been given life in 1989 after an armed gang shot dead an off-duty policeman during a failed security-van raid. One of his co-accused had been a Scot from Port Glasgow, Charlie McGhee, who was notorious within the prison system for attacking officers. Sadly, Charlie died in jail before his release. Perry was a real gentleman for whom I had a load of respect, and he kept telling me, 'Fucking Warren's nuts, but in a good way, the sort of guy you can trust.'

I told my story about Warren to another friend, Young Doc from Cranhill, whose girlfriend was pregnant. They were fascinated by the tale and they told me, 'If the baby's a boy, we'll call him Warren.' It was, and they did.

A few days after the Warren incident, I was moved to Long Lartin for no apparent reason. I was still in agony when Billy Whitfield, a Glaswegian who had moved to Manchester and whose drinking had resulted in him being tagged 'Billy the Fish', invited Perry, me and another guy into his cell. We were chatting away, me proudly wearing my Rangers top, when this big mad Taffy walked in demanding to know if we had any drink. When we told the Welsh guy no, he started getting cheeky with Perry, who could box a bit, and I told the gatecrasher, 'Hoi, don't talk to him like that.' The Taffy asks me, 'Who are you?' and I told him, 'Never mind who I am, you're a cruiser.' I'd just made this term up on the spot. He said, 'What's a cruiser?' At that, I opened the door and said, 'Somebody who's poncing drink. Now get out.'

Later that night, Taffy came back with three cronies, tried to punch me, and we steamed into them. I kept smashing the Welshman over the head with a honey jar. There was blood everywhere, and when I slipped in it, Taffy took a running kick at the shoulder Warren had punched. By the time the screws intervened, Perry had lost two teeth and Billy the Fish was covered in blood. I was bent double and every one of our opponents had been injured. As we walked along the corridor to the surgery, I heard one of the screws laugh and tell a mate, 'Fucking hell, that must have been some battle. It was like something out of a Wild West movie.' I was taken to hospital under armed escort. My shoulder was X-rayed and found to be dislocated. The doctors strapped it in a sling, but I refused to let them cut off my Rangers top. Five days after this, I was moved to Belmarsh and Perry to Winchester, the prison authorities invoking a rule saying we had been in breach of good order and discipline.

You might think that Rangers top would have been like a red rag to a bull as far as the IRA prisoners were concerned, but it wasn't the case. I got to know and like a lot of these guys really well. Men like Joe O'Connell, Eddie Butler, Harry Duggan and Hughie Doherty, who had taken a couple hostage in their flat in Balcombe Street in London in 1975, giving up after a six-day siege. Hughie was a gifted artist, who spent a lot of his time painting away in his cell, and he gave me one of his works, which I handed to Sheila during a visit. His brother Pat was vice president of Sinn Féin, the political wing of the IRA.

I used to visit the Irish guys, and others would ask, 'How are you allowed to sit in their cells when you're wearing a Rangers top and they're all Catholics and IRA?' I'd say, 'Because they like me. I'm not an Orangeman. I'm not bitter. All we do is sit and talk about our families and about Ireland and Donegal. They all know Glasgow well. They've stayed there, in the Gorbals.' Once they got to know me, they told me they knew John Friel well.

When we chatted, we would often be joined by Vincent Wood, an Englishman who supported the IRA's aims. Vinnie had been jailed for 22 years in 1993 for allegedly minding explosives and weapons for the movement.

At the time, Rangers were on a roll and I had a standard bet with Eddie, Joe and Hughie for a box of Cadbury's Roses chocolates from the canteen on the outcome of every Old Firm match. Because Rangers hardly lost a game, I was getting fatter and fatter. After the results were announced, they used to come round to my cell, where I'd be lying on my bed, and they'd go, 'There's your box of Roses, you Orange cunt.' I knew it was all said in fun and would shout, 'Hoi, you've forgotten something,' before leaping out of bed and giving them a single chocolate each. 'You bastard,' they'd say.

In 1998, when we were at Long Lartin, they were transferred under the Good Friday Agreement to prison in Dublin and said their goodbyes to me. I was watching television one day and saw them being welcomed at a Sinn Féin conference by Gerry Adams, Martin McGuinness and Pat Doherty. Adams described them as 'our Nelson Mandelas'. It was then I realised just how high was the esteem in which the guys from whom I'd been taking Roses chocolates for years were held.

Joe was married to a schoolteacher from Glasgow who knew Sheila through her sister Claire. Sometimes the two women travelled together to visit Joe and me, proving what a very small world we live in.

In 1997, I was called over and introduced to another Irishman, from Belfast, who said his name was Pat Martin. Pat had just been jailed for thirty-five years for blowing up electricity substations, although his sentence was later cut by seven years. We were of a similar age and got on really well.

'When I get out, I want you to come to Belfast and I'll introduce you to the family,' he told me.

I laughed and said, 'Pat, there's no chance of that.'

He looked surprised. 'What do you mean, there's no chance of that? I like you.'

'Pat, I'm a Rangers supporter. You'll put one in my nut.'

His reply surprised me. 'It's not like that. I've got a brother-in-law who's a Rangers supporter.'

One day, he asked me, 'Would you give me a loan of your Rangers top?' I told him I thought this was an odd request and asked what he wanted it for. 'I want to send a photograph of me in your top to my pals in the Maze prison,' he said. 'They'll see all that as good craic.'

I asked, 'Won't you get a bullet in your nut?', but he assured me, 'Nah, they'll all be laughing their backsides off.'

'OK, Pat, be it on your own head,' I said and handed over my top.

Pat had his photograph taken wearing it and a couple of weeks later he shouted me over in the exercise yard. 'I sent them the picture and they're in hysterics over in the Maze,' he said. 'They all think it's as funny as fuck.' He was roaring with laughter, but I found the whole episode incredible.

The Balcombe Street gang had been members of a six-man IRA unit that included Brendan Dowd, who was also later given life. Brendan was a nice guy who kept himself to himself, mostly remaining in his cell. I was shocked to hear him described as being at one stage the top terrorist organiser in Britain. One of his fellow volunteers, Sean Kinsella, on the other hand, was forever running around the exercise yard. Sean, from County Monaghan, was another lifer, having been convicted of the 1974 murder of Billy Fox, a member of the Senate, the upper house of the Irish Republic's parliament.

Not all the terrorists I met were members of the IRA. Nawaf Rosan was a high-ranking Iraqi intelligence officer who led a hit team that tried to assassinate Shlomo Argov, the Israeli ambassador to Britain, in a gun attack outside the Dorchester Hotel in 1982. The target survived, despite being shot in the head, but was paralysed. Rosan was caught and jailed for 35 years. We used to play soft tennis and badminton together and kept in touch after I left prison.

The crimes of some inmates led them to be regarded by the public as crazy, but none of them was as daft as Charles Bronson. Charlie is a legend, often described as the most violent prisoner in Britain, with his sentences being increased for fighting prison officers and other inmates. I was at Long Lartin chatting to pals when he appeared, steaming with drink. Somebody said, 'Give us a dance, Charlie,' and he stripped naked, apart from his boots, and started doing a mad dance on the tables. The screws were petrified. Eventually, he was persuaded to go back to his cell to be locked up for the night, but an hour later came noises of windows being smashed and someone roaring like a lion or tiger. 'That's mad Charlie. He's smashing up,' somebody said. The next morning when he was opened up, there sat Charlie wearing warpaint and looking like a Red Indian. He leapt up and ran along the landing whooping like a redskin. He grabbed a screw and said, 'I want a cleaning job.' They went along with it, but when he went back to his cell at midday, the riot squad moved in and dragged him off to solitary. I had seen Charlie on one of his rare appearances in general circulation.

I kept in touch with events back in Glasgow through Ma, friends and the newspapers. In 1995, I learned how Tam Bagan, who'd gone to work with Fergie for the Godfather after I turned the job down, had been jailed for 12 years for armed robbery. In jail, he tried to expose police corruption and, while he got nowhere, there were many who shared his views.

Gerry Rae was among them. He had never forgotten the beating he'd suffered in the raid on his home, and in 1997 he won a private prosecution against seven Strathclyde Police officers. A year later, while they were on trial for perjury, I read with sadness that Gerry had been found dead in his car in Yoker, surrounded by bags of heroin. The official version was that he had died from an overdose, but even now doubts linger over how he died. One suggestion that keeps cropping up in underworld circles is that a millionaire heroin dealer and police informer arranged for Gerry to be forcibly overdosed with smack.

Another death that year left me sad, that of Dessie Cunningham. I sympathised with his family in a letter to them, and they were kind enough to reply with an open invitation for me to visit. Dessie's pal Joe Collins, another of my friends, was good enough to write and tell me he'd bought a wreath on behalf of us both and that there was a huge turnout at Dessie's funeral.

I hadn't had any contact with Fergie for a long time, but in 1997 I read that he had been arrested in London and charged with gunrunning. After months in prison on remand, he was finally jailed for ten years, but then that was reduced on appeal to seven years. I knew that, like me, Fergie would be given a category A rating, and I wondered if we'd end up together. I looked forward to our meeting if it came.

No matter who or what a man was before, in jail everybody was equal, regardless of whether you were worth ten million pounds or ten pence. Many, especially the wealthy, found it hard to open up to others. Mostly, it took five or six years in the category A grades before you were sufficiently trusted by these rich guys for them to admit their feelings and fears to you. I'd sit with them and say, 'So you've got ten million – tell me about your lifestyle,' and they would talk of starting off in the East End of London, gradually moving upmarket, having second and third homes abroad, a yacht, flash cars, and being able to afford thousands of pounds for a suit.

'So with all that money, why didn't you retire?' I'd ask. The answer was always the same: 'Because it was so easy.' Then I'd say, 'If it was so easy, why are you sitting in this cell?' Usually, the reason was because they had made one phone call too many, the one that was overheard by the police, even if they suspected their homes and telephones were bugged and had driven miles to use a telephone kiosk.

I knew that after my visits they would lie awake through the night pondering on how they should have called it a day and retired with their millions safely invested. They couldn't spend their fortunes at the prison canteen. When I asked, 'Would you give up all your money if it meant you'd be released tomorrow?', every one of them said, 'Without a doubt, yes.'

Maybe there was a slight difference between us, though. When they came into my house – you called your cell your 'house' – they'd get a chocolate digestive. But in their own pads, despite all their riches, those miserable cunts would only ever give me a plain digestive.

21

Ronnie O'Sullivan

I WAS CHATTING IN my cell with James Healy when Ronnie O'Sullivan chapped our door. He had on his housecoat and was carrying a towel. 'I hear you two are the Scots boys,' he said, trying to imitate a Scottish accent, something he often did when chatting to us or other Scottish inmates. It was all done in good fun. We told him, 'That's right.' He was always very friendly and carried on, 'My mother's Scottish.' I thought he was winding us up. 'Bollocks,' I said. But he told us, 'Shettleston, Easterhouse,' and I thought, 'Fucking hell, he might be telling the truth here.' So I said, 'Aye? Your ma's from Shettleston?', and Ronnie replied, 'She's got a fucking better accent than you, and she's lived in London for the last 50 years.' I told myself, 'He's talking a lot of shite here,' and I could tell Ronnie knew I was having doubts. He said, 'Aye, mate, all right, no bother. Don't you believe me?' To me, there was no way anybody would have retained their accent after all that time, so I said, 'Nooooo, I don't. Not after 50 years. It's a long time, Ronnie, isn't it?' So he said, 'I'm off for a shower. I'll see you later and put my ma on the phone to you.'

Now, Ronnie was never off the telephone. You were meant to have no more than ten minutes at a time, but he always had a fistful of phone cards and sometimes seemed to speak to the whole of London, making one call after another. I'd have to go up to him and say, 'Ronnie, come on, get off that fucking phone. There's other guys here needing to phone the missus.' This evening I was

180

hanging around as Ronnie was talking, and I heard him say, 'Got these two Glasgow guys here, they don't believe you still have your accent.' Then he turned and said, 'Ian, come on.'

So I took the receiver and a female voice said in a clear Glasgow accent, 'Ian, isn't it?' and I replied, 'How are you, Mrs O'Sullivan?' She went on, 'How are you doing, son?', and I told myself, 'She's got a better fucking accent than me.' And she did. I couldn't believe it. We had a chat, and when I put down the phone, I looked around and there was Ronnie with a huge grin. 'I told you so,' he said.

Ronnie was well liked. When I'd first read he had been given life and then heard he was joining us, I expected him to be some sort of flamboyant multimillionaire who would get his son to come in and play snooker with the screws so they'd make life easy for him and help him get an early release. In fact, Ronnie was a good guy who had stayed out of trouble until the incident in the club that had landed him in jail. He was clearly proud of his son, but he didn't go around shouting about how good the boy was and how much money he was making.

'Ian, I got him one of those wee snooker tables when he was five,' Ronnie said.

I told him, 'I had one of those.'

'Aye, but you were probably shite,' he said, and we both laughed.

That was how Ronnie was – didn't mess about, got straight to the point.

'By the time the boy was ten, he was going into snooker clubs beating men twice his age. I was jailed when he was 16, so I've missed so much of what's happened to him since.'

Ronnie's was a real rags-to-riches story. He told me how he'd worked as a cook and then a cleaner at Butlins, where he met his Sicilian-born wife, Maria. He moved on to washing cars and was then offered the chance to take over a London sex shop. It meant risking all the family savings and taking a loan, but he took a chance and never looked back as one shop became a string of businesses. The incident that landed him in prison started as a row after Ronnie felt rude remarks had been made to a woman and intervened on her behalf. The victim was black, and Ronnie was given a savage 18-year tariff because the prosecution at his trial made out there was a racist element to the killing, something Ronnie and all those who knew him always denied.

The two of us went to the gym together to play soft tennis, and Ronnie would say, 'I don't know if I'm English or Scottish.'

'I don't care what the fuck you are, I'll beat you anyway,' I'd tell him.

One day, when young Ronnie was visiting him and Sheila had brought Daryl to see me, Ronnie said, 'Get a picture of the boys together,' but Daryl didn't want to be photographed with young Ronnie, and it ended up with the snooker star photographing Daryl and me instead. But I also made sure I had my picture taken with young Ronnie.

I've always enjoyed cooking and the top-security prisons allowed inmates to do many of their own meals. Most guys would team up in groups of three or four and form what were known as 'food boats', basically the same sort of arrangement featured in the hit gangster film *Goodfellas*. The make-up of the food boat obviously changed as you were moved around from jail to jail, but at one stage Ronnie, James Healy and me were three-quarters of a food boat.

The fourth member was Eddie Richardson. Eddie had already completed a long stretch imposed at the time of the notorious torture trial in 1967. 'Mad' Frankie Fraser was jailed for ten years at that same trial, where it was claimed he used pliers to pull out the teeth of victims. In 1990, Eddie was given another 25 years for a drugs offence. In prison, he discovered he had a talent for painting, in much the same way that Jimmy Boyle did in Scotland with sculpture. At one time, under the Michael Howard prison reforms, painting classes were withdrawn, the excuse being that the prison system needed to save money. And Eddie even had his paints taken away, the supposed reason this time being that they constituted a fire risk. He had to fight to get them returned. He loved painting in his cell, did a few pictures for friends and gave me signed photographs of some of his works, including one showing a foxhunt. It is one of my proudest possessions.

Eddie was also a keen cook. His mum used to visit him but his brother Charlie never came after they fell out over a series of business deals. Lord Longford, the well-known social reformer, would see him occasionally.

Eddie gave me the most astonishing piece of advice I think I've ever had. In Long Lartin one day, as I was approaching the eighth year of my sentence, he suddenly asked me, 'Ian, what are you going to do when you get out?' It reminded me of the conversation I'd had with his former great enemy Reggie Kray. I said, 'Eddie, I'm not thinking about freedom, just getting through my sentence.' He said, 'You're still a young man. You'll only be about 40 when you're released. What sports are you into?' So I said that while I'd been in prison I'd taken up mainly badminton and soft tennis. He asked, 'Why don't you take up skiing when you get out?'

I was amazed. 'Skiing?'

'Yes, skiing. It's a great sport,' said Eddie.

'Isn't it dangerous?' I asked, working out that he had been in his mid-50s when he came into prison for the drugs offence, and so must have been skiing at that age.

'Not for a young man,' he said. 'And you get a good suntan while you're doing it.'

But I wasn't convinced. 'It sounds too dangerous for me,' I told Eddie.

James Healy was listening to this conversation and going, 'Oh, aye,' while Ronnie was roaring with laughter.

The four of us would put ten or twelve quid a week into our food-boat kitty, and I usually worked out what meals we'd have. While I'd been at Full Sutton, I had enrolled for a food technology health-and-hygiene course and had been credited with an HND from Beverley College in Yorkshire. What I'd learned was useful for preparing menus. I would plan what we were going to eat each day, write down what we needed from the canteen – so many chickens, tins of tomatoes, bags of rice, chops, spices and so on – then order the stuff. Some guys just lay around during their spare time, smoking or watching television, but I enjoyed planning the week's dinners. Eddie and James usually cooked during the week, and I made a couple of meals at weekends. Ronnie wasn't a cook, so he normally did the washing-up. He was good at breakfasts, though, doing a great fry-up on Saturday and Sunday mornings.

Each wing had a communal kitchen, while every landing had big fridge-freezers. After collecting your order from the canteen, you put it into sacks with your name marked on them and stored them in these fridges. There was usually a rota for using the kitchen, so when it was your turn you simply took out what food was needed and cooked it. We ate with plastic cutlery, but if you needed a sharp knife for preparing the food, you asked the screws for one and it would be handed over. The knife had to be signed out and back in on a big board, so the screws could see at a glance who had knives. I could have stabbed anybody with one of those kitchen knives, but that never occurred to me because I was too interested in the food. We'd stick all the tables together and have a sort of dinner party, watched by the screws, who probably went home to egg and chips.

If you didn't fancy cooking, or wanted something different, then it was possible to taste the finest cuisine. Prisoners came from all countries and walks of life. There were drug dealers from Colombia, the Orient and India who had been expert cooks before being caught. Behind bars, they made a business out of preparing meals for other inmates. David Poole, jailed for his part in the £60-million 1987 Knightsbridge safety-deposit-box robbery, made meals that could have won *Masterchef*. Yardies from Jamaica served up the most delicious jerk chicken with rice and black-eyed peas. At Long Lartin, a group of Indian guys made better Asian food than I have tasted in any fancy restaurant. It was all takeaway, but you had to eat inside! You needed to stick your order in for chicken bhuna, lamb curry or whatever with naan bread a couple of days in advance.

No meal is, of course, complete without a drink to accompany it. No problems there. Booze, in the form of illicitly brewed jail hooch, positively flowed, especially in jails holding category A men. You needed to stick your order in for that, as well. So, come Friday, you'd head off to collect your takeaway meal and then it was on somewhere else for a couple of litre bottles of hooch. Back in the cell, I'd have a few drinks then heat up my curry.

Sometimes, I'd ring home and ask Ma, 'By the way, what have you had for dinner tonight?', and she'd maybe tell me, 'Just the usual, chips and beans,' and I'd say, 'Well, we're having steak with peppercorn sauce followed by Black Forest gateau and ice cream,' and she'd go, 'Piss off.' After I was in a few years, Ma used to meet people in the street and when they asked, 'How's Ian getting on?', she would tell them, 'How's Ian getting on? He's an alcoholic. He's in a holiday camp.'

At Full Sutton in 1995, I spotted the arrival of Rab Carruthers, who had been jailed for 15 years for running a heroin operation in the Manchester area. Rab was originally from Glasgow and was very well respected both there and in the north-west of England, where he had been a major player. I welcomed him, made him a curry and then tried to arrange for him to join us on our wing. But they didn't like having many friends close together and, like most of us, Rab was there one day and gone the next. Those controlling the system enjoyed flexing their muscles from time to time, to show who was boss, moving you around from prison to prison for no apparent reason.

Of course, the fact that there were so many different cultures could cause problems. I'll give you an example. John Bullivant joined my food boat. He was a great friend, a big man from Birmingham who had been jailed for 18 years in 1996 after being found guilty of being the getaway driver for a half-a-million-pound armed robbery on a security van. We were grilling our breakfast sausages one morning when a Muslim inmate who had been a top crack dealer on the outside demanded to know whether the bangers were beef or pork, protesting that if the answer was pork then the fat would drip onto where he and his mates were going to cook their chicken. If any fat did drop down, it would only be a tiny amount, but he jumped about and shouted as though it was enough to kill him. Eventually, I told him, 'I don't know what the fuck they are,' and he went off muttering.

That afternoon, over a few drinks, I kept thinking about how this guy had annoyed me and went back to the kitchen where he and his pals were cooking. 'Do any of you object if I put a pig in the oven?' I asked, but instead of anger this produced only laughs.

'Fuck you,' I said. 'I'm going to worship King Vodka.' I went down on my knees, kissed the floor twice and tottered off. When the rest of the boys asked where I'd been, I told them what had happened.

'This guy was noising me up this morning asking what the sausages were made of,' I said.

'Why didn't you tell him?' they asked, and I said, 'I had a hangover.'

There was never a shortage of booze, despite frantic efforts by the screws to find our hiding places. Some was smuggled in, but mostly it was secretly brewed in buckets, using yeast nicked from the kitchen and a couple of bags of sugar poured in with potatoes or fruit, anything that was to hand. The finished product could be really potent, especially if it was made with potatoes. The experts reckoned it should have been allowed to ferment for ten days, but after five I used to sample the brew and a couple of cups were enough to leave me steaming.

At Long Lartin, lifer Mickey Davey and I made so much hooch that we announced the opening of an unofficial pub, the Tartan Arms. Mickey used to say to me, 'I'm Scottish, Ian. I was brought up in Corby surrounded by Jocks.' Our 'pub' was soon well established and we sold drink from our neighbouring cells, taking turns to conceal the supplies.

In addition to doing a roaring trade, I have to admit to sampling the wares too often. One night, the comedian Jasper Carrott gave a concert in the visiting room. Along with most of the audience, I smuggled booze in, and by the time the show was halfway through we were sozzled and shouting. Carrott must have thought his gags were going down remarkably well, but the best part of the performance was the drink.

Sometimes booze could lead to unexpected problems. A near

neighbour in Full Sutton was Jimmy Collingwood, a double lifer from Liverpool. He had been having severe debt problems, and one morning I heard guys saying they couldn't open his cell door. This wasn't especially unusual, because sometimes we put wedges behind the doors to stop screws getting in. But I liked Jimmy and wanted to make sure he was OK, so a couple of us barged the door open. The cell was in darkness and Jimmy sat in a chair, motionless, wearing only his underpants. A screw arrived and announced, 'He's hanged himself.'

I knew Jimmy had been worried over owing one guy a tenner, and somebody else piped up, 'He owed me for two chickens.' I thought, 'For fuck's sake, the guy's hardly dead and you're moaning about the price of a couple of chickens.'

But that's how it is in prison at times: if it wasn't so tragic, it would be funny. That night I had a drink then went to the window and started shouting that Jimmy had been murdered. The next day, the prison staff tried to reassure everybody Jimmy's death was suicide, but I told them, 'Liars,' and was taken to the segregation block. A governor told me that Jimmy had hanged himself by putting wire around his neck then lying back in his chair, but I told him, 'That's not what I saw.' A couple of days later, I was told that if I stopped making my claims, I would be allowed back into my cell. I knew there was a party that night in the wing, so I agreed, but after a few drinks I was again claiming that Jimmy had been killed. The prison arranged for me to meet a relative of Jimmy's. I was still drunk, and when the man insisted on shaking my hand, I felt something in it. I believed it to be hash, but it was a tiny cross. 'Dirty wee bastard,' I thought. Finally, at an inquest at Hull, the coroner told me that Jimmy had left a note, so I left it at that. But, to be honest, I only ceased my protests and came out of solitary because I wanted a drink.

About once a month, before mandatory drug testing began, Friday was Ecstasy night. Time to eat pasta for energy, because there would be no sleep. Four of us were being supplied with smuggled Ecstasy, so at four o'clock in the afternoon I'd wolf down my pasta, at five I'd swallow the tablets and at six, when the door was unlocked for evening recreation, I'd be out on the landing whooping in front of demented screws who knew that the absence of testing meant there was nothing they could do to prove I was on drugs.

Other inmates would complain, 'Ian's on the fucking Ecstasy,' and I'd shout, 'I'm going to be raving all fucking night!'

Banged up back in my cell, my CD player blaring full blast, I'd transport myself back to Glasgow, imagining I was in the Tunnel nightclub, dancing and surrounded by women. I used to get an incredible buzz out of this.

The next day, guys would ask, 'How can you take an Ecstasy, Ian? We'd be thinking of our wives.'

I'd say, 'I'm thinking of everybody else's wife.'

22

Freedom Calls

ONE MORNING, FIVE years after I had gone to prison, I woke up and told myself, 'Now at last I can handle this.' It was as if somebody had flicked a switch and light flooded into the black tunnel that had seemed to be the future. I got up, went to work, went to the gym, did the cooking, chatted, and suddenly there were no black, brooding thoughts. 'I'm not in prison, I'm in a community centre,' I thought. And, oddly enough, much of the bleakness that had weighed me down seemed to have been lifted because a few months earlier Sheila had told me our relationship was over. That sort of thing happens all the time in prison, and most guys take it badly. It had the opposite effect on me. Often, I had told men starting their sentences, 'Don't think about the outside. Your life is in here.' I hadn't always followed my own advice, but now I felt able to move forward.

During the early years, every Friday night I'd lie back and think of all my pals going to pubs and clubs and worry about Sheila. She was my woman, the only woman. That's when I wanted her and only her. If Miss World had walked into my cell on those nights, I'd have told her, 'Turn around and shut that door on your way out.' Why? Because she wasn't Sheila.

It had ended in bitterness and rage, though, after I rang her one night from Full Sutton. 'How are you doing, Sheila?' I asked. I had been drinking and will never know what she said, but her words made me smash down the telephone. A screw asked, 'Are you all right?', and I told him, 'Aye, yes, just an argument.' Midway through the next morning, I called her again. 'What are you doing phoning?' she asked. I thought she was being cruel, but she went on, 'Didn't I make myself clear last night? We're finished, Ian. I can't take any more of this.' And I went, 'You bastard.'

There is good and bad everywhere: good coppers, bad coppers, good screws, bad screws. A good screw realised something was wrong, probably because he had been monitoring the telephone conversations, as they were allowed to do. He came to see me and said, 'Ian, I know what's happened with Sheila and your wee laddie. I feel sorry for you. But I feel sorry for her, too. She's doing the same time as you.' I realised he was right, but told him, 'Aye, but she shouldn't have done that.' The screw, a senior officer who came from Liverpool, paused and said, 'Listen, every woman needs a man to be there for her. Is it fair for her to have to wait all these years? You've done the crime, she's done nothing.' I warmed to this guy and said, 'Right.'

But it took me six months of talking to James Healy and the others to get the want for her out of my system. There were times when I thought back to our plans for a new life in Spain. I'd still hankered after that, even taking Spanish lessons in prison. But then that morning I awoke and thought, 'Right, Sheila, got you out of my mind, don't need to go back to my cell at night worrying who you're with. Go with who you want.'

Sheila was also Daryl's mum, though, so we stayed in contact. Then one day Ma told me on the telephone, 'Sheila's met a millionaire. The guy has a Rolls-Royce and he's bought her a big house in Bishopbriggs. Daryl's there.' My only question was 'Will Daryl be all right?', and James took the phone to reassure me. 'They're going all over the world,' he said. Sheila was with Ma and James at the time, and she asked to speak to me. 'You know I've met a new guy?' she asked and I said, 'Sheila, good luck. Just so long as he's not one of my pals and Daryl is having a good time.' And that was how I came to hear of Pat Sweeney, a wealthy married businessman.

A couple of months later, I called Sheila to see how my son was and she asked, 'How would you like to meet Pat?'

I told her, 'You're having a laugh. How would I like to meet Pat Sweeney in the jail?'

But she said, 'No, I'd like you to meet him.'

I told her I needed to think it over and mentioned the conversation to pals. Some of them told me, 'You must be daft,' but the older, more mature guys suggested, 'Why don't you meet him? Maybe it'll get Sheila out of your brain altogether.'

By this time, there had been a sort of delayed reaction to our break-up and I had begun asking myself, 'Do I still love her?' After all, Sheila had been such an integral part of my life. Ours was the strongest love–hate relationship I would ever experience. I knew I needed to test myself. Was I over her or was I going to come out the nick and chase her? I didn't want that to happen.

Eventually, she began putting me on the phone to Sweeney. He sounded a nice enough guy, but then Sheila returned to the subject of us meeting. I talked it over with Ma, who said, 'It's up to you, Ian.' In the end, I made the decision for myself. I had to learn whether after meeting him I'd go back to my cell and start thinking about her all over again or whether I'd just say, 'That's it.'

So I told her, 'Let's go for it.' They came down one weekend to Long Lartin in a Rolls-Royce, much to the amusement of the screws. On the eve of the visit, some of my mates, among them Londoners Paul Bryant, Olly and Ronnie Parry, told me I was stupid for allowing this. But within five minutes, I knew the magic had gone; Sheila no longer attracted me. I quickly sensed, though, that Sweeney was jealous, and no wonder. Sheila insisted on holding my hand as we sat at the table with him, and then she ordered him to get us tea and coffee. 'This is wrong,' I thought. 'She shouldn't be doing this. No matter what she has been to me, he's her man now.' The way she looked and acted with me wasn't right. She sensed it and so did he, but later on Sheila told me, 'The first thing that struck me about you was how good you looked.'

When they left, I felt relieved going back to my cell because I knew I wouldn't be trying to cut my wrists or spending the night mooning over her.

'No problem,' I told friends who asked how the visit had gone.

'Fantastic,' I told Ma and my sister. 'I'm actually looking forward to their visit tomorrow.'

Was part of my satisfaction the result of knowing, deep down, that Sweeney wasn't happy? I knew that if there was jealousy, it ought to have been from me, but it was from him. They came back next day, but this time there was no hand-holding.

We had always convinced Daryl that the place where he was visiting me was a big pub. By now, he was seven, and Ma said she thought it was time for him to know the truth. She brought him to see me.

I told Daryl, 'Right, this isn't a pub. It's a jail.'

'Prison?'

'Yes, prison, Daryl.'

He thought for a moment, looked at me and asked, 'But where's your ball and chain?'

I said, 'You're watching too many American movies.'

Then he nodded and said, 'Oh, right. There's bars, and they're policemen.'

He never liked the screws because they would take his toys from him when he visited.

'What are you in for?' he asked.

'A bank robbery.'

'How much did you get?'

'Nothing.'

'Nothing?'

'Nothing.'

'Nothing? I could have planned that,' he said. To add insult to injury he'd arrived wearing a Celtic top.

Each year, I had asked for my AA rating to be lifted, and the answer was always the same: 'No, you remain a danger to the public.' I was pretty pissed off about this, but I realised that the thumbs-down was almost certainly a throwback to the gun plot and a number of battles over the years with screws.

Finally, in 2000, along with James Healy, I applied for parole. The popular conception of a parole application is that a prisoner appeals in front of a board of examiners, the type of scene shown in films such as *The Shawshank Redemption*. In my case, I was assessed by the prison, given a medical to see if I was fit and healthy, and then interviewed by a member of the parole board, in my case Erica Norton, a battleaxe who had been an assistant chief constable with the Leicestershire police.

Before she arrived, I was a nervous wreck, and John Bullivant offered to help. John schooled me in what was likely to happen. He wrote down all the things I'd probably be asked. They'll ask you this, this is what to say, he would tell me. Say this about your family, tell them you're rehabilitated. So I wouldn't forget, he wrote it all down. I took my notes with me when I met Erica. She was so sharp it was unbelievable. There was no fooling her. As soon as the interview began, she asked, 'Do you mind my asking what the paperwork you have with you is?'

I said, 'Things I've written down that I think may answer your questions,' and she said, 'Well, you won't mind if I have a copy, will you?' I said no, and she took them and went off to get them photocopied.

Nothing more was said about the notes at the time, but later, when I was given a copy of the report she had made to the parole board, I read, 'Mr MacDonald has been coached by another prisoner for his parole hearing. He said it was his first parole review and you could tell he had been coached.' And it was true, I had. She was an old fox.

The interview lasted about an hour, and she went through all my offending, from being a 15-year-old up to the bank job. 'Why did you rob a bank?' she asked. I told her, 'For financial reasons,' but she retorted, 'No, greed. Greed,' and I had to sit there and agree that my motive was greed.

'I see you've done a couple of jewellery robberies,' she said. 'What was the reason for these?' I knew how this would end, but nevertheless I told her, 'Financial reasons,' and waited for that word. When it came, she leaned over the table and hissed it. 'Greed,' she told me again. 'It was greed, wasn't it?' Once more I had to agree.

How did I spend my time in prison, she wanted to know. Did I have hobbies? Did I read? 'Yes, I read a lot,' I told her.

'What book are you reading now?' she asked, and I told her, 'You won't believe this: Harry Potter.'

'Harry Potter? That's a strange choice,' she said. 'Why Harry Potter?'

'When I used to phone my son Daryl I could hardly get two words out of him. I told this to my sister one night and she said Daryl was a real Harry Potter fan and once he got his head into a Potter book he hardly looked up. My sister suggested I get a Potter book and read it, so Daryl and I would have a mutual interest we could chat about. I went to the prison library, read a section of a Potter book, chatted about it with Daryl, and then did that night after night.'

I felt a bit of a twat telling her this, an adult reading Harry Potter, but Erica clearly thought it was a great idea. I saw her scribbling away on her notepad, and in her report she praised me for swotting up on Harry Potter to enable me to improve the conversations I had with my son.

Before the interview ended, she asked if I was going to offend again. No, I told her. 'Obviously you're going to say that,' she said, and this time I leaned towards her. 'I mean it when I say no,' I said.

But I came out of that meeting dreading the outcome. I told John Bullivant, 'She's tippled about the papers.' He said, 'What?', and I said, 'She took them from me and copied them. She knew I'd been coached.'

I waited to hear whether I would be paroled, but wasn't hopeful. Then one day James was called to see the governor, who asked him to sit down and told him, 'I have good news. Your parole has come through. You'll be out in five days.'

So we were all happy for him, and now all the guys from London, Manchester and Liverpool whom I had known for years were telling me, 'You're next. You'll get parole, Ian.' And I was beginning to believe it, as well. I thought I was as good as home and dry when a social worker came to my cell and said, 'You'd better start thinking you're going to get out.' And then I was downgraded to category B. The signs were good.

It was a scorching hot day in August 2000 when James came to my cell. 'Ian, I feel guilty about leaving you,' he said. We'd been together in a few jails. 'I don't want to go,' he said. I told him, 'Don't be daft, James, you better go,' as loudspeakers began calling him to reception.

One morning not long afterwards, I had just collected my newspaper when a screw handed me a brown envelope. Inside was a letter from the parole board, and it said I had been knocked back for another year. 'You dirty bastards, you didn't even tell me in person,' I thought.

There were moments when I wondered if I'd ever get out. Earlier that year, Charlie Kray had, but only to be taken to a hospital near Parkhurst on the Isle of Wight. My worst fears over his health were realised when he died in hospital. At least Mickey McAvoy got his parole.

Then, in September, came more bad news from Glasgow. Tony McGovern had been shot dead, despite wearing a bulletproof vest. I knew that would start an underworld feud, and the prospect of my being on the streets when that happened might encourage the police to tell the parole board not to let me out.

A month later, Reggie Kray was dead too. He'd been freed on compassionate grounds to spend his last weeks in a hotel bed getting life and food through tubes. 'Freedom is too precious not to enjoy,' I thought.

At least my security category had finally been downgraded. I asked the screws one day, 'I'm category B now. What about rehabilitation? I've stayed out of trouble for four years. I've been a model prisoner.' They looked at one another and said, 'You're only staying out of trouble to con us, Ian.' I told them, 'That's rubbish. Cards on the table, where do I go from here? Are you sending me to an open prison for rehabilitation?' One of them said, 'Ian, you are not rehabilitation material.' I thought, 'Cheeky bastard,' then said, 'Well, I'll move to Scotland.' And I put in an application for a transfer.

I'd had nine years and two months of being locked up at nine o'clock every evening, of having my light switched on and off throughout each night just so somebody could check to see if I was still in there, of waking up every morning wondering if they'd suddenly announce I was being moved somewhere else. Nine years and two months trying to get a downgrade so I could move through the system towards freedom. Why hadn't I tried to get a move to Scotland earlier and be nearer my family? Lots of people have asked that and the answer is that the family didn't want me transferring to Scotland because they thought there was a greater chance of my getting into trouble in my homeland, joining in riots or rooftop protests and ending up with an even greater sentence. The fact was, too, that even in top-security prisons in England, among international gangsters and terrorists, the atmosphere was relaxed. Most of the prisoners were gentlemen, taking a sensible attitude and intent on doing what was necessary to get home. In Scotland, they'd stab you for half an ounce of tobacco. Scottish jails are barbaric, primitive, in comparison to those in England.

My transfer was approved and in November 2000 I was driven to Saughton in Edinburgh and told a place was being sought for me at privately run Kilmarnock prison. At Saughton, having had a cell to myself for more than nine years, I didn't take kindly to being made to share with a stranger and protested, but to no avail, although I was happy when I found my cell mate was my old friend Caff from Cranhill. Kilmarnock never transpired and instead, in January 2001, I found myself at Shotts, where I met up again with Andy Rodger, who had also been transferred to Scotland.

There, I once more asked about rehabilitation, a move to an open jail and days out to see my family, only to get the same response. 'We've looked at your record and are not moving you' was the reply. The refusal to rehabilitate me, to prepare me for freedom, was a big bone of contention.

At least I won my parole at the second time of asking. I was tipped off that my application had been approved, but I decided

I'd only believe it when I'd been told officially. The next day, I was called into an office, where everybody was smiling. 'Ian, your parole has come through. You go in six days. You'll no doubt be happy,' they said.

I told them, 'I'm happy. But I'm unhappy at being put through the system without rehabilitation.' I felt I was entitled to the same treatment as others doing fifteen years, who after five were moved to open prisons and given home leaves.

But at least I was going home. And on 15 November 2001, Ma came to take me there.

23

Tenerife Tap

I WAS DRIVEN AWAY from my prison nightmare drinking champagne in a stretch limousine and with a £40 discharge grant in my pocket. But I nearly didn't make it because of a mobile telephone. A friend, Terry, paid £200 for it to be smuggled into Shotts by a jail worker. Having it was magic. I was kept so up to date with everything going on outside that it felt as if my parole had arrived early. Of course, no instructions had come with it, but I worked out how to turn it on and off. However, each night, as more and more pals got to know my number, the sound of the ringtone was constant. I didn't know how to turn down the volume. My next-door neighbour asked, 'Have you got yourself a phone?', and I lied, telling him no. 'Well, I'm hearing a ringtone,' he said, and I told him, 'Oh, that's coming from a television advert for mobiles.' He said, 'OK, then,' but I was pretty sure he didn't believe me.

A mate tried to explain how to alter the settings, but I told him, 'I can't do this. The phone is like a computer to me.' So I had to own up to my neighbour. 'I need this on silent to stop the sound of the ringing,' I pleaded, giving him the phone. 'I knew you had one, Ian,' he said, smiling. Now, whenever I took it from the hiding place behind a wall panel in the cell, I watched for the little screen to flash, a sign someone was calling.

Two days before my release, we had a party to celebrate. I was wrecked with booze and had taken hash, knowing that even if I was drug-tested, by the time the result came through I'd be long gone. The next morning, I woke up to the sound of the door being unlocked and was horrified to see my phone lying on the floor. I was petrified and silently prayed that the screw wouldn't see it. If he did, my parole would certainly be withdrawn; mobiles were strictly banned. My luck was in that morning, and just before I left prison, I gave the phone away to another inmate.

On my last night, I heard the key lock me in for the last time and paced the cell silently, asking, 'Fucking hell, this has gone by so quickly. Is it really finished already?' For so long, all I had wanted was to be free; now I felt scared at the imminent prospect of getting out. For the past ten and a half years, everything had been done for me; there was nothing to worry about, no mortgage, no bills to pay. No 'Who's going to feed me? Where will I get money to go for a drink?' For the past decade, my family had been there for me, doing all those little but so important things that helped me survive. Sending newspapers, stamps, ten pounds a week for the food boat. Most guys didn't have that kind of support. How would I manage now?

Those torments melted away as I slept, and when morning came the world seemed a brighter place. No more regimentation, no more orders, just freedom to choose. Tongue in cheek, somebody asked, 'Ian, you want a bowl of porridge before you go?' I said, 'No, thanks, I think I've done enough porridge.' A new outfit had been handed in for me. I'd forgotten how to knot a tie, but I turned down an offer from a screw to fix it for me. 'I'll do it myself,' I said. They had refused me rehabilitation, the chance to be prepared for freedom, so now I'd reject their help. It might have seemed petty, but I looked on it as a victory nonetheless. Then it was through the gates, with ten years of catching up to do. I'd missed a lot, but nothing so much as watching Daryl grow up.

My first appointment was with my social worker. The second was with pals, who told me, 'We're taking you out to get drunk.'

'You'll find that hard to do,' I promised them.

We toured wine bars in Glasgow, where I was introduced to Smirnoff Ice and Bacardi Breezers, baffled about their potency. I sampled Aftershock from fancy coloured bottles, all the while hearing a cacophony of mobile ringtones.

'I've had stronger drink in prison. The IRA made the best hooch,' I told my friends.

'Aye, right,' they said, and I knew they didn't believe me.

But the proof of the booze was in the drinking. I drank and drank, but didn't get drunk. I met up with Kathleen, who had visited me in Shotts, and we spent the night together in each other's arms. Let's just say it went well; everything came naturally.

Two days later, I went to Victoria's nightclub. It was as if I'd never been away. A guy who'd managed it before I was jailed was still there.

'I saw you were out, Ian,' he said. 'That was quick.'

'What do you mean, quick?' I asked. 'I was in ten and a half years.'

'Well, it seemed like five,' he replied.

'Well seen you weren't doing them, then,' I said.

I started clubbing regularly, returning to my routine of a decade earlier. In one club I was invited to stay after hours so often that I started to take late drinking as a God-given right. Others attached themselves to me, following me in and staying late. I was like a miniature John Friel.

At the start, the relationship with my social worker had been amicable, but it soon began to deteriorate. He had refused my request to let me holiday in Tenerife after my release. Now he made it clear he didn't want me going into the city centre. But I told him, 'I'm single, I have no ties, I've been away for a long time. I'm only going out to enjoy myself. I'm not breaking any rules.' He grumbled but had to leave it at that.

So I carried on. I was taking Ecstasy, being offered lines of cocaine. Eventually, Ma asked, 'Ian, are you going to settle down? You're out four or five times a week.' I told her, 'I'm enjoying myself.'

I'd stand in the middle of the dance floor and pour two bottles of Budweiser over my head.

'I'm having a Bud shampoo!' I'd shout.

'You're off your nut!' the other dancers would shout.

One night, a member of the family that owned the club banned me from staying after hours for a party. I told the messenger who brought news of the curfew, 'Take a fuck,' and joined the guests up in the piano bar. I saw a crowd of guys and told a pal, 'Now I know why I wasn't wanted – it's the serious crime squad.'

At the bar, I ordered drinks. A girl wandered over and asked, 'Do you know who these people are?' I told her, 'Aye, probably the polis,' but she said, 'No, take another look.' I did, and saw them grumbling and muttering to themselves that we were the serious crime squad. Then I realised who the guests were and was embarrassed because one of them was a one-time Rangers star now managing a Scottish football club. And the guys with him weren't the police but his team.

Word spread that the nightclub was being sold to Paul Ferris and me for six million pounds. That wasn't true, of course, but because I'd been in there so often during the five months since I'd been released I felt as though I did own it. The story reached my social worker, who asked, 'Do you and Paul Ferris own it? This office is awash with rumours.' I told him, 'I tried to steal six million, not spend it.' Relations with him were getting strained. I needed his approval to rent a house in Bishopbriggs, but he refused it, although he did let me rent a little flat near the Kelvin Hall.

Having fun costs money, and I'd been having fun from the day I left prison in 2001. So where did the money come from? The truth was that, after so long inside, I had resolved to take a year off from crime. Guys I'd met in England had offered me chances to take part in jobs, major crimes that would probably get me another 16 years if they went wrong. Mostly, I had politely turned these down, but I had done a couple of turns and made enough to afford to continue going dancing. I certainly wasn't going to put any of it in a bank.

There were parties galore, including a memorable one when friends and I booked a £450-a-night suite at the Moat House Hotel and turned it into a discotheque with the help of pals who arranged music systems and flashing lights. We were told it was the same suite that Kylie Minogue had once stayed in. The party started around lunchtime but at three in the morning, following a series of warnings that police were about to be called after complaints from other guests about the noise, the manager kicked us out.

I'd been seeing Fergie regularly since his release from Frankland jail in January 2002, usually meeting at the Counting House in the centre of Glasgow – which, ironically, was a former bank that had been converted into a bar-restaurant – and chatting about crimes, prisons and people we knew. And about money. And it was money that led me to meet up again with Tam McGraw. At last, I had been given permission from the social worker to have a holiday on Tenerife, but he stipulated that Ma and James had to go along. Nothing had been said about who else could go with me, and I invited Steff McVey. He stayed a week and once he was gone I met McGraw in a bar in Los Cristianos. The subject was the one million pounds I wanted him to give me. And who arranged the face-to-face? None other than one of McGraw's most trusted allies, Billy McPhee.

Only a handful of our closest friends knew Billy and I were pals. It was because of him that very little went on within the McGraw empire without my being told. I'd got to know Billy because he used to visit Sheila and Daryl at the house in Bishopbriggs bought for them by Pat Sweeney, sometimes taking along his mate Gordon Ross, who was probably McGraw's closest pal.

I'd called from prison one day, and she said, 'I have a visitor who wants to talk to you.' When I asked, 'Who is it?', she told me, 'Billy McPhee.' I said, 'Billy McPhee? I've heard of him but I've never met him,' and Sheila explained, 'He's related to Pat Sweeney.'

That was the first of many conversations with Billy. To me, he was a brand-new guy, I couldn't say anything bad about him, and he was very good to Daryl.

After I was moved to Shotts from England, Billy asked if he could visit me and arrived with a mate, David Hughes, who I'd known for a long time. David is unfortunately serving life after being convicted of murdering a guy in a Cumbernauld garden centre. From then, Billy arranged for me to be supplied with hash in prison and he also got me loads of top-up vouchers for my mobile phone. He was very kind to me. Much of the time, I swapped the hash for phone cards, which I then traded for sweets. Friends were regularly buying vouchers to top up my mobile phone credit.

I knew how close Billy was to McGraw, but that didn't bother me at all because I had no issues with Tam. Billy told me McGraw was going to Tenerife for a short holiday, so I arranged my holiday to make sure I'd be there at the same time, and, through Billy, organised a meeting. The two of us spent about an hour together having a drink and talking.

I told him he had benefited financially very considerably as a result of Paul and me being in jail and therefore not taking over his rackets. 'Paul is looking for a million pounds,' I told him. It was a tense meeting, and I had a nagging worry that we might be spotted together, because there are a lot of Scottish people with properties on Tenerife. I particularly didn't want word getting back to my social worker, because he might have twigged I'd only used the excuse of going on holiday as a cover for seeing McGraw.

Tam's attitude was that, no matter how we felt, it was nothing to do with him. But I repeated, 'You owe Paul a million.' There were no threats; it was left at that for the time being. McGraw didn't mention Billy or ask how I came to know him. But the issue of money would not go away. I'd finger somebody else for cash: Pat Sweeney, because I reckoned he owed me.

Sometimes Billy and I had spoken about Sweeney. One day, in Shotts prison, I had been playing badminton a couple of my pals from Govan came running in. 'Blink, what's this about you offering a fortune for a hit on Pat Sweeney?' they asked, and showed me a newspaper in which there was a story claiming I had put a £50,000 contract on Sweeney's life. I couldn't believe it, and when Alan visited me, he asked, 'What's this about the 50-grand hit?' I told him, 'Fucking hell, Alan, 50,000 quid? I don't have 50 pence.'

Billy was gutted after being told it was his relation Sweeney who had planted the story in the paper. 'Why would he do this?' Billy asked me, and I told him, 'I can't understand it. I had no problems with him, and he was good to Daryl.'

Sheila hadn't helped by telling Sweeney, 'Blink knows IRA guys and London gangsters.' The story sprouted arms and legs. Three guys were supposed to have gone to his door and asked, 'How do you want to die, Pat? The swimming pool or a car crash?' Then three Liverpool gangsters were said to have turned up at his workplace looking for him. It was claimed Sweeney had managed to get past these people to his Bentley and driven off like a bat out of hell. A story like this could have destroyed my chances of parole, but it was another of my friends who found a solution by doing me a really big favour.

One of my neighbours in Shotts was James Hamill, who had been jailed for 18 years in 1997 for a drugs offence. Jim spoke regularly to an old friend of mine, Frankie Donaldson, and one night Frankie asked Jim to put me on the telephone. By this time, Frankie had become a very successful businessman and was involved with Raith Rovers. I met him once in the 1980s in Tenerife, and the pair of us got into an argument with a security guard outside a club. Frankie was a good fighter and was about to punch this guy when I told him, 'Don't, Frankie, he's got a gun.'

As soon as I picked up the phone, Frankie said, 'That Sweeney carry-on, Ian, the word is going around clubs that there's money on offer for anybody doing you in when you're released.'

I said, 'Frankie, I've no intention of touching Sweeney. The story about the contract is rubbish.'

Frankie said, 'Can I do anything to help you?'

'I don't think I'm going to get my parole because of this and I was really looking forward to getting out,' I said.

Frankie told me, 'Leave it to me.'

A couple of days later, Jim Hamill came into my cell. 'Frankie's got some good news for you,' he said. When we spoke again on the phone, Frankie told me, 'Listen, Ian, I've got hold of Pat Sweeney. He's agreed to see your lawyer, Joe Shields, and I'm taking him to Joe's office. He'll swear an affidavit confirming the story about the £50,000 contract is rubbish, that you've never threatened him and that he has actually offered you a job with his firm.'

I said, 'OK, great, Frankie. Can you get me a copy of the affidavit so I can send it to the parole board?' Frankie promised he would and, typical of the man, kept his word. I've always been grateful to him for what he did to resolve what could have been a very difficult situation for me. But that finally ended any chances Sweeney might have had of being included on my Christmas card list.

24

Refusing an Offer

IT WAS TIME to turn up the heat on two fronts. Sweeney had nearly cost me my freedom and, now I finally had it, I reckoned that if he wasn't going to wave an olive branch, he could at least hand me a bag of readies.

I rang him up and told him, 'You almost cost me my parole. I think you should compensate me.'

'What do you mean?' he asked, and I said, 'I don't think one million pounds would be an unreasonable sum.'

There was a silence at the other end of the line, and then he said, 'You'll not get that kind of money off me.'

He must have been in touch with Sheila about that, because she spread a story that I'd met Sweeney in a café in Byres Road and a holdall containing £440,000 had been handed over to me. It wasn't true about the money, but it reached the newspapers and one night I happened to be in Victoria's when one of the bouncers said, 'Fucking hell, Ian, that was some turn you had, eh?' What made them believe I really had been given a payoff was that by chance that night I had a few hundred pounds on me and was buying champagne.

Did I meet Sweeney? No, not him, but one of his associates had met with me in a Byres Road café. Was money handed over? That would be telling.

After returning from Tenerife, I had another couple of meetings with McGraw. Billy arranged them, and he was there at the first, in Waxy O'Connor's in the city centre. Gordon Ross joined them for the second, in Candy Bar, a pub in Hope Street. I remember thinking how Tam, for all his wealth, all his supposed millions, looked scruffy in a faded blue denim jacket. It was only much later that I was told it had an expensive bulletproof Kevlar lining.

During the first meeting, I repeated what I'd told McGraw on Tenerife: 'Paul is looking for a million pounds. You owe him a million.' He snapped, 'I owe him nothing.' At the second meeting, I said, 'For a guy rumoured to have 20 million, you dress like a tramp.' Tam laughed and said, 'Oh, that's because I'm skint.' He asked me, 'How are you getting on, Blink?' and I told him, 'Brilliant.'

'Well, then,' he said, 'how are you getting on for money?' I told him, 'I'm getting by. I'm just enjoying myself. After ten and a half years inside, I'm not going to worry over money. As long as I have enough to go dancing, I'm happy.'

He looked at me and said, 'I find that strange,' but I went on, 'No, it's not. If you were in jail for as long as me, you'd realise your freedom is all that matters. The cops have their eye on me now, because they think I'm up to something with Paul, but all I want to do is have a good time.'

At that, McGraw turned to Gordon and said, 'Give Blink whatever he wants,' and I knew what he meant by that, which was to give me as much coke, smack or hash as I wanted. But I never took up his offer.

I found McGraw OK then, but as time passed my view of him changed. I started hearing that he was slagging me off, especially to women. I thought, 'I'm going to kick your balls in. I won't need a gun.'

The meetings had been secret and seemingly friendly, but word about them leaked out and it was being said I'd been given £350,000 by McGraw.

Then something happened that made me wonder. Fergie had only been out a few months when a report from Strathclyde Police claimed he had been associating with criminal types thought to be plotting drugs deals and had been in a vicious fight with McGraw, and as a result he was hauled back to prison. I ought to have taken more notice of the chain of events. Not long after he was back inside, I had even greater cause to question just who could be trusted.

I was in Bar Cini one night with James Healy when I had a call to say the CID had been to Ma's looking for me. They'd scared Ma to tears by telling her, 'Watch how you open your door. You never know who might come through.' She had asked what was behind the comment but was told, 'Oh, never mind. Tell Ian to ring us right away.'

When I called the number they'd left, the police refused to tell me what it was all about. 'You could be anybody,' they said. 'Come and see us. You'll be out in five minutes. We know where you are anyway.' I thought it was a strange remark.

I told James I was going to meet the police. 'Enjoy your half-cooked breakfast in the morning,' he said, meaning he reckoned I'd be kept in.

Five detectives were waiting for me. 'Your life is in danger,' they said, and when I asked what they were talking about they said, 'It's not an idle threat. It's a serious threat. We've got good intelligence that somebody is going to kill you.' I asked the obvious question – 'Who?' – but was told only, 'We can't tell you that.' And when I asked what they were doing about the threat, the reply was 'We can't tell you that either. Our advice is to change your routine.'

As I was leaving, they told me where I had been and who was with me. 'Enjoy Victoria's, Ian, and don't be staying there too late,' they said, and I thought, 'Fucking hell, they even know where I'm going next.' I'd just had my first Osman, a formal warning that my life was in danger. It wouldn't be the last.

Who was behind the threat that forced the police into giving me my Osman? I thought it was definitely McGraw, trying to frighten me, because Paul had just been recalled to prison and this was the time when we were looking for a million pounds from him. Had he got rid of Paul only for me to be still around? Was it an attempt to frighten me off?

Then I began thinking hard. In Victoria's one night, a guy had come up and said, 'Stewart Boyd is going to try and take you out. He believes you and Paul will try taking over the security business.'

Stewart 'Specky' Boyd was a dangerous major player suspected of organising a host of murders, mainly over drugs. He had ambitions to go legitimate by carving out a chunk of the extremely lucrative security business, supplying bouncers for clubs and watchmen for buildings and sites, and his camp was close to the McGraw faction.

I told this guy, 'I don't know what you're talking about,' but he said, 'I know this for a fact.' I told him, 'Well, if Specky comes here, he'll not get out alive.'

Then not long after this, the gossips had it that I wanted to take over territory reckoned to be controlled by the McGovern family. I'd known the McGoverns for years and got on well with them. It was one more tale based on fiction, but it could have had deadly repercussions for me.

I discussed the threats with Billy, who told me, 'Don't worry, Ian, you're all right. Tam's not going to make a move against you. It's up to him to sort this out with Paul when he comes out.'

And when Paul was released, he and I got together. 'I hear you've been meeting McGraw,' he said, and I told him that was true. He said, 'Well, where's my money?', and I asked, 'What money?' He said, 'The money he gave you.' I asked, 'Did you believe that story about me getting money?', and Paul told me, 'I don't know.' So I said, 'Paul, I got fuck all. I did you a favour by going to Tenerife to pull him for a million, but that never came off and I never got any money.' At that, Paul said, 'OK, so you never got any money. Good to see you again.'

So Paul and I fell out, and not for the first time. Fergie and I had been pals for more than 20 years, and I regretted the break-up of our friendship. We'd had disagreements before, but now I knew he thought I was holding back the truth about my dealings with McGraw, keeping a secret from him.

We'd become friends again after I'd done him a big favour. It involved saving him from a bleaching, a bad beating, because when he was jailed over the gunrunning episode a number of guys, including many of the IRA inmates, wanted to attack him. They, like others, liked Mick Healy and had been appalled to hear how Fergie had once, with the connivance of Gibby Lobban, threatened to shoot Mick. I intervened and told them the problem with Paul had been sorted.

After I'd stepped in on his behalf, Paul started writing to me. We were kept apart on the prison circuit and held in different jails. Some of his letters were downright cheeky, and at one stage I wrote to tell him, 'Look, Fergie, you're still the same wee boy that I remember coming to my ma's and who was pals with Alco. It means nothing to me what you've done while I've been inside.' He had written back, saying, 'Nobody's ever spoken to me like that in my life,' and I replied by telling him, 'I'm speaking to you like that because I know you.'

In his letters, Paul had discussed his plans for when he was released, telling me, 'I want the security to kick back into shape the way I had it, and believe me it was an excellent set-up.' Everything had been and would be totally legitimate, he said, and he promised there would be a place for me in his businesses if I wanted to join him. He told me, 'The indications I got were that you would come in with us if and when we got going into a new venture and that's fine by me as we can make up for the stupidity and stubbornness of us two and get back to how it was and forget the whole bollocks that went on. I have a confession to make and that is I sometimes sent you letters to wind you up and got back a decent reply that showed me you lost none of your fire and brimstone.'

In any case, after *The Ferris Conspiracy* was published, I read the account of the shooting of Arty. The book said:

> But The Apprentice's contract was for the son, not the old man. He shot at young Thompson's head. The first bullet caught Arty on the cheek, spinning him around and dumping him on the ground. Arty whimpered, scrambling on his hands

and knees towards his own house. The second bullet shattered his rib cage, puncturing a lung. The third pierced his anus, travelling through his stomach and into his heart. The Apprentice paused for a second, considering a close-range headshot. The man was dying and the silencer hadn't been that silent. Time to go.

Despite all, I was glad when Paul's recall was scrapped after a few weeks. It was shown that the police claims about his alleged activities were largely fictitious.

I continued to keep in touch with Billy McPhee. One night, while we were having a drink in the Counting House, I asked him if he fancied a couple of hours at Victoria's club. He looked at me oddly and asked, 'You're having a laugh, aren't you?' I told him no, and he said, 'Ian, I'd love to go there, but I wouldn't be welcome. There was a murder there a few years back and they reckoned I was involved. I'm barred for life.'

I realised that, despite doing my best to keep up to speed with what had happened in Scotland, I had missed so much. In 1994, a guy had died after being stabbed inside the club. Billy had gone on the run, even spending some time in Tenerife, but eventually gave himself up and was arrested, although he was never charged. Two Moffat brothers, Stephen and Alan from Easterhouse, were convicted of the murder and given life, but many doubt if they were guilty, and Billy told me, 'They didn't do it.'

My friendship with Billy gave me one of the most unlikely nights out of my life. I was out with the family when I had a phone call from James Healy.

'Ian, Ian, I need to talk to you,' he said.

'You sound distressed, what's the matter?'

'My dad's been stabbed.'

'Who did it?'

'I know who it was,' he told me. 'When can I see you?'

He came to Ma's house and said his dad and three of his dad's pals had been stabbed in a pub in Shettleston Road. He named the person responsible and said, 'He's linked in to the McGraw crowd. This needs to be sorted. I know you know Billy McPhee.'

I told him I did, and James asked, 'Can you meet him?' I asked why and he said, 'I don't want any trouble.'

I told him, 'But, James, this is your father.'

He asked what I would have done if my dad had been stabbed, and I told him, 'I hate my dad's guts, but if I liked him I'd go ahead. Look, I'll back you up. I'll get all our pals and we'll back you up against McGraw and his crowd.'

But he insisted, 'I don't want any trouble,' so I asked, 'James, what is it you want me to say?'

James told me, 'I know Billy trusts you. Tell him this from me. I'm not going to seek a revenge attack. My girlfriend is pregnant. They know where I stay in Carntyne. And the most important thing is that I don't want you getting into trouble and going back into prison. I appreciate what you're saying, that you're going to back me up, but will you meet Billy McPhee and tell him this?'

I agreed and rang Billy. 'James doesn't want any trouble,' I said, and Billy told me, 'That's great.' I asked, 'Can you meet me?', and he said, 'Can I bring Gordon Ross and the guy who did it with me?' At the time Tam, Gordon and Billy were like glue, stuck together, inseparable.

I said, 'Look, Billy, am I going to be all right? There are stories going around that Paul Ferris and I are going to start a war with Tam McGraw.'

He said, 'Of course you'll be OK. It's me you're talking to.'

So it was agreed that Billy and the others would pick me up at Ma's house. Billy said, 'We'll go to a pub and Gordon'll tell you the true story of what happened to James's dad.'

Despite the reassurances about my safety, I told my brother Gary, 'If I haven't rung you by ten o'clock, it means there's something wrong. But I trust Billy. I've met Gordon, but not the other boy they're bringing, and I don't know if Tam's going to appear.' Gary asked if I could rely on Billy's word and I told him, 'I trust him implicitly,' but all the same he insisted, 'Remember to phone me so I know you're all right.'

REFUSING AN OFFER

On the dot of eight, I heard the sound of a car horn and looked out to see a Mercedes at the gate, the engine purring. Gordon Ross was driving, with the third member of their group in the front. I joined Billy in the back. To tell the truth, I experienced a wee shudder when I got into that car, because I was thinking, 'I could be taken away here and killed.'

Billy made the introductions, we shook hands and there were smiles on their faces, which put me at ease. I was sure things would be fine. They asked where I wanted to go for a chat and I suggested John Harvard's, a pub in Bishopbriggs. There, I felt even more comfortable, that I was among friends.

We sat down with drinks and Gordon wasted no time. 'Right, Blink, let's get this sorted. I know you are here for James Healy.' I told him, 'Yes, he doesn't want any trouble.' Gordon said, 'Neither do we. Do you know why his dad got stabbed?' I told him I had heard only gossip and didn't know the truth.

The third member of their group was the guy who, according to the word on the street, was responsible for the stabbings, and he didn't deny that this was the case. But he said trouble had kicked off over a five-pound debt to a moneylender. This put the matter in a new light. Somebody else in the pub at the time had begun the argument that had led to bloodshed. It sounded typical of the many incidents that start over nothing and result in tragedy. I told Gordon, 'I didn't know about the moneylending,' and he said, 'Look, we know where James lives and that he's your pal. We don't want this to go any further.' And that ended the discussion. We began talking about mutual friends, and Gordon explained how he used to visit Sheila and Sweeney with Billy.

Before long, we were sneaking into the toilet to takes lines of cocaine. I thought, 'This is fucking great,' and felt totally relaxed. When ten o'clock came, I thought, 'I can't take my phone out or go outside, because they'll think I'm setting them up.' So I didn't bother calling Gary and switched it off.

At midnight, Gordon asked if I fancied going dancing. 'Aye,' I told him, and he said, 'How about the Cube?' I'd been away out of circulation for so long I'd never heard of the place, but he told me, 'It's a nightclub. We know the bouncers.' When we arrived, there was a long queue, but we simply walked past and into the VIP suite. Any thoughts that I might be getting done in were long gone by then. The time went by quickly. It was three o'clock and I was thinking of going home when Billy asked, 'Do you want to go to a party?' I thought, 'Why not?', and found myself at a house in Sandyhills. George McCormick, a taxi driver and relation of Billy, turned up.

Even that wasn't the end of the entertainment. At seven in the morning, Gordon took me to the home of a witness to the stabbings. We went in George's taxi, and the witness repeated the story of how the trouble had begun over a few pounds.

I had a couple of joints to cool down and at ten that morning Billy said he was going home and asked, 'What did you think of the night?'

When I told him, 'Memorable,' he stuck 500 quid in my pocket.

It was then that I realised I hadn't rung Gary to tell him I was safe – the call I should have made 12 hours ago. 'Too late now,' I told myself, and went home to bed. At four that afternoon, I switched my mobile phone back on and discovered more than forty missed calls from Gary and pals worried about me. When I rang Gary, he said, 'I was going to kick McGraw's door in. I thought you were a goner.'

25

A Doomed Man

THE MEETING WITH Gordon Ross was my second but also my last with him. In September 2002, he and Billy wanted to watch a televised football match over a few drinks, but the Barrachnie, the Mount Vernon pub in which they had met, couldn't get the necessary channel. So they went on to the Sheiling bar in Shettleston, a few hundred yards from the spot where the bodies of Joe and Bobby had been left more than a decade earlier. Not long after they'd arrived, Billy went home, leaving Gordon, who became involved in an argument with another customer. Shortly afterwards, Gordon was told someone was outside wanting to see him, and when he went out into Shettleston Road he was stabbed, dying later that evening in hospital.

Billy took the murder particularly badly. In 1998, at the High Court in Edinburgh, Billy and Gordon and nine other men, including McGraw, had been on trial accused of smuggling hash from Spain in holiday coaches. Most had walked free from court, either because they'd been acquitted or because the charges had been found not proven. Three had been jailed, including Arthur Askey lookalike Paul Flynn from Liverpool. Not long after entering prison, Paul died from a heart attack. Trevor Lawson had been cleared and went home to his farm near Dunipace, Stirlingshire. One night in April 2002, a fight started in a local bar and, fearing something more sinister was about to happen, he ran off, only to be knocked down and killed by a passing car. Now

Gordon became the third to die, and Billy was never the same man. He seemed to think that everybody who had been in the dock was now being taken out in one way or another. 'They're dropping like flies. I wonder if I'll be the next,' he told me.

Billy felt naked without Gordon and I sensed tension between him and McGraw. At one stage, there was a rumour that Fergie and I were behind the deaths, and then gossip had it I'd been in a scrap with McGraw and stabbed him. None of it was true, but I wondered how this was affecting McGraw.

At least I knew another wealthy man who was having a bad time of it. Poor old cheating Pat Sweeney had been dumped by Sheila, divorced by his wife and ordered by a court to pay his ex-missus £745,000.

Then Lady Luck smiled in my direction. I began a serious relationship with a lovely nurse from Kirkintilloch named Lynn. I'd been introduced to her by mutual friends while out clubbing one night, and we quickly became an item. Every Sunday, after clubbing with DJ Vance at Victoria's, we'd go back to the home of Danny and Catherine in Carmyle, where we'd meet up with Michael, Spike and Zeta.

Mentioning meetings, another about this time was one I'd never forget. My pal Steff McVey and I had gone into a hairdresser's in Duke Street for haircuts, and as we sat waiting our turn in walked Ford Kiernan, one of the stars of the popular television comedy series *Chewin' the Fat*. The young woman hairdresser dashed out to buy a camera, and when she rushed back in asked Ford if he'd have his picture taken with us. He agreed, and as we smiled for the camera, he joked, 'I hope you two aren't a pair of gangsters!' For once, I was lost for words.

Not long afterwards, a series of events began that led me right back to a prison cell. My brother Gary and I were in Victoria's nightclub when I had a row with my new girlfriend and bouncers intervened. A couple of weeks later, the police raided Ma's home, looking for me over this incident, and then Joe Shields, my lawyer, telephoned to advise us to hand ourselves in. 'Gary will be fingerprinted, photographed and let out to appear in court the next day, but you'll be kept in because you're on licence,' he told me.

I thought, 'This isn't fair. Gary has as many convictions as me.' But I told Joe, 'OK,' and we went to the police station, where two young cops took photos and fingerprinted me. One said, 'Oh, Blink, we've not heard of you before apart from what we've seen in the papers,' and I pointed out, 'Well, no wonder. I've been away for ten and a half years. In any case, I'm not doing anything.'

Then one of them said, 'Can you give us a turn?' He was asking me to become a police informer, a grass. I gave them a turn all right, because I spun right around. I was raging and warned him, 'If you ever ask me that again, I'll punch fuck out of the two of you.'

Gary had been promised he would be allowed home that day, but because the coppers didn't appreciate my remarks he was kept in. However, when we appeared in court charged with assault and breach of the peace, he was bailed and, much to my surprise, so was I.

I kept my head down and made a real effort to stay out of trouble. Lynn was apprehensive, because my name was regularly appearing in the newspapers, but finally she introduced me to her parents and all seemed fine.

Then, out of the blue, came a real blow. I was still on bail when newspaper headlines screamed out that Fergie and I and a mutual friend, David Santini, had come up with an amazing scheme to supply £10-million worth of heroin and cocaine every month from a base at Kirkintilloch. We'd supposedly be smuggling the gear into Scotland in a bogus AA van.

I wasn't even speaking to Fergie at this time, but what was embarrassing was that the story appeared the day before David and I were going to the funeral of a good friend, Tommy Porter, from Ayrshire, whom I'd met in Shotts prison, where he'd been doing 14 years for hash smuggling. Tommy had been released pending an appeal but sadly contracted cancer and died. After the funeral, people were coming up and joking to us, 'Can we get a kilo of smack at 16 grand?' or, 'How about a kilo of cocaine for 17 thousand?'

That ridiculous story effectively sealed my fate. Before that point, friends were betting that I'd be recalled back to prison. It had happened to Paul Ferris, they said, so the same was sure to happen to me. I protested, 'All I'm doing is trying to enjoy myself. I can't stop people making up stories.' Days later, the police again swooped at Ma's, looking for me. I wasn't there and they raided the homes of Lynn and my brother Gary. Actually, at the moment this was going on, I was walking up Byres Road in Glasgow, a sports bag on my back, heading for the gym and unaware of the dramas elsewhere. Sheila was in Spain, and when the newspapers got wind of that, they put two and two together and came up with ten, claiming I was with her popping champagne.

This was all nonsense, but unknown to me Strathclyde Police were collating a file on my so-called activities. I knew they wanted me off the streets, not least because keeping an eye on me was taking up a chunk of their manpower, but I didn't realise just how desperate they were to achieve that end. They clearly hadn't learned a lesson from their attempts to put Fergie away by accepting that you need to gather facts and not fiction. In due course, I would discover just what the constabulary's finest had come up with.

Remembering Fergie's recall had lasted just a few weeks, I decided to get the process moving by handing myself in, reasoning that that should also stop the cops hassling Ma and the others. I just didn't trust the police, though, so I bypassed them by going straight to Shotts jail, where I chapped on the door.

A screw appeared, looked at me and asked, 'Aren't you supposed to be on the run? What do you want?', and I told him, 'To come in.' He said, 'You can't just turn up and demand to get into prison. You want to visit somebody?' I said, 'No, I want a cell.'

'I'll have to get the governor,' he told me, and disappeared. Audrey Park, one of the governors, arrived. 'I thought you were in Spain. You've got a beautiful tan,' she said, then asked, 'What is it you're here for?'

I told her, 'The tan is from a sunbed shop in Duke Street. The police are supposed to be looking for me, so I thought I'd hand myself in here because I was released from Shotts.'

Audrey said, 'Guys like you are supposed to be trying to escape, not wanting in. I've never been asked this before.'

By now, I was literally begging her, 'Please take me in.'

She thought for a while, then said, 'OK, but don't be ringing your bell after ten minutes to be let back out.'

'Not me,' I promised. 'I'll be out in a couple of weeks when all this is sorted.'

It felt as though I was booking into a bed and breakfast.

The next day, Audrey said, 'You were only here an hour when the serious crime squad showed up saying I had no authority to hold you and ordering me to produce you so they could take you to a police station.'

'What did you say?' I asked.

'I told them you were sleeping and I wasn't waking you up.' She said the police had then left.

'Thanks very much for doing that. That's a big drink I owe you, but I can't take you to Victoria's for it when I get out,' I said, and meant it.

I thought how Fergie had been recalled and then freed a few weeks later and expected I would only be held in prison a few months. But nothing happened to suggest my case was progressing and time began to drag. Then, in March 2003, came awful news. Billy McPhee had gone to a bar-restaurant near his home to watch a rugby match on television. The place was packed, and as he sat with a drink, a man pushed his way through the Saturday teatime crowd up to Billy and stabbed him repeatedly in the neck, head and body. A couple of customers tried to save him but had no chance, and he died almost immediately.

Billy had been a good friend. He'd once tipped me off that McGraw suspected Paul and I were going to do him in and had ordered a £30,000 hit on me as I left the European Cup final between Bayer Leverkusen and Real Madrid at Hampden Park in May 2002. I'd taken a different route home.

I knew Billy had been fearful that something might happen to him. He had survived being shot in the face a few weeks previously. I had seen a photograph of him at Gordon's funeral, and he had the look of a doomed man.

As I was getting over the shock of his murder, Strathclyde Police produced another in the form of an 'intelligence report' that was sent to the Sentence Enforcement Unit in London. This body could recommend to the parole board that I should be recalled to jail. According to the cream of the police investigators, Fergie and I were plotting to distribute heroin; my pal Steff McVey and I were forcing club owners to let us have lock-ins so we could snort cocaine; I was arranging with Martin Brown to help him control the drugs market in Torquay; and, most bizarre of all, my friend Gary Moore and I had been overheard in Sauchiehall Street discussing a plan to assault or kill somebody who had attacked my younger brother Alan.

This report would have been laughable had it not had such potentially damaging consequences for me. I was due to appear in court the following month over the Victoria's rammy. Normally, a prison sentence gave the parole board an excuse to recall, even ordering somebody to serve out the entire remainder of a sentence, although that didn't always happen in Scotland. However, if the board took the police report seriously, it could scupper my chances of appealing against a recall. I informed my London lawyer, the excellent Vicky King, of the situation. Because I was on parole from the sentence imposed in England over the bank robbery, it would be the English Home Office that would oversee any recall, and Vicky's firm had been representing me while I was in jail. Joe Shields would be appearing with me in court and came to see me with a copy of the police report. 'Everything in it is wrong,' I told him.

At Glasgow Sheriff Court in April, the prosecution offered to drop the assault charges against me if I'd plead guilty to breach of the peace. I gambled on avoiding a recall and agreed. Standing in the dock in handcuffs, I listened while Gary's convictions were read out. They sounded horrendous. He admitted two assaults and a breach of the peace by battering two bouncers. The sheriff told him, '£500 fine plus compensation,' and I thought, 'Brilliant, what a result. I'm going to get admonished, which gives me a better chance of getting out.' But the sheriff looked at me and said, 'Mr MacDonald, being out on licence, you should have known better. I'm going to give you 30 days' imprisonment.' While I served that, the parole board revoked my licence and told me to complete the entire remainder of my original sentence.

Now Vicky fought my corner with the parole board. As the weeks turned into months, I refused to work (although my offer to act as barman in the prison officers' social club was rejected). By August, when the board met in London, we had totally discredited the allegations in the intelligence report, in particular the reference to Gary Moore and me.

Cleared of the Ice Cream Wars murders, Gary had escaped two more murder raps. The victims in those cases were Glasgow prostitute Diane McInally, in 1991, and Jimmy Boyle's son Jamer three years later, when Gary was actually convicted of culpable homicide and jailed for eight years. But not even he could have got himself to Sauchiehall Street the day the cops said they'd overheard us talking, because he was in Kilmarnock prison at the time. The trouble was the breach of the peace conviction was always going to drag me down, and it did, the parole board saying I'd have to stay in jail.

I was gutted, and so was Lynn, because I'd told her I was confident of getting out. She'd visited me regularly while I awaited my court appearance, her first experience of being inside a prison. She was seeing me one weekend when I heard that Specky Boyd was dead, killed with five others in a head-on car smash in Spain. Well, at least another threat had gone.

In November, I was sent to Castle Huntly open prison, where I'd been a quarter of a century earlier. The following year, I got a job working with the Salvation Army, something I loved doing, and finally we persuaded the parole board to let me go.

I got out on April Fool's Day 2004 and vowed that there would be no more clowning around with my life. It was impossible not to admire and respect the gentleness and selflessness of those working with the Salvation Army, but I knew their way of life was not for me. Lynn picked me up outside Castle Huntly prison and, as she drove me back to Glasgow for a reunion breakfast at the Counting House, I told myself, 'I'm coming out with a vengeance, and I'm ploughing right back into crime. No more little turns to keep the wolves from the door. From now, it's big time, it's party time.'

I had seen the way things operated in Glasgow and how different the scene was from nearly a decade and a half earlier. Gangland then had been run by people who were respected and feared by underlings. Now there were too many petty idiots running around, their stupid antics attracting attention to themselves. They lacked skill and had no influence. I had contacts, wasn't messing about and within two days was pulling my first turn. I had decided when I was 16 to become a career criminal and now it was time to put that into serious practice. I had thought long and hard about this in prison, telling myself, 'I missed out on six million and came out to fuck all and a crooked police report. I paid for nothing with more than ten years of my life. It's time to get something back.'

The prospect of doing a legitimate job, a nine-to-five in a suit or an eight-to-four in overalls, never entered my thoughts. When I'd first gone to prison, I'd vowed never to get into trouble again, but as time had passed that had changed.

I teamed up with a couple of people in England and also did jobs on my own. Money rolled in, and I splashed out on an eye-popping, high-powered Audi Quattro, a car I'd long wanted, and a top-of-the-range caravan. I'd always promised myself I'd make it up to my family for standing by me. There were watches and hotel stays for the family, and a pink stretch limousine to take Ma out on her birthday. I treated myself to a Cartier Roadster watch. I moved to Kirkintilloch, where I discovered my next-door neighbour was a policewoman, so I took a sumptuous flat in the West End of Glasgow, near the Kelvingrove Gallery. I took Lynn to Turkey. We were really fond of each other and I even thought of asking her to marry me. It was the closest I ever came to breaking my vow to marry at 70 and get divorced at 70½.

It was just as well I didn't take the ultimate step, though, because as 2005 sped by we realised that, as a permanent fixture, our relationship had run its course. However, we'd always remain friends, and I made sure Lynn had my number.

I wasn't footloose and free for long, because I met Kirsten McFarlane, an air hostess 14 years younger than me, and we quickly fell for each other. But ours would be a love–hate relationship, as time would show. I'd always found it difficult to be completely faithful to any woman. Temptation often came along, because Kirsten's job would mean her being away for days at a time, and it was during one of those absences that I invited Lynn to join me at the Dunblane Hydro. I had long wanted to stay there, but the visit proved memorable in a way I could never have expected. After dinner, we went into the bar to find it mobbed with smartly dressed men and women with tiny identification badges hanging around their necks.

To my horror, one read 'Yorkshire Police' and another 'Garda'. I told Lynn, 'Fucking hell, we're surrounded by coppers.' There was worse to come. A woman started chatting to Lynn, telling us the sort of work she did. I looked at her badge, which showed she was with Strathclyde and gave her speciality, and I realised she had probably been involved in compiling the bogus report on me. Obviously, most of these people hadn't a clue who I was. But not everyone, because I saw a guy staring at me from the opposite side of the room and recognised him as a detective inspector. He beckoned over two young guys in suits, spoke to them and suddenly they were at our table whispering to those with whom we'd been chatting. A few seconds later, Lynn and I found ourselves alone.

Clearly, Glasgow's answer to Inspector Morse had detected the presence of a crook and warned the others to treat us as though we were lepers. Lynn asked if I wanted to leave, but I told her, 'No way, we've paid good money as well, even if it was stolen.' Half an hour later, I spotted one of the cops who had been at the Chinese restaurant the night I was arrested.

I was determined to sit the night out and fancied another drink but didn't want to have to push through the crowd around the bar, so I asked Lynn to go instead. She looked magic in a pencil skirt and tight top. She disappeared for 20 minutes, and I had visions of young cops chatting her up and was raging by the time she returned with our drinks.

'Who were you talking to?' I demanded, and she said, 'They told me they're the people who solve the crimes others can't.'

'You were flirting,' I accused her, but she insisted, 'They all wanted to tell me about their police work.'

When Kirsten flew back, I was waiting for her. She had no idea what had happened in her absence, and we resumed being a normal, devoted couple. But I couldn't cut the cord that still held me to Lynn. One night, I left Kirsten to buy milk from a nearby garage and on the way took a call from a pal who said Lynn had been assaulted and was asking for me. I shouldn't have gone to her, but I did, taking her to hospital and then back home. Her door had been smashed in and she was afraid to be left alone, so I stayed the night with her, turning off my mobile phone. I knew there would be hell to pay when I went back to Kirsten the next morning. There was, but I told her the truth. After that, from time to time I'd look in on Lynn to check she was OK. 'You owe her nothing,' Kirsten told me, but I said, 'Yes, I do, I owe her a lot. She stood by me when I was in the nick.'

I split up briefly with Kirsten and went off to Tenerife to visit a pal from Glasgow who was on the run. In a nightclub at Veronica's Strip, I felt a hand on my shoulder and turned around to see a smiling Malky O'Halloran, who was over there with pals.

Back in Glasgow, Kirsten and I made it up. There were trips to Sandals on St Lucia and then to Egypt, where I climbed the pyramids. Mick Healy had been released and rang me from London. 'I'm in Chelsea. Come down for a couple of days,' he said. We checked into a hotel next to Stamford Bridge and discovered Celtic were playing there the next day. I bought a Chelsea top and had 'Blink 1' printed on the back. There was a lot of trouble in London that day between supporters of Celtic and Chelsea.

We looked up Nawaf Rosan, who had been in jail with us. At Harrods, we had a good look around but didn't splash out on anything expensive, just ice creams, and as we wandered down Knightsbridge licking them I asked Rosan if he had heard from a mutual friend from prison, Yilmaz Kaya. Yilmaz was one of the founders of the Turkish Connection, a highly organised group that smuggled heroin from Afghanistan. Most of this at first made its way to Liverpool, from where it was distributed throughout the UK, including Scotland, but as the business increased so the markets expanded into Spain, Holland, Germany and Italy. Banks in Scotland and northern Cyprus were used to invest part of the proceeds. Yilmaz had links to John Haase and his nephew Paul Bennett. In 1995, after the gang was caught as a result of a long surveillance operation, Kaya was jailed for 20 years and had £200,000 confiscated. Rosan had no news of our friend.

Then he told us, 'My social worker gave me a telephone, but I think it's bugged and he's a policeman.'

'You're right there,' we said and told him in all seriousness, 'He's not a social worker, he's with MI5. Don't use it. It's probably bugged to fuck.'

26

Pain in Spain

IN PRISON, I had stayed clear of hard drugs; now I was taking cocaine with increasing frequency and I felt shattered. I took Kirsten to Benidorm for a weekend break to help me recover. A few days in the Spanish sun might also help us to decide if the cracks in our relationship were too wide to heal.

'Don't carry any cocaine,' she had said, but I ignored her command, telling myself, 'I won't use it if she behaves.' It was difficult to bring cocaine into Scotland, but I was aware from past experience how easy it was to smuggle it into Spain. I knew how to hide things so they wouldn't be found even if I was given a body search. So I had no trouble getting through security at Glasgow airport.

As we were heading for the departure lounge, I met Jim Brown, a friend who ran Bar Cini. Jim asked where we were going.

'Benidorm,' I told him, adding, 'The last time I was there, I got arrested coming off the flight.'

'Just enjoy yourself. You'll not get nicked this time,' said Jim.

The holiday started brilliantly on Saturday evening with a romantic meal, and midnight found us in a pub with friends. That's when it all began to go wrong. Kirsten and I began arguing. It was trivial, over nothing, but spiralled into name-calling and then a full-scale row, which continued as we walked back to our hotel.

'We're finished,' she told me.

'You'd better believe it,' I said.

She sat in our room, watching as I defied her by producing my cocaine. 'You bastard,' she screamed but I told her, 'No, you're the bastard. If you'd behaved yourself, I wouldn't be going to take this.' I took a big line, snorting the powder into my nostrils through a banknote, ignoring her loathing.

'Look at you,' she said. 'You're nothing but a junkie cocaine bastard.'

Her words meant nothing to me. 'I don't care a fuck what I am,' I retorted.

The drug was mixing with my anger in a cocktail of defiance. I downed a glass of San Miguel beer and went out onto the balcony, where the stars twinkled, seemingly enticing me back out into the night. A voice from within me whispered, 'Fuck this. You're in Benidorm. Why are you still here? The night has just started. Get yourself out.'

I took another line of charlie. Kirsten warned me, 'I'm going home. I'm disgusted with you,' and I said, 'I don't care a fuck if you are.'

From the little safe in our room, I took 600 euros and pocketed the rest of my cocaine, then left wearing just flip-flops, a T-shirt and shorts. My thinking was warped; I was obsessed with plotting revenge on her. Two taxis sat at the rank. The driver of the first was middle-aged, the second in his 20s. My plan required the help of a younger man, so I paid the first ten euros to let me take the cab behind.

The maddest night of my life was beginning. I asked the young driver, 'Can you take me to a brothel?' This would be my way of getting her back for arguing. 'Yes, but it's on the outskirts of Benidorm,' he said. That freaked me out a little. Was I being taken into a trap to be robbed and battered? 'Will I be safe?' I asked, and when he promised I would, I gave him 60 euros. 'Wait for me. I'll want you to take me somewhere else,' I told him when he pulled up at a house from which lights showed despite the hour.

Inside, a Kylie Minogue lookalike, showing me a smile that said, 'You know I'm worth it,' began chatting. 'Oh, aye, you'll do for me,' I thought. I only wanted to stay long enough to do the damage, cheat on Kirsten by having sex with another woman, any woman, then get out of there. In my haste, I was hurrying Kylie. 'How much for you?' I kept asking, but she would only answer, 'No, no,' and then when an older woman appeared and asked, 'You go with her?', I realised this was the house madam, who negotiated the price. 'You have a drink first?' she offered. I told her, 'Yes,' and asked Kylie if she'd join me. I ordered two vodkas with Coca-Cola and with the drinks came a demand for 80 euros. It was a lot, but I paid up. I was being ripped off, but I wasn't giving a fuck because I was about to get one.

'We go now?' I asked Kylie.

'Calm down, calm down,' she told me, probably hoping to stretch things out to another vodka.

I asked her boss, 'How much?', and she told me, 'That depends how long you want to stay.'

'What's the shortest time?' I asked, and when she said, 'Half an hour for 150 euros,' I handed over the money. I didn't want half an hour, just five minutes to do the deed.

Kylie led me into a room where I took off my shorts and she bathed me. She handed me a condom, and, as I stood there, I gazed into a huge mirror and wondered if thugs were about to leap out from behind it and rob me. Kylie lay on the bed, naked, and it was over in a couple of minutes. No soft words, no kisses, no emotion. 'Is that it?' she asked, and I tipped her 20 euros.

My taxi driver was waiting. 'You have a good time?' he asked, and I told him, 'Fucking hell, I met Kylie Minogue in there,' but he didn't understand.

I asked him, 'Can you take me to a rave?' He looked baffled. 'An all-night party,' I explained, adding, 'And can you get me Ecstasy?' The answer was yes to both, and I promised, 'You'll get a huge tip.'

Back in Benidorm, he produced four Es at a very reasonable ten euros apiece. I paid up and tipped him another 100 euros. Now I had fewer than 200 left. It was around three in the morning when we arrived at the rave in a club. I swallowed all four Ecstasy tablets and danced away on my own, a forty-five-year-old man, old enough to be the father of most of them and a grandfather to some. I still had my cocaine. I left at seven, then went to a pub, where I met an Irish couple in their 50s. 'You're up early,' I said.

Three English guys who worked there were playing pool and I joined their game. One of them tumbled to the fact that my frequent visits to the toilet were to snort cocaine. 'Where have you been all night?' he asked, and I told him, 'I fell out with my girlfriend, went to a brothel, met this wee bird who looked like Kylie Minogue, treated a taxi driver, got these super Es and went to a rave.'

He said, 'You look out of your fucking nut.'

'And I've been taking coke,' I added.

'You got any left?' he asked, so I gave the three of them a couple of lines.

'That's good stuff, better than we get here,' they said.

'Away ye go.'

'Where's it from?'

'Glasgow.'

'Wow,' they said.

By mid-morning, I decided to go back to the hotel. One of the guys drove me, so I gave him a couple of grams of coke. I still had a gram and a half left. As I walked through the entrance, Kirsten was standing there.

'Oh, aye,' she said.

'Oh, aye what? I thought you were going home,' I told her.

'I just saw you in that car with a guy. Is that your boyfriend?'

Refusing to rise to her sarcasm, I said, 'What if it is? We're finished.'

Now the fun was about to really kick off. I had intended going straight up to our room on the 16th floor, but she began shouting, 'So you're not giving me my stuff?' The foyer was busy with groups arriving and leaving. She'd had hours to get her things together and could have sat and waited for me at the pool, anywhere. Instead she'd decided to make our disagreement public. The drugs made me feel cheeky and I told her, 'You're getting fuck all.'

At that, she stormed over to the reception desk to complain. 'He's not giving me my stuff,' she said, and so I joined her, telling the manager, 'You know what, mate, get the police.' None of this was his fault. 'Cool down,' he said. I told him, 'Cool down fuck all. Get the fucking police.'

Then I walked towards the lift and as I reached Kirsten passed the stupidest comment I've ever made. 'If the police come up to that room, I'm going to batter them,' I said. Instantly, I knew it was a mistake, and in the lift I told myself, 'I've just said to her that if the police come up to that room, I'm going to batter them. Ian, if the police come up to the room, you'll need to batter them or she'll think you're a shitebag.' I knew there was no way I'd back down, lose face in front of her.

Back in the room, I paced up and down, just as I had in my prison cells. I knew Kirsten had every right to be angry, but she'd agreed we were finished, and when I'd walked out of the hotel earlier that morning it was as a single guy. 'I could do with another line of coke,' I thought, then decided, 'If she comes up with the two security guards, I'm going to tell her to just come right in and get her stuff. But if the police come with her, I need to attack them because I've told her that's what I'll do.'

I took another line of coke, then rang a pal in Glasgow and explained the situation.

He said, 'It's Sunday morning. Why've you phoned me up?'

I said, 'Show a bit of sympathy.'

'You're not going to attack anybody?' he wondered, and I told him, 'I probably won't.'

'Well, if you've any more stuff left, flush it down the toilet in case the police find it.'

I promised I would, but I treated myself to a final line to finish it off and felt like Superman. I was determined to batter any police who showed up, and when a knock came on the door, I was right up for it. This was crazy. You just don't argue with the Spanish police, but by now I felt I could fly. I opened it, took one look, and said, 'Oh no.' Two policemen in their mid-20s flanked Kirsten, with two hotel security guards behind.

The policemen carried guns and wooden batons and asked, 'Can we please come in, get her belongings and then we'll go?' They were polite and friendly. 'No,' I said. They asked, 'What?', and I demanded, 'Have you got a search warrant?' Now their vocabulary seemed limited. 'What?' they asked, so I told them, 'Fuck off,' and slammed the door.

But as I went back inside the room the door opened again and there stood the police. Now they didn't seem so friendly. And Kirsten was still there too. In my eyes, it was as though she was daring me: 'Come on, big man, you've said you'll attack the police, do it.' I was out of my head, the extra lines of charlie kicking in, and I thought, 'It's now or never.' This was like the days of the jewellery robberies: do it now or you'll lose your nerve.

'Calm down,' the police ordered. I said, 'Calm down fuck all,' grabbed a table lamp, shouted, 'Fuck you, fuck you,' and threw one of the officers into the middle of the room. As we rolled around grappling on the floor, him trying to pull out his gun, his colleague attempted to intervene. I saw his pistol emerge from its holster, then I cracked one of them over the head with the lamp. Blood ran from the wound and the two security guards joined in. Within seconds, I was lying helpless on the balcony, my hands cuffed behind my back. 'If they knew my history, they'd throw me off,' I thought.

What happened I've pieced together from my own memory of what went on during brief spells of consciousness and from Kirsten's description of the Battle of Benidorm. The two policemen produced their batons. Suddenly, I knew there was nothing wrong with their English as one told me, 'OK, hard man, this is where the fun starts,' and I knew what to expect. I'd gone through all of this before too many times in police stations and prison cells when coppers and screws had demonstrated on me their version of fun. There was only time for me to shout, 'Fuck you, fuck you,' before the batons began descending.

I saw Kirsten standing there watching. 'You want to hear me scream out in pain,' I thought. 'No way will I give you that satisfaction.' The drink and drugs were encouraging my defiance, and I yelled, 'Harder, harder,' as the police smashed fuck out of me. I was told later that they stopped at one point, but I don't remember that, because I was unconscious. Some of my fingers had been broken in the attack, too.

Friends have since wondered, 'She was still your girlfriend. Didn't she shout for them to stop?' But if she did, then I didn't hear, because I was out for the count. When I came to, I was on the balcony and the handcuffs had been removed. I think the truth is that the police realised they had gone too far and decided it was in the best interests of everybody, not least their own, to let me go.

Kirsten told me later what had happened, describing how I lay there crumpled, blood running from my head, face and hands, fortunate not to have suffered life-threatening injuries. All I can remember was coming to, seeing her with the police and security guards and then taking a running jump into them. This time, there was no need for another beating. Had I not done it, the whole thing would have been forgotten, but I brought upon myself the trouble that followed.

I was handcuffed again and taken downstairs in the lift. Despite the blood, I felt no pain, but I was screaming with rage, telling the police, 'You two are a pair of cunts. You're bastards.'

They shouted back, 'Shut up, shut up!'

'You're a pair of faggots, poofs, homosexuals,' I spat.

At that one of the officers said, 'I've had enough of you,' and put the barrel of his gun in my mouth.

It was the first time anybody had done that to me, and it was the most terrifying moment of my life. Not even the drugs could prevent terror making my body shake. As the gun was in my mouth, he mocked me, saying, 'You think you're a hard man?'

On the ground floor, I decided I'd had enough and ran away but was tripped up. Other police arrived and I was pushed into a van. Inside, I bashed my head against the side of the vehicle time after time. I was driven to hospital, where a doctor decided against examining me, announcing instead, after a cursory look, that there was nothing wrong with me. So it was on to a police station and a cell, where, the next day, an officer told me they had been in touch with the police in Britain and knew I had convictions for armed robbery and possessing a gun. 'You'll be charged with two police assaults,' he told me. In fairness, they didn't lay a finger on me, but perhaps they were worried about the possible repercussions of the extent of the beating I had already endured.

I was put into a cell with six others. It was baking hot, and as the effects of the drink and drugs wore off, the bruises began to throb. I asked for water, but a jailer told me, 'You're getting fuck all,' so I had to beg one of my fellow captives for a drink. 'What are you here for?' the others wanted to know, but I simply told them, 'A domestic row.'

However, as the hours went by, these guys tried to get cheeky, clearly thinking they'd have some fun at my expense and that I was some simple tourist who'd never seen the inside of a nick before. 'You'll go to the local prison. It's full of Moroccans who will have you,' they mocked. The aches were worsening, making me irritable and angry. 'Nobody's having me. I've done 16 years for bank robbery and I've carried guns,' I shouted.

At this time, Spain was constantly being rocked by bombings and assassinations committed by ETA, the feared Basque nationalist and separatist organisation. 'See all your mob, ETA? I sit with the IRA. My friends in the IRA train your ETA terrorists,' I said. Suddenly, their vocabulary became limited. 'What?' they asked, and I repeated, 'My friends train ETA. I'm not an idiot, so fucking shut it.' They understood that.

The next day, I appeared in court and on the way there remembered the words of Jim Brown at the airport about not getting arrested. A young, female Spanish lawyer came to see me and told me Kirsten would not make a statement against me. The lawyer said, 'OK, you are going to prison today,' and I told her, 'Yes, yes.' I was prepared for all of this, but when she said, 'Eight months,' it was my turn to ask, 'What? Eight months? Eight months? That's a joke.'

However, the effects of the drink and drugs had not worn off completely and I cheered up. I told the lawyer, 'OK, I go to prison today for eight months. In the mornings, I lie in the swimming pool and the prison officers bring out sangria with my breakfast.' The 'What?' habit was spreading. 'What?' she said, and I continued, 'The jail has a swimming pool and you get sangria with your breakfast. In fact, it's so good I might tell everybody back home to come over here and get the nick.' She asked, 'Which prison is this?' and I told her, 'The prison in Benidorm,' but she said, 'No swimming pool there.' I'd heard, though, that there were prisons in Spain with pools.

I asked, 'Well, what's in the Benidorm prison?', and she told me, 'Rats, maggots and faggots.'

I told her, 'Wait a minute, this is just a domestic. I'm not a football hooligan.' As soon as she mentioned faggots, I tried to play the seriousness of the whole thing down.

I began whinging about my treatment by the police, describing in great detail the beating I had been given. 'So the police did that?' she asked, and I said, 'They could have killed me.'

Clearly this put a new slant on the matter. 'Have you any convictions?' she asked. I told her, 'Does Big Ben tell the time?' and began listing my history.

She stopped me: 'Be quiet. I want to know if you have any convictions in Spain.' I told her no and realised that as far as the Spanish authorities were concerned I was a man of good character.

The lawyer told me, 'I can get you a suspended sentence. You'll pay compensation to the policemen and walk out.'

Later in the day, I was taken into a room in handcuffs to face a number of men and women sitting around a table. My lawyer whispered, 'It's all sorted,' and I thought, 'Fucking hell, I'm walking out of here.' I heard someone telling me they proposed dishing out an eight-month prison sentence suspended for two years with six hundred euros compensation to be paid within thirty days. 'Do you understand?' I was asked, and I nodded.

That night, I was released. Somewhere between the prison cell and the court, my flip-flops had vanished, so I trudged barefoot back to the four-star Hotel Melia. The manager, whom I'd been shouting at a couple of days earlier, was there.

'Where is she?' I asked, and he said, 'Gone. She went yesterday.'

'Did she leave anything?' I asked, and he handed me a soap bag with shampoo in it and 50 euros.

I went to the pub across the road, where I met a guy I knew and told him the story. 'You're lucky you're not dead,' he said.

I spent a few euros on some new flip-flops.

There was a flight later that night, and I phoned Ma, who arranged to pay for my ticket. Ma and James were waiting for me at the airport and said Kirsten had visited them. 'She said she had never seen anybody act like you, that you were like a wild animal,' said Ma. 'She said you were on the cokey-wokey,' and I admitted that this was true.

I said, 'Ma, tell me this. I'm this wild animal, taking coke, I've hit the police and so on. Did she tell you what she did? Did she tell you how she noised me up?' I called Kirsten. I felt like killing her, and when we spoke she said she was terrified I'd have her slashed, but I said, 'No, Kirsten, I'd never do anything like that.'

One of my friends told me, 'If you ever go back to her, I'll never speak to you again.' And I vowed it was all over. But a while later Kirsten telephoned and asked, 'Ian, are things all right?' I told her, 'Of course,' and went to see her. We talked, and the longer we were together the more I realised I missed her and wanted to get back together with her. I convinced her nothing unpleasant would happen and said, 'I still have feelings for you,' and she told me, 'I still have feelings for you.' And we ended up together again. So much for the pain of Spain.

27

Two Square Goes

MOST OF THE crooks in Glasgow came to party in my West End flat at some time or other as I did my best to recover from the nightmare in Spain through a blitz of booze and charlie. In my heart, I knew Kirsten and I would get back together. I'd written the Audi off when it had overturned while I was on my way home to pack my bags for a trip to Tenerife with a good friend, John Jackson, and Kirsten had talked me into spending £26,000 on a brand-new black Mercedes 180 Kompressor, which we nicknamed 'the Blinkmobile'.

With Kirsten, I visited the north of Cyprus, which had at one time been a haven for another of my pals, Rifat Mehmet, who was jailed for 18 years in 1983 for the armed robbery of a security van in London. Three years later, he escaped when an armed accomplice ambushed a prison van taking him to a court hearing about access to his daughter. Rifat ended up in northern Cyprus, which did not have an extradition treaty with the UK. There, he ran a beach bar and even acted as a United Nations interpreter. He sneaked back into Britain to see his daughter and robbed a building society branch, but he was caught when police stopped his car because he wasn't wearing a seatbelt.

We stayed in a five-star hotel, and nearby was a bungee jump over the sea, which fascinated me. I longed to have a go, but I didn't dare because of the shoulder I'd dislocated in prison years earlier. I told Kirsten, 'Do the jump and I'll give you £1,000 cash.' She told me, 'Ian, I wouldn't do it for £100,000.'

Within a few days of returning to Glasgow, I discovered Arthur Thompson's favourite drinking place, the Provanmill Inn, was up for sale at £99,500. It had been firebombed and only the lounge remained, but I wondered whether to buy it. If I did, then it would be in direct opposition to the Ranza, run by the Morrison family. The Provy stood in a staunchly Republican area and, being a Rangers supporter, I'd have bought it for devilment, just to noise up all the Celtic supporters. Pals were warning, 'You can't turn it into a Rangers bar,' but I told them, 'I can do what I want. If people don't like it, they can lump it. It's my money.' That last bit wasn't true, of course. Finally, though, I abandoned the idea. It would have taken a lot of money to rebuild, and I'd have needed someone to run it for me. With my record, there was no way I'd have been granted a licence.

Money was simply no object. I was on a mad adventure, spending money made through robberies, up to my neck in criminality. I had enough to do things I'd only dreamed of while I whiled away the lonely prison nights. It was spend, spend, spend, buy, buy, buy. Kirsten and I went to the Gleneagles Hotel for a few days, and to Gran Canaria. I gave friends money, took others to expensive restaurants, paid £1,400 for a family gathering at the Ubiquitous Chip in Glasgow, footed the bill for Christmas dinner for 18 at the Grosvenor Hilton, took Kirsten to Tenerife for four days to get her a Cartier watch, even though I'd already bought her one for her birthday. We stayed at the five-star Scotsman Hotel in Edinburgh; I took her to Durham just so we could walk around outside Durham and Frankland prisons, the insides of which I knew so well. I had a first-class credit rating and a Mercedes credit card with a £7,500 limit that I cleared four times. When it was announced that luxury flats were to be built at Hogganfield Loch, I paid somebody to get first place in the queue so we'd have our pick of the new buildings. We put down a £1,000 deposit for one and then, when the sales representative said the development would include duplex flats, I told her, 'I'll have one of those as well,' and handed over another grand. It was just like buying Maltesers.

Of course, money can't buy love, and gradually Kirsten and I began slipping apart. We split up for a while, then got back together and I took her to Thailand, stopping off first in London, where we stayed at the Waldorf Hilton and watched Don Johnson of *Miami Vice* in the stage show *Guys and Dolls*.

There was an ulterior motive to this break in the journey. For six months, three associates I'd met in prison and I had been discussing a raid on a depot in England. My role would be to act as muscle. After my previous experience of a major robbery, I'd told them, 'I hope this is 100 per cent,' and they said, 'Ian, nothing's ever that certain.' But these guys were good at what they did, and I was going to go ahead with it. The haul was expected to be up to three million pounds. We had a number of meetings, usually in the north-west of England, roughly halfway between Glasgow and their base. I never drove there in my own car in case the police were watching. Now, in London, I sent Kirsten off shopping and met my friends in a West End bar. They told me, 'Ian, we need to call this off. We think we're being watched. And we think you're being followed.'

During the 12-hour flight from Heathrow, I couldn't sleep because of what they'd told me. We stayed at the highest building in Bangkok, the Baiyoke Sky, for five days, then it was off to the island of Koh Samui. After getting the nick in Benidorm, and suspecting the police were tailing me, I couldn't get out of my mind the fear of ending up in the Bangkok Hilton, the notorious Bang Kwang Central Prison, which housed death-row inmates and where food was so scarce that cockroaches and rats were regarded as delicacies. Despite my fears, the holiday went smoothly, and when we got back home I continued doing turns, with the result that the money flowed in. Our trip had cost £5,000: a drop in the ocean to me.

Not everyone in Glasgow appreciated my determination to enjoy myself and help others do the same. One by one, club owners barred me, and so I stepped up the frequency of parties at my West End flat. I'd go to Asda, buy a £200 carry-out and take it back home. My home became party central, with the back bedroom resembling a Haddows off-sales. Everybody came, even lap dancers from Seventh Heaven club. There was unlimited cocaine on offer for anybody who wanted it. I spent £3,500 on charlie in one frantic five-day binge. 'Have a wine and a line,' I'd tell my guests.

There was just one house rule. 'Start any trouble and you'll be lobbed out,' I'd say. My good friend George Redmond, who headed the Pulp Fiction crew (so called because they reminded me of the mobsters in the Quentin Tarantino film of that name), would ask, 'Can we come up with a few pals?', and I'd say, 'You can bring anybody, but you're responsible if there's any trouble.'

And there never was, although one day a trendy young couple who were neighbours rang the bell and asked, 'Can you keep the music down? Our bedroom is directly over your living room.' I asked, 'Which night?' and they said, 'Every night.' I told them, 'I'll try, but I'm promising nothing,' so they said, 'We're moving.' Frankly, I had no intention of doing anything, because I didn't give a shit.

Christine Brown – sister of Shug O'Donnell, my good friend from borstal years earlier – visited the flat and gave me a lecture about my lifestyle, saying, 'Ian, you need to slow down.' Christine married Tommy Campling in Shotts jail, and they put my name down on the guest list, but the prison refused to let me in. Tommy received a life sentence with a 25-year recommendation after a pal turned Queen's Evidence.

The knock-back was a familiar scenario. I had more chance of getting into the National Westminster bank at Torquay than any club in Glasgow. I had public rows with a couple of club owners who obviously had the ear of the police, because when I went along to a Saints and Sinners Night at Hamilton Racecourse the cops stopped me. 'We have intelligence that you are going to assault a nightclub owner,' the police said. They were right. I'd gone there with the intention of doing him in.

Shug O'Donnell was there and he took me into the VIP area. As we were driving out of the racecourse in the Blinkmobile, the police waved us down and told me, 'Straight home to bed, Ian.'

'I'm not on a fucking tag,' I told them, and drove back to a party at a restaurant in Bothwell with Shug.

He told me later, 'I can't believe you get all this hassle,' and I told him, 'This is an everyday thing for me.'

I took Daryl and his friend Gary to Portugal for a week. The holiday gave me a chance to reflect on my life. I knew I was my own worst enemy, partying continuously and taking cocaine. When one party ended, someone would be asking when I'd be having the next one. I just couldn't say no.

A couple of months after returning from Portugal, I began hearing that Tam McGraw was badmouthing me. One of the claims he was supposed to be making was that if he came across me he'd kick me up and down the street. My anger was increasing, and then a good friend from the past turned up to say rumour had it that McGraw and one of his pals had offered money to have me whacked, murdered. My friend had been approached and asked, 'Do you want to do something to Blink? There's good wages in it.'

I knew McGraw was a silent partner in Glasgow Private Hire, the huge taxi firm based in Edinburgh Road and run by Stevie Malcolm. During a party at home one night, while I was high as a kite, I rang the taxi company number and told the girl who answered, 'I don't want a taxi, I want two square goes.'

She asked, 'Is this a wind-up call?'

'No, it's deadly serious. It's every man's right to ask for a square go.'

She asked who I wanted to fight.

'Tam McGraw and Stevie Malcolm,' I said. 'Tell them I'll be round at the office at ten.'

She asked, 'Who will I say is coming up?'

'Ian MacDonald.'

She then said, 'This call is being recorded.'

I told her, 'Tam's an idiot and Stevie's a bam.'

While I was laying down my challenge, the party continued, with the lines of cocaine getting bigger and the music louder. But at half past nine the next morning, I changed into my shorts, put on the shirt I'd bought from the Chelsea football club shop and slipped into my flip-flops. My guests were sitting around taking more lines. 'Where the fuck are you going?' they asked, and I told them, 'Edinburgh Road for my two square goes.'

I did 30 press-ups, picked up a rave CD and drove off. A friend who was still at the party rang and said, 'Come on back,' but I simply turned up the music in my car and switched off the telephone. I was about to start a chain of events that would have long-lasting and horrific consequences.

At the taxi base, I walked into the office and asked for McGraw and Malcolm. I was ranting and raving, 'I'm here for a showdown.'

A man introduced himself as the manager and asked, 'Are you serious? I know who you are.' I told him, 'Deadly serious.' He said, 'I'll phone Stevie,' and returned a few moments later to say he had been instructed to ring the police. He told me, 'I don't want to do that,' but I insisted, 'Phone them. Tell them it's Blink and they might come quicker.'

I went outside to calm down, but when I tried to go back in, the doors had been locked. I waited, then drove back to the flat. 'They didn't turn up,' I told my friends.

It never rains but it pours. That same morning, my phone rang and a man identified himself and named three people I knew as 'the New Kids on the Block'. He said he was a go-between and they wanted to meet me. But I named one of them and said this individual should come alone, and the caller agreed to that. We arranged an immediate rendezvous for a coffee shop near my flat.

Still in my flip-flops, I sneaked out and ran through pouring rain to the café, where I bought myself a latte, sat down and waited. One of the men, who it had been agreed would stay away, appeared at the window, as if he was taking a ringside seat for what was about to happen.

I wandered to the front door of the café and realised the New Kids on the Block had all turned up. And then it all happened in a flash. One of them grabbed me and tried to punch me on the back of the head. Another ran in front of me, raising his fists in a boxing stance. Screaming customers, among them a party of

American tourists, were watching this free entertainment, and suddenly we crashed into tables, sending coffee cups and breakfast plates flying. The two attackers fled. The place was in uproar and I was asked to leave. 'No, I've lost my watch. It cost me £4,000,' I said, and began looking for it.

Suddenly, the police were there, asking me, 'Excuse me, can we have a word?' I told them, 'Hang on a minute, I've lost my watch,' and a voice said, 'Oh, fuck, that's Blink, he's not going to say much.'

I asked what they wanted and they demanded, 'Who were you fighting with?' I told them, 'Randall and Hopkirk.' They said, 'Who?' and I said, 'Randall and Hopkirk. Ghosts.' *Randall and Hopkirk (Deceased)* was a popular television series about two private detectives, one of whom had died and who reappeared as a ghost giving advice to his partner.

Before leaving, they took my name and my ma's address, because I didn't want them to know the whereabouts of my flat. I gave the coffee shop manager my phone number and asked him to call when he found my watch. He said, 'Sir, before you go, you're barred.' I wanted to get back to my flat but couldn't because the police were hanging about, so I had to wander about for an hour and a half before they went and I could get home.

In the flat, my friends wondered where I had been. They asked, 'Why didn't you get out before the police came?', and I told them, 'Because I wanted to find my watch.' One of them pointed to it. I'd left it behind in the flat.

Word spread that I had been battered, with my nose and jaw broken, but a few days later came a different version, saying my opponents had come off worse. Friends, including George Redmond, visited me, asking what had gone on, and when I told them, they offered to kill the attackers. 'No, I can handle this,' I said.

A few days after the bust-up in the café, Jake Devine was murdered in Cowlairs Park, Glasgow. Jake had taken his dog Chico there for a walk. It was three days before Jake was found, dumped in bushes, and throughout that time Chico never left the side of his dead master. I thought, 'If only human beings were so decent.'

At the end of that month, McGraw went for a routine hospital check and, after returning home, died suddenly of a heart attack. Now five of the eleven were dead. In some quarters of Glasgow, people celebrated his passing, me among them.

The next day, what was left of the body of Billy Bates turned up in an oil drum in the River Clyde. There were rumours that Billy had been involved in the shooting of a barman in Bishopbriggs. I'd always liked Billy. Once, at Ma's house, he'd become fascinated by a huge fish I had that kept leaping out of its tank. Now, sadly, Billy had been sent to sleep with the fishes.

The dust from the spat with the New Kids on the Block would never settle, but I wanted only to get on with my life. What others did was their affair.

In November, Kirsten and I got back together and moved to the new homes at Hogganfield Loch. Mine was a duplex, but we stayed together in hers, a penthouse. I called mine the Bird Sanctuary, because I was determined to live quietly and put an end to parties and wild nights. I had taken a step back from crime and my crazy spending was beginning to catch up, with funds starting to run low. I was down to my last £30,000 and happy to settle for taking my dog Lucky for walks, reading and going to bed early.

The bonds that had tied Kirsten and I became loose then parted altogether after I heard on the grapevine she had been dating an associate of one of the New Kids on the Block and felt betrayed. She announced she was switching to long-haul flights, meaning that she could be away for weeks at a time, and we called it a day. She moved out of the penthouse and went to stay with her mum in Baillieston, leaving me on my own. The duplex stayed empty for a year and a half. I used to give pals conducted tours of it and should have got round to renting it out but never did.

28

Bugged

IN MAY 2008, my beloved Rangers reached the final of the UEFA Cup. It was to be played at Manchester, and there was no way I was going to miss such an event. Everybody who was a Rangers fan wanted to be there, even if it was just to watch the final on big screens near the City of Manchester Stadium, home to Manchester City football club, where the Gers would meet Russian side Zenit St Petersburg.

The day before the game, I took the Blinkmobile to Blackpool with Daryl and my pal Alex Manson from Carntyne, a cousin of John Lynn. We'd tried getting accommodation in Manchester, but the entire city and its surrounds were booked up, and in the end, along with about 30,000 other supporters, we'd gone to Blackpool, 55 miles away, where we booked into a bed and breakfast.

That evening, we went out on the town in Blackpool, and in each pub we seemed to meet friends who joined us, until we had a crowd of around 30. At one stage, we were joined by a good friend, Alex McGaughey, who ran a pub in the Gorbals. We ended up bevying the night away in a hotel. There was absolutely no bother from us at all.

The next morning, because we were going to be drinking all day, we decided to leave the Blinkmobile in Blackpool and paid £80 for a taxi to Manchester. When we arrived in the city centre, the place was heaving with football fans from all over the world, determined to have a good time. It was one gigantic party, with everybody in a good mood and optimistic for a Rangers win.

At first, everyone was buying carry-outs. Then a few simply went into a supermarket and walked off with cartons of beer. Others, seeing them get away with it, followed suit. And so did I, telling the petrified security staff to piss off as I vanished out of the doors. Stores like Sainsbury's were mobbed. People were wandering about boozing and the police seemed in good spirits. I even had my photograph taken with a policewoman. The atmosphere was great. There were an estimated 175,000 Rangers fans in the city that day, laughing, singing and enjoying themselves. I met literally hundreds of pals. The last thing I was expecting was trouble, but it came when I bumped into the guy Kirsten had been seeing.

Before Kirsten and I had broken up, I had been told she'd been seeing him, but this had nothing to do with our split, which had been on the cards for a good while. Somebody had spotted the pair of them in Karbon nightclub, but I could say with complete honesty that I wasn't at all bothered by this. Like me, she was free to go with who she wanted. However, somebody intent on making mischief and a few quid at the same time had told a newspaper I was furious, my anger made all the worse because the guy was much younger than me. This just wasn't true, but it gave the gossips something to mull over, and suddenly he and I came face to face in Piccadilly Square.

We looked at each other, then, without warning, he punched me in the mouth and ran off as I shouted after him, 'You cowardly bastard!' I was wearing flip-flops; they seemed to bring trouble every time I wore them. I'd hardly had time to recover when he reappeared with pals and they all piled into me. What saved me that day was that my opponent wasn't wearing a Rangers top. He had on a yellow shirt. I was trying to fight the lot of them, but I found myself on the deck being booted around like a ball, doing my best to parry kicks and blows.

When I managed to get to my feet, my face was covered in blood, but it looked much worse than it was, the blood coming from a little cut to my head. What made me go ballistic was that I'd lost my flip-flops. I'd lost a pair during the fighting in Benidorm, now I'd lost another pair in Manchester. Rangers fans were coming up saying they'd stepped in to stop the attack. I thanked them, then said to Daryl, 'I'm getting a knife. I'm going to stab this coward,' but he pleaded, 'Please don't.' I stormed around the centre of Manchester hunting for the guy, my blood boiling, but he was nowhere to be found.

To make matters worse, Rangers lost the final 2–0, and all the supporters were on a downer. Before the start, we'd been arranging to meet up after the final whistle to celebrate, but now all we wanted to do was drink our sorrows away. It seemed everybody was trying to get out of Manchester, and Daryl, Alex and I hung around for hours before finally managing to get a taxi driver who would agree to take us to Blackpool. He was a grasping sod who could see we were desperate and demanded £120. When he dropped us off, I didn't give him a tip but told him, 'You're a greedy bastard.' I had a shit night.

The next day, after breakfast, we headed back up to Glasgow. I was fuming and telephoned a friend who knew loads of people. I reckoned she would have the number of the guy I'd fought with before the match. She asked why I wanted it, and when I told her what had happened in Manchester, she passed it on to me. But he had already been in touch with her. She said, 'I've spoken to him and he wants to talk to you.'

So I phoned him and told him, 'I want to take you a square go. What happened was out of order. You punched me and ran away and then came back.' His version was that, as the fight began, 'A lassie was going by with a pram and we fell over the pram and all the Rangers supporters kicked fuck out of the two of us.' I told him, 'Try coming up with a better story than that. My son saw you. You and your mates were kicking fuck out of me. The only reason it stopped was because the Rangers fans saw me wearing a Rangers top and decided this wasn't right.' But he said, 'None of that is true.'

I told him, 'Listen, a woman would hardly be likely to be

walking around pushing a pram among 175,000 people. I want a square go. I'll meet you tomorrow,' but he insisted he wanted an end to the ill feeling, saying, 'I don't want to fight you. Can't we shake hands?' I wasn't shouting or bawling but trying to be reasonable and polite. I said, 'Another thing: you were nipping Kirsten,' referring to the story that he had been spotted kissing her in Karbon. He said, 'I've had a lot of flak over that. Listen, Ian, I have a young girlfriend and I haven't pulled Kirsten.' I said, 'This isn't about Kirsten. We've moved on from that. This is about me and you and Manchester and kicking fuck out of me with your pals.'

He continued to insist he had not attacked me, that the kicking and punching was done by others, but I repeated, 'My boy watched it. It was lucky for you I wasn't with all my pals or you'd have been done in.' He asked, 'Can't we resolve this?' and I told him, 'No,' so then he said, 'OK. You want to meet me tomorrow for a square go. How do I know you won't turn up with your mates?' Quick as a flash, I said, 'Listen, that's rich coming from you.' I was determined then that if I came across him again I'd attack him, but with the passage of time the animosity has faded away.

Shortly afterwards, somebody viciously slashed businessman Paul Fitzpatrick across the face as he was getting into his car in Queen Street, Glasgow. Huge pools of blood lay on the pavement for days afterwards. I was detained and questioned by the serious crime squad over that attack, but I was released without charge.

That same month, my friend Eleni Pachou was butchered at Di Maggio's in the West End of Glasgow, where she worked as restaurant manager. Just four days earlier, Star Keenan and I had been greeted by Eleni when we went there for a meal with Daryl and his pal Aidan. She was a lovely girl, killed for the day's takings by a cowardly waiter, Juan Carlos Crispin, who was later jailed for life.

Following the attack on Fitzpatrick, events began taking a series of very sinister turns. The serious crime squad stepped things up a gear, hounding me, continually stopping and searching my car, claiming to be looking for drugs, when both they and I knew they were really searching for weapons. My answer was to park up the Blinkmobile and use hire cars.

One night, I had been drinking in a pub on Great Western Road. I'd had at least four lagers and three vodkas, and when the police stopped me for going through a red light and announced they would breath-test me, I knew I was over the limit. I made a half-hearted go of blowing into their device. The police made a call over their radio, then, without looking at the reading, told me, 'You've passed. You can go.' I drove off, certain they were trying to pin more serious matters on me.

Not long after this, I was driving into the car park beside my flat at Hogganfield Loch when I saw the police. Star Keenan was with me and so was Colin McKay. Colin was a friend from way back who had been very close at one time to Frank McPhie, before a sniper murdered Frank outside his Maryhill home in 2001. Colin instinctively reacted as he always did when he saw the police, by bolting. Star and I met the two uniformed officers, who asked if they could 'have a word, sir'. I took them up to the flat, where they said my life was in danger and responded to the usual 'Who is it?' with the customary 'Can't tell you.' Numerous Osman warnings would follow in the months ahead.

In July, my old friend Perry Wharrie was jailed for 30 years in the Irish Republic after police there smashed a £350-million cocaine smuggling plot. He and his gang might have got away with it had it not been for their misfortune when the boat bringing the coke ashore suddenly sank.

Lady Luck, on the other hand, decided to smile on me. Star had by chance got out of his bed at 1.30 in the morning and glanced outside to see a pair of legs sticking out from underneath his car. His wife, Mary, woke up and the two of them went downstairs. The sound of their door opening alerted the mystery mechanic, who took to his heels, pursued by Star, who looked up the street and saw two more people, a man and a woman, apparently keeping a lookout. They too disappeared.

As soon as it was light, Star examined his motor and discovered a small black box hastily attached underneath. He turned up at my flat to tell me about it. He had thrown the device into his garden and it was still there when we returned to his home. Star told me, 'I don't know who's behind this, the police, crooks or whoever. Is it a bomb?' I told him to sling it into the back of my motor and set off with it to see a friend, who said, 'Leave it with me and I'll ring you in a few hours to tell you what it is.'

Five hours later, the caller told me, 'It's a sophisticated tracking device capable of letting six to eight cars tail you when it's up and running. It's expensive and the type of equipment used by the police.'

The Blinkmobile had been parked outside my flat and Star and I searched it but found nothing, so I told Star I'd take it to the main Mercedes dealer the next day for a professional check. But that night Star and Colin were again with me when, as we drove out of Star's street, two police cars suddenly blocked us. I call Colin 'the Road Runner', because the instant I came to a halt, he was out, sprinting away, vainly chased by a cop. Star's family and neighbours had watched this and began running towards us.

The police were clearly scared, eager to get away, and told me, 'We have a warrant to search your car.' As soon as they said it, I realised they knew what had happened to the little black box. They wanted it back and were convinced it was in my motor. Not just that, but I wondered if they'd also planted one under my car and, realising the garage was sure to discover it, had decided to remove it. I told them, 'Why not search the car here and now?', but they ignored my offer, insisting I go with them to Baird Street police station and promising, 'You'll only be there a few minutes. You can watch while it's searched.' But the police refused to let me drive my car there.

Then I realised why the police were so interested in me. During their questioning of me about various altercations I'd been involved in, they had told me, 'We don't want your situation spiralling out of control. We don't want another Daniel and Lyons turf war kicking off.' These were two well-known north Glasgow families who had been engaged in a long and dangerous feud. There were many in the underworld who were convinced it was only a matter of time before it resulted in dead bodies. The word was that enemies of mine had got wind of Colin's association with me and were frightened because of his reputation. But what concerned the police was that they knew none of us would back down.

At the station, it was obvious the police wanted to do a thorough examination of the Mercedes without me being there. So they announced I would be strip-searched, which took around 20 minutes, after which I asked to watch their check of the car. At that, an officer walked in and said, 'Here are your keys. We've searched your car. We've found nothing in it.' When I protested at not being present during the search, they said, 'Come on, Ian, what are you worried about? We've found nothing.' I was dying to tell them that I knew they were taking their device back out and looking for the one they'd planted in Star's car, but I said nothing. Of course, the box Star found was still with my pal. We got it back from him and fixed it to a truck going to Holland.

In September, I was due to appear on a speeding charge at Dumfries Sheriff Court, but I sent in by recorded delivery a note from my doctor saying I wasn't fit enough to appear. Due to an administrative bungle, the sheriff was never shown the letter and issued a warrant for my arrest. Later that day, as I drove through Glasgow to keep a dental appointment, an unmarked car with four men in it suddenly drove up to me and began flashing its lights as if wanting me to stop. Remembering the police warnings that my life was in danger, I sped away, eventually stopping, leaping out and running off. One of the guys from the chasing car tripped me up and my face smashed into the road. I thought my nose was broken. Then I realised they were policemen. 'You're a coward,' I told him. I was taken to London Road police station, blood streaming down my face, and a sergeant asked me three times what had happened. 'Nothing, I did it myself,' I told him.

Naturally, I wanted to know why I had been chased by four detectives in an unmarked car, and the excuse was that they were executing the warrant issued by the Dumfries sheriff. What I found odd was that within two hours of the warrant being issued, it was being served, a process that generally took two weeks. I later told a pal, 'It must have been one of the quickest warrants ever served in Scotland.' Then, when I asked why the police hadn't simply knocked at my door to serve it, there was no response. I was kept in custody over the weekend and on Monday appeared at Dumfries charged with speeding and failing to appear at court. I pleaded not guilty to both charges and suddenly the recorded-delivery letter I'd posted turned up. It had been lying in a file while I was being chased, having my face smashed and being thrown into a cell.

Just before the case began, two members of the serious crime squad walked into court. I was fined £250 to be paid at £10 a week, but I asked the sheriff not to impose a driving ban because my life was in danger and I needed a driving licence. To back up my case, I pointed to the two coppers. They were ordered to stand up by the sheriff but said they were there for another case. I got a three-month ban.

Trouble seemed to follow me around. In October, Grant Mackintosh and I went to visit a good friend of ours, Stephen Logue, in Glenochil jail. Stephen was waiting to go to court accused of stabbing two guys outside Karbon. The incident had attracted a lot of publicity because two of the witnesses were footballers Nicky Butt, the England midfielder, and the legendary Rangers defender Craig Moore. At Glenochil, Grant recognised a prison officer and began arguing with the guy. I joined in and next minute the officer had ordered all the gates to be locked and the police to be called. We couldn't understand why he didn't simply order us out and stop the visit. Grant went quietly, but I told the screw, 'If I knee you in the bollocks, they'll come through your eyes.'

When the police arrived, we were strip-searched to see if we were concealing drugs. Grant was allowed to go, but I was arrested and charged with a breach of the peace. As I was being led out of the prison gates into the police car, Grant shouted, 'Where are you taking him?' and the cop said, 'Stirling police office.' He called, 'I'll be there,' and I thought, 'Fucking hell, I'm the one who gets arrested, but it was you who started it all.' But he came to the police station and waited six hours for me to be released.

I later accepted a £200 fiscal's fine and, to rub salt into the wound, the Scottish Prison Service told me I was banned from visiting any prison in the country. My options for going anywhere were fast diminishing.

29

Bombed

GEORGE REDMOND AND John McGuire were shot outside the Waldorf Bar in Cambridge Street, Glasgow, in October. George died soon afterwards in hospital, but John survived, although it was touch and go for a while. I looked on them as being among my closest friends.

I was at home reading when about midnight the phone rang and one of their crew came on the line in hysterics with news of the shooting. I couldn't believe it. There had been a rumour that there might be a hit on them, so they'd stayed in a rented pad in Canniesburn, never venturing over the door for at least a week.

I was soon able to put together what had happened, and it was obvious a major player had spent a lot of time and money planning to murder both men. It was just like a plot from a gangland movie. The targets were invited for a meal to a bistro, in this case Gizzi's in Cambridge Street; they had hung about for most of the day, gone for a drink to the Waldorf that night, and when they went outside, George to take a phone call and John accompanying him to have a cigarette, they were blasted from a passing car. The killer obviously knew when they'd be outside and had waited nearby for a message, probably from a spotter watching the Waldorf through binoculars from the window of a hotel opposite, to say they were in view. A number of names were being mentioned as being behind it. I knew who the gossips were talking about. And I knew the names of two others suspected of setting up my friends to be shot.

John was taken to Glasgow Royal Infirmary, and a few hours

after the shooting I went to see him. At the hospital, uniformed police barred my way and refused to allow me to visit him. George and John had never let me down when I'd needed support, and there was no way the cops were going to stop me. 'This isn't a prison,' I told one of the coppers. 'I have human rights like anybody else.' He was adamant I wasn't getting in, so I rang the squad investigating the shootings and told them who I was. 'Cool down. We're on our way and we'll make sure you see John,' I was told. Clearly, the police thought John might tell me what he wasn't telling them. They were as good as their word, and within a few minutes a team of suits arrived. 'On you go,' they told me, but a policeman carrying a machine gun was having none of it. 'I don't want him in here,' he told them, but the suits insisted, 'Well, he's coming in,' and the guy said, 'I'm not too happy.' I looked at him and said, 'You've just been outranked.' Now he looked really unhappy.

He was left to sulk while I was taken to meet with John. He'd been shot just below the heart, and when he'd realised what was happening he'd dived to the pavement. George had been shot in the back. The suits and another guy with a gun hung around the room, earwigging. I asked, 'You going to go away?', but they said, 'No, we're going to listen to everything you say.' After ten minutes, I said to John, 'Can't get talking to you.' I shook his hand and said, 'John, do you know your brother George is dead?' and he said, 'Yes, I know, I'm gutted.'

The police were especially keen to find George's mobile telephone, which had disappeared. They wanted it to see whether there might be a call or a message from whoever had arranged the meal with them. They were hassling George's friend Tam McGoldrick, who had been with them that day. Tam and his wife, Heather, are good friends of mine and I took them to George's funeral. Tam told me, 'I had the feeling something wasn't right. George was getting lots of phone calls throughout the day and stayed in Cambridge Street.'

What lay behind the shooting? Although we were close friends, what they did was their business.

BOMBED

The murder distressed me and I pulled no punches over my views as to what should happen to whoever was responsible. I said, 'I don't want George's killers put behind bars for 20 years and kept in a little cell. I want them in a box under the ground, and I want to be judge, jury and executioner.' Friends warned, 'Ian, you're putting yourself out on a limb,' but my attitude was that George, his nephew Barry and John had taken risks on my behalf, and I knew that if I had been the victim, George would have left no stone unturned hunting for the murderer. What worried a lot of people was that this had been a murder in a busy street in which bullets were sprayed about, putting innocent passers-by and bystanders at risk.

Who knows when the Grim Reaper will call? Paul MacArthur, a good friend to Nello Orsi and me, did. Paul didn't drink, smoke or take drugs, although he loved cars and clubbing, but then found he was seriously ill. He underwent dialysis for a long time, then rang me one night. 'Ian, I'll be dead in a couple of days,' he said. I told him, 'Paul, don't be silly. You're still a young guy,' but he told me, 'I just can't take any more of this.' Somehow, he knew he was about to die, and two days later Nello called. 'Paul's dead,' he said.

Now that the police knew where I was living, I was sure they'd use any excuse to call, and I was right. Towards the end of the month, I arrived back at the flat, having spent the night elsewhere, to be met by one of the neighbours. 'Ian, the police have smashed your door in,' he told me. 'They were about to kick mine in until I pointed out that if they were looking for you they were at the wrong flat.' Sure enough, my door and its surrounds were damaged, and pinned up was a note saying the serious crime squad had called, searched my home and fitted a new lock. What I found inside was bizarre. I'd gone out leaving my bed unmade and cutlery on the draining board. Now any hotel chambermaid would have been proud of the neatly made bed, while the cutlery had been stored away. When I checked, I realised the intruders had taken away personal documents relating to my mortgage and had gone through letters from pals in jails, as if they were looking for clues as to where my income came from. But it wasn't only the police who were taking an interest in my location.

Over the years, I'd had more than my fair share of hassle from the police. Now it was my turn to give them a taste of their own medicine. I was following a police van one day when I noticed one of the brake lights wasn't working. When we stopped at traffic signals, I jumped out and pulled up the driver for breaking the law.

'You think you're a smart alec, a fucking gangster. I'll have you,' he stormed.

'No, I'll have you. Get your light fixed,' I shouted back, much to the amusement of other motorists. But I was about to have a whole lot more unwanted dealings with the cops.

A television production company asked if I would take part in a series called *Dangerous Men* fronted by Danny Dyer. They arranged a preliminary meeting, and the night before it was due to take place, I sat up till about 3.30 in the morning writing up notes to remind myself of some of my more outstanding memories. At one stage during the early hours, I looked out to see a car driving into our car park, circling and driving away. It meant nothing at the time, so I went to bed and switched off the lights, leaving the flat in darkness. The next morning, my doorbell rang and when I didn't answer somebody put their finger on the buzzer and held it there. It was the sort of thing I expected when coppers came, so I still didn't answer. Then I heard my name being shouted and looked out to see a neighbour calling, 'Ian, let me in.' When he appeared, he looked upset and told me, 'There's something under your car.'

I remembered what had happened to Star Keenan and my immediate reaction was to tell him, 'It's a tracking device.' The last thing on my mind was that whatever was there could be a bomb. But when I looked I changed my mind. It wasn't the sort of small square box that had been fixed beneath Star's motor. Instead, there was a foot-long canister attached to the underside of the Blinkmobile. 'It looks like a bomb,' I told myself, and after another quick look added, 'It is a fucking bomb.'

'How did you know this was there?' I asked my neighbour.

'We're just back from a holiday abroad and my wife is still suffering from jet lag,' he said. 'She got up around 4.30 to make tea and saw an estate car coming into our car park.'

Later on, his wife gave more detail. 'The estate car stopped. There were three guys in it, and two who were wearing hoods got out and went around to the front of your car. I couldn't see what they were doing, but I thought they were car thieves. They were messing around for about ten minutes.'

She called the police and, as she did so, the visitors drove out. I was sure it was the same crew I'd spotted earlier. The police arrived and had a look about. But they were not told I was the owner of the car that had attracted interest from the hooded strangers. 'Everything seems to be OK,' they told the woman, and went off.

As her husband and I examined my car, he asked what I intended doing. 'I'm not phoning the fucking police,' I said. I was sure I knew who was behind this. But there was never going to be any chance of my naming names.

However, it was obvious that somebody was out to kill me. I hung about, holding my dog Lucky, wondering what to do. Bombs had been everyday events in Ulster during the Irish Troubles, but this was Glasgow, and not the work of any terrorist organisation. Bombs in Glasgow were a rarity. My mind went back to the bomb that had blown up Arthur Thompson's car, killing his mother-in-law. That had been more than 30 years ago, just around the corner from where I now stood.

I rang Star Keenan, who arrived, took one look and asked, 'What the fuck are you going to do, Ian?' I'd also called my sister Tracy, who showed up in a taxi. While I debated with Star what the next move should be, another neighbour appeared, and when I said I wouldn't call the police, he announced that he was ringing them.

I had been shocked by what I'd found, but now the realisation of what the bomb could mean was sinking in. Bringing Tracy could have put her life in danger, along with those of my friends and neighbours.

'I'm going for a shower,' I said, and at that the police arrived in strength, taping off the car park and telling everyone to leave their homes – everybody except me, and that made me very angry.

Star and Tracy gave in to my pleadings for them to go home, and when they did, Lucky and I were left. I could hear police calling at the other flats, advising the occupants to leave, but still nobody came to my door. I thought, 'Fuck it,' and said to Lucky, 'Come on,' and we went down to the car park. I was really annoyed at the police, and as I opened the main door and walked out, a voice shouted, 'Hoi!'

I yelled back, 'What?' and a policeman shouted, 'Come here.'

'Piss off,' I retorted.

I had the electronic car key in my hand and one of them screamed, 'Don't fucking press that.'

I said, 'Why not? You've said fuck all to me.'

They ordered me, 'Mr MacDonald, don't press that remote for your car. There's a bomb under it.'

I told them, 'I fucking know that. Why didn't you come to my door?'

Lucky and I began walking to the Blinkmobile and the police came towards us, shouting, 'Don't go near that car.' I knew they were trying to get me to hand over the key, but I was so pissed off I ran back to my home, ignoring shouts to 'come here'.

Back in my flat, I waited. Now a policewoman rang the intercom and said, 'Mr MacDonald, you were very foolish.'

I told her, 'It's my car. I've watched you evacuate everybody else, but nobody came to me.'

'That's correct. We thought the safest thing to do was to keep you in your flat.'

'That's stupid. If you think the neighbours needed to be evacuated because they might be in danger, then I'm no different.'

I was really pissed off and refused her request to be allowed to come into the flat.

'We've called in the bomb squad,' she said.

It wasn't just the police I was angry with. My car had been parked next to a duplex that was home to a young couple who had two children. The mum was pregnant. Whoever planted the bomb was recklessly and stupidly putting their lives in danger, along with those of all the other innocent people who lived in my block. I couldn't understand why, if somebody wanted to kill me, they didn't simply come to my door and do it themselves, instead of paying three kids in a car. Was the reason that they lacked guts? I was the easiest guy in the world to get at, not hiding away or surrounding myself with cronies. I walked around Hogganfield Loch every day, an open target.

While I debated my next move and downed a bowl of breakfast cereal, the buzzer sounded repeatedly, voices asking, 'Can we talk?' I ignored them, but then Tracy telephoned to say, 'Ian, you'd better get out of that flat.'

Eventually, I went downstairs again with Lucky to be met by police who ordered me to stay away from my car. An officer demanded, 'Where are you going?', and I told him, 'To my mother's.' He said, 'Stay where you are. Have you got the key to the car?', and when I told him I had, he reached out his hand for it. 'You're not getting it,' I told him. 'You've pissed me about. You never even told me you were evacuating everybody. Piss off.' He said, 'Well, you are putting the lives of everybody in danger,' and I told him, 'No I'm not, because there's nobody in the flats now. You've evacuated the whole place, everybody except me.' He said, 'You're going to make it harder for the bomb squad if they don't have the key,' but I stuck to my guns, saying, 'You're not getting it.'

I went to Ma's, where Tracy told me, 'Ian, just give them the key.' Finally, I saw reason. When the police came, I said to my sister, 'Here's the key, let them have it.' I sat and vainly waited for a phone call from the police to tell me the device had been made safe, but when none came, I returned to the flat around 10.30 to find everyone being told they could go back home and the car being taken away. Someone said the Army had used a robot to inspect the device and neighbours had been told that had the bomb been activated it could have destroyed half the block.

That night, I defied whoever had planted it by going out on a pub crawl in the West End with Grant Mackintosh and two other pals. I told them, 'Whoever has done it isn't keeping me away from my mates or a night out.' By the time I got home, I was steaming. There was a police car stationed outside the flats.

The next evening, the police asked if I would be willing to give a sample from my nails and hair for forensic examination. I asked, 'Am I a suspect in this?' But they said, 'Oh, no, this is normal procedure.' All the same, I thought it very strange, but nevertheless I agreed. They asked for details of my movements up to the point when I'd parked my car, and I told them I'd been shopping and had then stayed up late writing. But I never mentioned seeing the car.

30

Slashed and Nicked

'WHAT'S FOR YOU won't go by you,' I often told myself. Now friends were warning of rumours that a contract had been taken on my life and urged me to leave the flat. 'Get out of there. It's an assassin's paradise,' James Healy said. There was an unwritten underworld code that you didn't attack someone at his home where innocent women and children might become victims. I told him, 'James, all the people shouting they are going to get me have houses. I'm not going to their homes and it's out of order for them to come to mine. If they want to attack me, they can do that in the street.' I knew that if somebody was desperate to have me taken out, there was nothing I could do to stop them trying. So I carried on with my routine.

The police had continued their surveillance on my home for three days. On the fourth, Tuesday, 12 May 2009, I realised they were no longer there when I took Lucky for a walk around Hogganfield Loch. It flashed through my mind that nearly 20 years earlier the police had been keeping an eye on Bobby Glover, and on the day they withdrew their observation he had been murdered along with Joe Hanlon. Still, that was a long time ago. It was a beautiful afternoon, and as I sauntered along, licking an ice lolly, I noticed a car drive by. Inside were three young guys who seemed interested in me, staring as they passed. I thought nothing more of it, went back to my flat, but then decided to visit Ma, who had been holidaying in Benidorm and was due home.

261

On the way, I saw the car again, but I put that down to coincidence. I passed the house that had been home to Arthur Thompson, and the spot where Arty had been gunned down, then suddenly felt a blow to the back of my head and went flying. It was a very amateurish attack. In my younger days, if I'd been doing the business on somebody from behind, I'd just have walked up and made a proper job of it. I managed to stand up and found myself in the middle of the road, staring across at three guys. Dazed, I asked, 'Who the fuck are you?' They taunted, 'Come on,' and I said, 'Come on, then,' and began walking backwards. My mind was in a whirl. What the fuck was going on? Who were these characters?

I didn't have a weapon, not even a dog lead, but, to tell the truth, I wasn't scared because I'd been in these situations for 30 years. I could have run and would have got away from them. But I fell hook, line and sinker for one of the oldest tricks in the book, a challenge to my pride. Psychologically, they defeated me there and then just by one of the trio calling, 'Don't run. You're supposed to be a gangster.' One of his cronies took it up with, 'Aye, come on, big man, hard man, don't fucking run.' I sensed the three were frightened, wondering what to do next. They'd made a foolish move by hitting me from behind and not completing the job. Now they'd have to try again and I'd be ready. They muttered to one another, seemingly to boost their confidence, and then began circling around me like sharks about to move in for the kill. Suddenly, we were fighting, rolling down a slope, and we came up against the gates of St Paul's Church at the corner of the road where Ma lived.

One of the gang sat on my legs to stop me getting away and another asked, 'Who's going to do this?' I heard a voice say, 'Here, take this,' and now they were trying to cut my throat. I put up my hands for protection and felt my face being cut. I was struggling for life. 'They're trying to kill me,' I thought. 'I can't believe this is happening in broad daylight.' Then they were up and running away and I saw their getaway car. They'd clearly meant to do the job where I'd been struck from behind, allowing them to escape without their car being spotted. But because they had been too wary, their scheme hadn't worked out.

'You shitebags, you cowards,' I was shouting. I was holding my face, not aware of how bad the cut was or conscious of blood running from the back of my head. 'This is nothing,' I told myself. 'If they'd cut my throat, I would have been struggling. Four minutes and I'd have been dead.' Then the cops would have been looking for three murderers and their paymaster. I wondered if the hitmen had been told just to slash me but had panicked over being recognised and gone for a kill.

A woman motorist stopped and asked, 'Are you all right?' She had a child strapped in the back seat. Blood was pouring down my face and body, but I wasn't really bothered. Over the years, I'd dished it out and finally it had come to be my turn to be on the receiving end. I told her, 'I'm OK,' and she asked, 'Did you see who did it?' I said, 'Yes,' and she said, 'So did I. Did you see the car? Do you want the registration number?' and I said, 'No, no, I saw them.' By now, I reckoned she was thinking, 'This is getting too heavy for me,' and she drove away. She seemed a professional of some sort, upmarket, and I reckoned she was heading for the Robroyston part of Glasgow.

There were kids running around, and a few of Ma's neighbours who had heard shouting came out to offer help. There was blood on the street. Somebody handed me a towel. 'I'm all right,' I said. I walked to Ma's, knocked at the door and it was opened by my niece, who began screaming. I asked her to telephone Gary and then a neighbour drove me to Stobhill Hospital, where I realised for the first time that I had also been cut with a knife on the back of my head. Gary and some pals arrived, demanding to know who was responsible. I told them, 'I don't know,' but I had a detailed description of the attackers imprinted on my brain.

They were followed by officers from the unit dealing with the car bomb. They asked, 'We suppose you're going to say nothing?', and I replied, 'No, I'm not.'

'Well, are you OK?' they wanted to know, and I told them, 'Aye.'

That was it. I was never questioned, something I found strange. My T-shirt was soaked in blood and I expected the police to take it away so they could examine it to see whether there was DNA left by my attackers on it, but they took nothing. Their attitude seemed to be 'You deserve all you get', but then I was of the same opinion.

That night, I was transferred to the plastic-surgery unit at the Royal Infirmary, and the next day I underwent an operation in which 36 stitches were put in the wound that stretched from my eye to my ear. The skilled staff at the unit did a brilliant job. By now, I was much calmer, the shock wearing off, and staff who enquired about my welfare seemed surprised when I insisted, 'I'm fortunate.' And I was. I could have been murdered. Visitors offered sympathy, but I'd say, 'Don't feel sorry for me. I've given it out, now I've got it back. The only thing that surprises me is that I reached the age of 48 before it happened.' To be totally honest, I didn't think I'd ever be slashed, believing that was something that happened only to younger men. Mostly, I'd made my own way through life, but now I found myself in a gangland war, just as the police had feared.

What can I say about the three guys? They were in their late 20s and their accents told me they were Glaswegian. But that's as far as I will go, because I have an idea who they were. They were certainly paid. The bomb and my slashing were connected, of course. Why was I targeted? I don't know for certain. I am sure, though, that the three attackers were paid by the same individual who footed the bill for the bomb. They were lucky, because if I'd been carrying a knife that day, I'd have done at least one of them. Did knowing who was behind it help? Yes, it did. It would have been worse had I been wondering who was paying for this and why. But knowing the identity of the paymaster and his character meant I wasn't scared, especially after what I'd gone through during 30 years in gangland.

There was something else that gave me satisfaction. One of the codes in the culture into which these people had put themselves is that you do your own dirty work. You have to be seen to be doing something yourself; you can't continually send others to do it for you, because that not only makes you a weak link but them as well. You pay these people money to commit crime on your behalf, to steal, slash, shoot, kill even, but the danger is that once the deed has been done they will come back for more money and you find yourself being blackmailed. That was the situation in which Specky Boyd found himself. He paid others to kill for him but then became paranoid in case they stuck him in, and so he had to pay even more others to kill them. It was a spiral that could have gone on for ever. Now the individual behind the attack on me had put himself at the mercy of those he had paid.

Uniformed police remained at the hospital. I hadn't asked for protection and wondered whether they were guarding me. After my operation, I wandered along to the television room to find two coppers sitting there. I don't know what programme they were watching, but I switched the channel over to the news and one of the policeman protested. 'What are you doing?' he demanded, and I told him, 'What do you think I'm doing? It's my television.' He said, 'But we're watching another channel,' and I said, 'I'm the patient here, not you. What are you doing here anyway?' The answer came, 'We're not here for you. We're here to protect the nurses.' I told them, 'You're thinking somebody is going to come here to try and finish me off?', but there was no reply.

A news item referred to the car bomb, but the words of a senior detective who was interviewed by a television reporter infuriated me. 'Ian MacDonald is a well-known criminal in Glasgow,' he said. I was appalled and told the uniforms, 'Your boss is an arsehole just like you two.' I was so angry I telephoned Strathclyde Police headquarters and made a complaint. A senior officer arrived in the early hours. 'What's this all about?' he asked, and I told him, 'One of your guys has gone on television branding me a well-known criminal. He's appealing for witnesses. He's got a cheek giving out all my details.' He wrote it all down, went away and I heard nothing more about it.

I looked at myself in a mirror, examining my wound. I knew it would leave a 'Mars Bar' – Glasgow parlance for a scar. 'Fucking hell,' I thought. 'Well, at least things can't get any worse.'

I was wrong. Two days after the slashing I was released and collected my car, which was still covered in dust left during the search by forensic specialists for fingerprints and any other clues to the identity of the bombers. Then I went to Ma's and told anybody who would listen, 'I'm going to kill these cunts for doing this and for the bombing.' I knew who was behind it all. 'They're cowards,' I said. 'They could have done it at Hogganfield Loch or at the flat, but they chose a church beside my mother's. How would they like it to happen outside their mother's house?'

The next day, Friday, I was in a bar with Star Keenan when the police rang demanding to know where I was and saying they wanted to speak to me urgently. They wouldn't say what about, and I assumed it was to give me another Osman. That evening, I was back at my flat with Star when a team of detectives showed up. 'This'll be to give me the Osman,' I told Star. 'They'll be from the serious crime squad.' I was wrong on both counts. The officers said they were from the major crime and terrorism investigation unit. Seeing Star, they asked, 'Can we speak to you alone?', and I thought, 'Here we go, another warning I'm going to be killed.' Instead, they crowded around and I was told, 'We're sorry to tell you this, but we're here to arrest you.'

That hit me for six. 'What the fuck have I done?' I asked. They looked shamefaced and one replied, 'It's for an alleged breach of the peace three weeks ago outside Boho nightclub in Dumbarton Road, when you were shouting and swearing.' I asked, 'Are you having a laugh?', but they said, 'No. Put your hands out,' and put handcuffs on me. I was stunned.

First a bomb under my car, then slashed, now arrested. At Baird Street police station, I was asked about Boho, but I replied, 'No comment,' to every question. The police were clearly becoming frustrated by this tactic and began threatening that if I continued saying nothing it would jeopardise my chances of getting bail. But I knew there was no chance of that anyway. So I was locked in a police cell, and when they refused to give me the tablets prescribed by the hospital for my injuries, I began kicking the door to annoy them, so a police surgeon arranged for me to be taken to hospital.

On Sunday, I was back in my cell at Baird Street when three detectives visited. They weren't there to enquire about my welfare or offer to take me to church.

'Your car was firebombed last night outside your house,' they said.

'Where the fuck were you?' I asked. 'Is this true?'

The police response to that was 'We don't want a gangland war starting here', and I told them, 'Well, it's already fucking started. Look what's happened to me in a week.'

I'd left the Blinkmobile parked on the pavement outside the flat at Hogganfield Loch, and at one in the morning it had exploded in a fireball. Somebody didn't like me.

The next day, much to the irritation of the police, a sheriff granted me bail.

'At least,' I thought, 'I'm insured.' But the insurers refused to pay out, saying I hadn't told them about my firearm or robbery convictions. Friends said, 'Blink, get away from Glasgow,' so I took Daryl to Magaluf, where a pal took me for trips on his luxury yacht.

While I was waiting for my court appearance, John Friel died, and I went to his funeral in September. I thought of all the friends who had passed on. John had been among the best.

In January 2010, I appeared at Glasgow Sheriff Court and pleaded not guilty to the Boho breach of the peace allegation.

Joe Shields had advised me to admit the offence, but I said, 'Joe, over my dead body. I've already had a bomb under my car, been slashed, petrol-bombed and jailed. I'm going to prove my innocence.'

Joe said, 'OK, I'll give it my best shot.'

When it was my turn to give evidence, I simply told the truth.

'Not guilty,' said the sheriff. The verdict proved that yet again the police had lifted me off the streets for nothing.

The following month, another of my good friends, David Fitzsimmons, died at the age of just 49. David had moved to

Corby in Northamptonshire and invited his pals to his 50th birthday party. He never made it. He had bravely fought against drug addiction, but five days before the party he was found dead from an overdose in a house in Stirling. I was devastated by his death. Just before his funeral, I met his daughter Amanda and her husband, Martin, and David's brother Paul, together with the rest of the family, and I've stayed in contact with them, honoured to have them as friends.

A few weeks after his funeral, I received a message from old underworld comrades in London to say that Ronnie Biggs wanted to meet me. Ronnie was the Great Train Robber who had escaped from prison and gone on an amazing adventure that saw him living first in Australia and then Brazil. Eventually, his health declined and he was persuaded to return to the United Kingdom, where, frail and suffering the effects of a heart attack, he was thrown into prison but then released to live in an old folks' home in north London. He was in great form when we met. Unable to speak, he communicated by pointing to letters on a board. As I was leaving, Vic Dark and Eddie Richardson rang to wish me well.

31

Clocking Off

I HAVE NEVER SOUGHT out trouble; it just seems to follow me. In November 2010, I attended the funeral of my pal Gock Mackenzie's brother Homer. A lot of the mourners were appalled when I was attacked at the funeral.

A few weeks later, I was warned that somebody with established links to the Ulster Defence Association had hired former volunteers to assassinate me over the trouble at Homer's funeral. The sum mentioned was £20,000. 'Is that all?' I protested, but when the rumour began to spread it scared Ma. As if to pour salt into the wound, an explosion near Loch Lomond was blamed on ex-terrorists demonstrating bomb-making techniques to my gangland rivals.

It would be easy to dismiss all of this as idle gossip, but what gave the UDA rumour substance was the regular appearance at my local bar, the Princess, of police. There were daily checks inside the pub and I was tipped off that my movements were being monitored. Nobody would say what was behind this, but the word was that intelligence about UDA supporters being asked to whack me was being taken seriously. I simply went about my business as usual, too long in the tooth to let something like this bother me.

In between came more sadness. Maggie Steele died. Her sons Jim, Johnny and Joe are pals. Joe was wrongly jailed along with Tommy Campbell over the Ice Cream Wars murders. Then came a double tragedy, with the deaths, within three days of each other, first of my uncle Billy and then of Ma's sister, my aunt Chrissie.

As for me, there wouldn't be another Blinkmobile. The days when money poured from my wallet like rain from the sky were long gone and the insurers were immovable. At one time, I'd splashed out for a personalised number plate, 'B1LNK', but it had attracted too much attention, not least from the police, and so I'd moved it on.

I reached 50 and was flattered that so many friends helped me celebrate with a party, among them George Redmond's son Kyle, John McGuire, Barry Redmond, Sammo the Bear, Caff and James McGovern. As the fun progressed, someone poked his head around the door and there was James's brother Paul. When Sheila and I ran the Talisman, I used to think of Paul as a teenage Arthur Daley. I was very happy for him when he overcame major problems to become highly successful in the security industry.

And I am happy, too, for Michelle, who cuts my hair in Smithycroft Road under the shadow of Barlinnie. She and her fiancé, John, invited me to their wedding in January at the Garfield Country House Hotel. I'm sure their future will be a lot smoother than mine. I'm pleased also for my cousin Sharon in Australia, who is expecting her second child. Like me, Anne, Demi and Samuel are over the moon for her.

Mostly now my time is spent reading about other gangsters. Many of those with whom I spent time in jail stay in touch, mainly through Christmas cards or an occasional telephone call.

The small fry who tried to have me killed remain just that: small time, low on bottle, regarded with contempt by those who matter.

Some think I've wasted much of my life, and maybe I have. But I've lived a thousand experiences, made and spent fortunes, and learned a million lessons. I often think of those millionaires whose money and power came from drugs but who would cheerfully give up everything in exchange for freedom. The fact is that the drugs road has just two destinations, prison and the grave, and often both, for anybody crazy enough to journey along it.

As for me, if I had my time over, would I do anything differently? Yes, I'd buy Roy, the chief cashier at the National Westminster bank in Torquay, an alarm clock.